MY TEMPORARY LIFE

Book One of the
My Temporary Life Trilogy

Martin Crosbie

Dedicated to Bill and Bob.

Without them none of this happens.

CHAPTER 1

I think I first smelled booze on Gerald when we were eleven, and as far as I know he's been drinking ever since. We're thirteen now, almost fourteen, and he still carries a mickey to school a couple of times a week. I know how he does it. He told me once. He raids his parent's liquor cabinet and takes a little from every bottle, making up a toxic mixture of alcohol. He's small, and wiry, almost invisible really, so it's probably quite easy for him to sneak around his house, stealing things, unnoticed.

Once, he flashed me a rare sinister-looking grin and offered me a sip. "Try it, Malcolm. Try it. I cannae gie ye much, but try a wee bit of it." The taste was harsh and strong and had no flavour. It burned my throat and reminded me of the oil that we use in the big old heater that sits at home on our hearth. I politely gave him his little bottle back, hoping that he'd never offer it to me again.

He drinks his booze after we eat our twelve o'clock dinner. We always sit across from each other in the dinner hall, and when he's finished eating his lukewarm potatoes and dried-up meat, that Kilmarnock Secondary School provides us with every day, he sneaks away to the boy's toilets to drink his concoction. When I meet up with him later, on the school grounds, his face is red and his breath is foul. He says it makes him numb. It's what he likes, what he needs.

Although we're all students in Second Form and we're all twelve or thirteen years old, the Masters separate us into two

1

different sections. Form 2A has the regular children, the children that are easy to categorize. Gordon McGregor is in 2A, the tall, red-headed son of the local butcher, and so is Stuart Douglas, with his holier than thou smirk, and chin covered in pimples and peach fuzz. They run the school. Everyone is afraid of them, even some of the masters. McGregor is in charge, but Douglas is the dangerous one. He's the one who does the dirty work, and he's always talking, always *stating* something. He'll widen his fingers and raise his hands after one of his statements, challenging anyone to contradict him. Then he'll seal it off with a look over at his friend, Gordon McGregor, gesturing for his approval. McGregor always does the same thing. He smiles back at the frozen, waiting look on Douglas' face and says, "Aye, you're right. It's us against them Stuart. Always has been, always will be."

Sometimes he's alluding to the English and the tenuous relationship that the Scots have with them, or sometimes it's the Masters, and sometimes it seems to be directed at me, or those like me. I never have felt as though I'm a part of the "us" and I certainly never feel that I'll ever be one of "them," or at least not in their eyes.

Form 2B is my class, mine and Gerald's. We're the segregated children, the ones that the masters, and the school I suppose, don't quite know what to do with. In our class we have children whose mothers look young enough to be their older sisters, or fathers who are away, just away, whatever that means. And we have criminals, young criminals anyway. These are the

2

boys who are already legends in the school because of the violence and criminality their last names are associated with, boys who carry knives to school, and use the stories of what their big brothers and fathers did the night before to intimidate the rest of us.

The rest of us are from broken homes. That's how I ended up here. My mother left my father and returned to Canada four years ago. That's where she's from. She met my father while on holiday in Scotland, then shortly afterwards, I came along. Then, when she tired of Scotland, or my Dad, or me, I'm not sure which, she went home. So now I spend the summers with her in Vancouver, Canada, and my school year here in Kilmarnock, in Scotland, with my Dad.

I've never really been sure why Gerald is in 2B. He has a mother and father and although he's poor and his clothes often look to be in the same, unwashed state week after week, he's still no poorer than the rest of us. He's small though, very small, so perhaps the Masters thought that he wouldn't fit in with the regular kids. Perhaps they thought he needed to be segregated too.

Science class is packed. We always have Master Hextall's Science class right after dinner, and today it's crowded. It's never this crowded. The other Master must be busy or absent because Form 2A has joined us, and there are two class loads of students packed into my one little classroom. Usually they're good at keeping us divided, keeping us apart, but not today. Students are sitting on the floor, and doubled up at desks. Gordon McGregor and Stuart Douglas are even leaning against the walls. Master Hextall is scared of them. I can tell. He keeps looking out at the rest of us, ignoring the two of them, pretending that they're not there.

Hextall is always nervous, but today he's especially flustered. I can see it in his face. There are just too many wound-up, twitchy children in the classroom, and I'm sure half of us look as though we want to take a bite out of him. He's scanning the class, his greasy skin glowing from the classroom lights, as he tries to find a way to silence the murmurs, the restlessness. I know what he's looking for. He needs the same thing that all of us want. He needs to fit in, and the only way he knows how to do that is to offer up a sacrifice. He needs a victim.

Standing at the front, he's surveying us, deciding. He won't pick McGregor or Douglas or even one of the hard boys from my class. He doesn't want a confrontation, a fight. I know that. I know it by the way his beady little eyes are darting around, and the way he's furiously tapping his cane against the side of his leg, over and over again. My desk is behind Gerald's and there's no point in trying to hide behind his small frame. I'm too tall and gangly. Hextall can see me. I stick out too much.

I always do the homework, and usually, Gerald does too, but not today. I just know that he hasn't. I can tell by the way his body is slumped forward with his head leaning over his schoolbooks. He may as well have a target printed clearly on the front of his school shirt. Hextall sees it too, and makes his decision. He doesn't pick

4

on me or Angie Craven, one half of the Craven twins, who sits in front of Gerald. He picks the weakest person in the room.

"Mr Taylor, Gerald, tell me that you've read the assignment. Please tell me that you now understand that in all equations there is a problem, an observation, and a conclusion. Tell me your interpretation of the problem on page 74 please, and say it loud enough for all of us to hear, Mr Taylor." Hextall has a nasally irritating voice that runs its fingers through your hair and slaps you on the back of the head at the same time. He keeps staring at Gerald while nervously adjusting his glasses, just before they slide off the end of his nose.

It's worked for him too, because now there's only silence in the classroom. The nervous murmuring and noises from a moment ago have changed to a class full of children holding their breath, waiting anxiously for the blood to spill. From my vantage point behind Gerald, I can see my friend's face looking down, staring at his desk, at his jotter. There's a murmur of laughter, half of it at his expense I suppose, and the other half just relief that he's today's scapegoat. We're all watching him, waiting.

Hextall doesn't wait long; he too can smell the blood. "Can't you look up at me Mr Taylor? Have I said something that you find offensive, or amusing? Or are you deef? Are you hard of hearing today?" The old bastard is enjoying it. He's actually grinning and does nothing to silence the laughter that's coming from the rest of the class.

I can see the back of my friend's neck turning red as he raises his head to answer the teacher. I can hear the buzzing of the overhead lights in the classroom. I perch forward and crane my neck to the side, just a bit, trying to see what he's doing. He's opened his mouth. I can see that much. His mouth is open but no words are coming out. I don't understand what's happening right away, but then I get it. Then, I know.

His mouth is wide open, and he's probably trying to speak, but he can't. So the odour, that harsh, pungent odour of liquor is blowing all over the back of Angie Craven, and probably over anybody else who's sitting in the first couple of rows of the classroom.

Hextall must see the squeamish look on the girls face, or perhaps her eyes are darting around in anger as she's reacting to the smell of my friend's breath on the back of her neck. Either way, he isn't waiting. Seizing the moment, he leaps forward from the front of the class, and stations himself right in front of Gerald.

"Have you been drinking, boy? Is that alcohol that I smell on your breath?"

This time there is an answer. He pushes himself straight up in his chair and addresses the teacher, his mouth surely no farther than a few inches from Hextall's thick glasses. "Hardly," he mumbles.

Hardly. That's all he says, and that's all that he has to say. The classroom's laughter is now without restraint. I can hear Douglas and McGregor, and even the kids from our own class, repeating it over and over again. "Hardly. Hardly. Hardly's been hardly drinking."

And of course Hextall, the sadistic old bastard, has no trouble finishing him off. Not even bothering to hide his own delight, he pulls the newly christened, "Hardly," by the shoulders, and with very little struggle, lifts him out of his seat. "Very well Hardly, if that's the way you want it. Let's get you to the headmaster's office, and you can let him know what it's like to be hardly drinking."

He doesn't even try to subdue the class's laughter. He just pulls my friend towards the hallway and smiles back at the class, thinking I suppose, that he's one of them now and, that somehow, he's managed to fit in. When the door closes behind them, the taunts became crueller, clearer. The laughter is still there, but it's different now. It's the words that are important. The words pierce me every time I hear them. The crowd of two classes, who would normally ignore or taunt each other, are now banded together, chanting the word over and over again. Their victim is gone of course, so they have to settle for the next best thing.

I'm his friend. We walk to school together and spend dinnertimes walking around the school grounds, trying to find ways to be unseen, to be less of a target. So, it's me that McGregor and Douglas chant their "Hardly" taunts at. They're still leaning against the wall, but somehow it feels as though they're closer to me, pushing their faces into mine, their breath and spit spraying all over me, much the same way the teacher just did to my friend.

"Wilson. Malcolm. Look at me. Look ower here. Are you hardly drinking too? Is that what you two get up tae at dinner time? Are ye hardly drinking?" It's Douglas talking. I know that it's him, and I know that McGregor will be standing back, looking smug, waiting to join in.

I look around, wondering where Nan McHendry, my 13 year-old angel from 2A is sitting. Is she flicking her long dark hair back, chattering to her friend? Does she condone this? Or, is she looking down somewhere, her shy smile ignoring it all?

I'm used to being alone. I live with a father, who didn't intend to have a son with no wife, or I spend my summers in Canada, with a mother who forgets that I'm there. This is a different type of alone though. This is an alone where there's no relief, no escape. I have a decision to make, but in reality, I probably made it as soon as the door slammed shut and McGregor and Douglas turned their attention to me. It's self preservation and I have no choice. I have no escape. So, I join in. I chant back. I laugh and ridicule and make jokes about Hardly drinking and Hardly being hardly there at all.

There's a meeting that night with Hardly's parents, and the principal, and of course Hextall. They suspend him for a week, so it's not until the following week that he's back standing by the lamppost at the end of his street, waiting for me, so that we can walk to school together. He's standing sideways, his face half-turned, smirking, trying to look brave I suppose.

"I've stopped, no more booze. It's just not worth it." His voice has its usual shakiness, and as he walks, his short, thin frame doesn't seem to know how to control putting one foot in front of the other without stumbling. "I mean it. I don't want to go through that shite ever again." He pauses, and almost as an afterthought says, " Fucking Hextall."

We walk in silence for a few minutes and I don't know what to say. Just before we reach the main road that takes us straight to school, I realize that he's stopping every so often not out of clumsiness, but because he's limping, and favouring one side over the other.

I want him to stop. I want him to stop his nervous walking and tell me what happened to him but I can't, and I don't. I'm thirteen and my only priority is getting through as many days as I can without being mocked or beaten because of my wrong clothes or wrong haircut.

"Math was cancelled while you were gone. Fire alarm had us outside for almost an hour."

He stops and turns to me, and then I see it. The left side of his face is red under his cheek, and scraped, and his eye is bruised and has turned a sickly, grey colour. As he sees me staring, he turns away and we do what frightened, poor, thirteen year old kids do. We ignore it.

"That's brilliant. I wish I'd been there just for that. No Math, that's almost as tempting as no Science. Fuck." Then he seems to remember something and says it again, "Fucking Hextall." He speaks as though he's in a hurry, and his laugh is forced. He seems to be begging me to not ask. So, I don't. We just keep moving towards the school, him limping every few steps, and me trying to walk slow, waiting for him.

CHAPTER 2

Gerald's bruises heal and with the absence of booze he starts to look almost healthy. His skin still has a greasy unwashed look, but his eyes seem different somehow. Instead of their usual dull lifeless appearance they seem more alive now, always nervously searching around as though they're looking for something. His manner of speaking has changed too. He cocks his head up when he talks to me, and his eyes dart around, looking at me, and then immediately looking everywhere else. He's like a little soldier in a foxhole, alert and aware, waiting for the next bomb to fall. That's how we find the tree. We always knew that it was there, of course, but he notices it. It's his idea.

"We should take it, claim it as ours."

I know that he's talking to me, because there are only the two of us sitting on the grass by the entrance to the dinner hall. It's impossible though, to know what he's talking about, because his gaze doesn't settle on any one thing long enough for me to follow.

"The tree, Malcolm, the stand-alone tree. Nobody else even kens that it's there. I can climb it and I know that you can, so why not. Let's take it."

He's right. Nobody else ever seems to notice it. The tree stands by itself on a small green patch of land that sits adjacent to our school. It's almost as though the busy roads and the school itself have been built around the tree and nobody felt that they had the right to cut it down. So there it stands, tall and alone, a short distance from the back of the school.

"I don't know if you can just take a tree, but if you're talking about climbing it we can certainly try and climb it, Hardly..." The name is out of my mouth before I realize that I've said it, and, without looking back, he's off and running towards the stand-alone tree.

I know that I can catch him, or pass him even, but I don't. I run behind, letting him lead, wondering if I should be the only one in the school that still calls him "Gerald".

He's running so quickly that his short, frail body slams into the bottom part of the trunk, and he bounces backwards. I catch him, and putting his foot on my hand, leverage him upwards, trying to make it appear as though the plan was to work in conjunction all along. With one hoist, I have him up to the first branch, and then, groaning, he pulls himself upwards.

I'm taller than him, and certainly more agile, but it still takes all of my strength to grab the bottom limb, and swing myself up. By the time I reach one of the lower branches, he's scampered upwards and is sitting above me, peering through the leaves.

"It's perfect," he laughs. "Absolutely perfect."

I have to agree with him. From our vantage point, we can see the boys running around, chasing the ball on the school field. We can see the girls, pretending not to watch them, and we can even see the Masters pacing back and forth, as they distractedly watch the comings and goings of thedifferent students. And, they can't see us. The leafy old tree is a perfect camouflage. I don't think anyone saw us running towards it, and certainly no one is looking up at it now. He's right. It is perfect.

I lean back on my lower branch, and watch him as he cautiously moves from limb to limb, trying to find the perfect vantage point. His face is different now, more relaxed, mischievous even, and his eyes aren't darting around as much anymore, waiting for those bombs to land. Hardly and I have found a safe place.

The old tree becomes our refuge and nobody seems to mind, or if they do, they don't say anything. Hardly still gets teased and mocked, and Stuart Douglas or Gordon McGregor routinely bump their shoulders into him sending him sideways, as he walks down the hallways, but now he has something. We have something. Morning and afternoon breaks don't quite leave us enough time to get to it and get settled without anyone seeing us, but dinner time is different.

We quickly eat our school dinner of watery powdered potatoes and ground up mincemeat, or tatties and mince as they're known, and then as cautiously as we can, we run to our tree.

Some days we see nothing. Bored kids run aimlessly around the fields, while others congregate in little groups, cherishing the fact they have somewhere they belong, somewhere they feel safe. Other days there are things happening. There is activity, arguments, shouting. And there are fights. There are always fights.

The main objective when it comes to fighting at Kilmarnock Secondary School is to grab your opponent's hair and pull their head down, so you can kick at it. Then, get as many kicks in as you can, before the master pulls the two of you apart. This usually involves an initial kick to the groin or the knee to unsteady your adversary and then a clutch for their hair. The crowd of children circle around of course, hoping that the fight gets to the head kicking part before the master who is on patrol, can intervene.

The teachers have different methods of separating the fighters. Mr McRae, the Physical Education Master, athletically pounces in and gets between the two before any harm can be done. Others manage to intervene before the grab for the hair, and separate the two. Hextall is different though. He waits until one fighter has over-powered the other, has his opponent's scalp firmly in hand and has applied a kick or two, before moving in and breaking it up. I'm not quite sure if he wants to see the blood or if he's just afraid of being hurt himself in the scuffle.

It's a day without fights, when we can see little activity from our vantage point, that Hardly starts asking me questions.

"Why are you here anyways? Why aren't you in Canada with your mother or somewhere other than here? Why would anybody want to be here?" He tries to spit, but the saliva slips from his mouth and dribbles down his chin. He's gesturing towards the school grounds, looking over the playing fields at the faded grey walls of the building with disgust.

I pause before saying it, although I know the answer, and think about it every day of my life. "She didn't want me. We got to Canada and she decided that she didn't want me. So, she sent me back here to my Dad."

I don't look up at him as he sits on his higher branch, but I know that he hasn't moved. I know that my answer hasn't really answered him at all. "It's complicated. It's not easy to explain. They split up. She was never really happy here I guess, always wanted to go back to Canada, that's where she's from. I'm half-Canadian."

14

He sniggers sarcastically. "Mine is easy, not complicated at all. Neither of them want me and they remind me of that every day, actually, probably more like every minute."

I resist the urge to look up, and I let him continue talking.

"My old man is just an angry old fucker, hits, hits, hits. Hits everything. That's his answer. Just hit till the noise all stops. And her, my ma, she takes it, and then hits me to show him that she agrees with him. And then they send me to this shit hole five days a week, one big, happy fucking family."

He's still staring at the old building that looms in front of us. "You should have stayed in Canada, Malcolm. You should have found a way to stay there. Look at this place. I mean it's supposed to be 1976 not 1936. Anything's gotta be better than this."

He isn't just talking about school of course. He's talking about all of the things that make up our lives. He's talking about the things that eat us up inside and make us run and hide in a big, safe old tree every opportunity we get.

Living with my father is living with silences. It's living with a shared sadness at being left. I get my height from my Dad, but where I am thin and boney; he's broad and strong with the muscles that come from building other people's houses year after year. We're a strange pair, I suppose, this big, strong, quiet man and a scared, passive, almost-man living together and apart at the same time.

"My Dad's okay. He just doesn't say anything. My mother though, she's different. She talks. She talks to everybody."

He wants more. I can tell from his silence, so I give it to him.

"She moved us into a motel, in Vancouver. That's in Canada. That's where she used to be from. There was one big bed, and we shared it." I wonder if he's sniggering again. "I was ten then. I wouldn't do it now. I was just a kid," I say, underlining that fact that I'm 13, three long years from being a ten year old.

"There were sparkly things on the ceiling. They were embedded right into the plaster on the ceiling, and they'd shine even in the dark. They were amazing; they looked like little diamonds that someone had left there. I got this idea that if I could pry those diamonds out of the ceiling, I could sell them and get back to Scotland."

This time he does laugh, just a small, short snicker.

"I was ten, remember." I almost laugh myself and it helps me for a moment to forget how much pain there had been that day.

"She was out in the hallway, talking to a man from another room. She was complaining about my Dad, about Scotland, telling him things that I didn't remember, things that just didn't make sense. The other man was laughing and being nice to her. I couldn't see them, but I could hear them. I could hear everything."

"So did you get the diamonds? Is that how you got back here?" He's laughing now but it's a kinder laugh, the type that invites you to join in.

"I suppose in a way I did, yes." I stop to think about that day again, and I can remember the look on my mother's face as she came back into the room to find me unsteadily teetering on a chair, trying to reach the ceiling.

"She threw herself on me, before I could reach them, and we both landed on the bed. Then she started hitting me, over and over. They weren't hard hits," I say, remembering the beating that he'd endured from one or both of his parents. "She was just frustrated I guess, and tired. We were both tired, just really tired."

"I told her that I wanted my Dad. I told her that I missed Scotland."

"You missed this? How could you have missed this?" I look up and see him perched forward on his branch now, peering down at me.

"It wasn't *this* that I missed. I just didn't know how to say what I meant. It was her and him and me that I missed. It was us being together that I missed. It was "normal" that I missed. She just didn't understand."

Plans were made quickly after that. She told me that if I missed that 'boring old Scotsman', then I could go back to him. She made arrangements to send me back before the school year began, and said she'd see me in the summertime, by then she'd be settled. It would be better by then, better for both of us.

I was at the airport four days later, and held my face hard and rigid, determined not to show any feeling. She was carefree and friendly to everyone around us, and made it sound as though I were going on an adventure, and that I should be happy. After all, I was getting what I wanted.

I was through the first line-up, and with my small carry-on bag in my hand, I looked back, hoping to see some kind of remorse from her, some kind of reaction, some kind of anything. It took a minute before I spotted her in the crowd, leaning over and flicking back her long blonde hair, and smiling. She was talking to a man, oblivious to the fact that I was about to fly halfway around the world.

"She wanted me gone. So, I was gone, back here. I told you it was simple."

We sit in silence until the bell rings and then make our way down the tree. I sometimes feel as though he's going to fall when he jumps and lands on the ground. He doesn't though. He rights himself just in time, somehow staying upright. Then, he stumbles forward, and runs reluctantly towards the sound of the bell, and back to school.

CHAPTER 3

We're almost always able to reach our tree during dinner hour. In order to get there undetected, we have to be amongst the first students to leave the dinner hall. To accomplish this, we quickly eat whatever they serve us, and then make our way across the yard to our safe haven.

It's a routine that's become familiar to us. Hardly leaves first, dropping his plate into the large metal bucket, then runs to the door, as I trail a few feet behind him, trying not to look quite so anxious. Sometimes, a few heads turn and there's murmurs of, "Hardly," or "Hardly drinking," but we still make it. We almost always make it. There's only one day that we have obstructions.

We follow our usual routine, but once Hardly is outside, he's met by McGregor and three of his cronies, and they quickly corral him into a corner. I stop in my tracks, and sit at an empty table, dropping my head, pretending to be engrossed in the design of the table top. The door to the dinner hall is propped open, and I can see him, through the opening, cowering in a corner. My forehead sweats, but I'm not sure if it's from anger or fear, or just frustration at being held up, and not able to get to our tree. I can hear McGregor's booming voice. He speaks, then pauses, waiting for the inevitable laughter from his lumbering sidekicks.

"Is that why you walk funny, Hardly? Are ye always on the booze?"

Hardly doesn't answer. He just keeps staring down, shuffling his feet and trying to walk between them. They keep it going, not wanting to let him off the hook, as they bounce him back into the corner as though he's a ball and it's all a game. I look up occasionally, from the safety of my table, looking for Stuart Douglas, wondering why he isn't with them, involved in their performance.

McGregor is tall and bulky, but Douglas is the fighter. Douglas has a litheness and arrogance that make the rest of the school fear him. He has an unpredictability and rage that can erupt without provocation. I've seen him amble down the halls, swinging his gangly arms, only to start slapping or even punching the heads of boys that he passes. From our vantage point up the tree, I've seen him fight too. He attacks with no warning, running towards whatever boy seems to be in his disfavour that day, and mercilessly beats him. He has no qualms about size either. He routinely picks boys who are as tall and broad as him or even larger. Douglas is the one that I'm really afraid of. He's the one who'll hurt you just for the sport of it.

McGregor is still being entertained by Hardly and keeps pushing on, showing off for his crowd. Nan McHendry brushes by them, leaving the dinner hall with her girlfriends, trying to take no notice.

"Nan, luk at this yin. I've found me a drunk in oor school. Come and see me kick his arse." The son of the butcher is larger than life now, and Hardly is reduced to just standing, pinned against the wall, staring, once again, at the ground.

She refuses to encourage McGregor, and backs away, grabbing her girlfriend's arm. "Leave him alone, Gordon. He's no daeing you any harm, none at all."

For a moment, I think she might be looking back at me, and then back at her girlfriend. I start to stand, and I'm sure that I have every intention of doing something, anything, when I hear Douglas' voice, coming from beyond them, out in the yard.

"Right, Gordon, it's done. We're right as rain, mate."

I don't know what they're talking about, nor do I care. All that matters to me is that I've avoided yet another confrontation. I wait until McGregor and his cronies saunter towards Douglas, dismissing Hardly as though he's a piece of litter lying at the side of the road, before I make my way to my friend, trying to make apologies for my tardiness.

"It's fine. You can't do anything anyways. There's too many of them. There's no point in both of us getting into it with them." He knows. He might not have seen me cowering back at the empty table, but he still knows.

We don't have enough time that day to reach our tree unnoticed, so, we spend it in our previous manner, walking from open space to open space, trying to be invisible to the Douglases and McGregors of the school yard.

The next day I'm excited, anxious to get back to our routine of watching the world while sitting hidden from the rest of the school. Our schedule has been disrupted, and I feel as though I've missed something. I need to get back to the safety and security of our stand-alone tree. We glance at each other while wolfing back our dinners in anticipation. Hardly has an earnest look on his face, and when he does look at me, he smiles, sharing in our secret.

Thankfully, there are no obstructions at the door this day, and we quickly make our run across the open grass. It feels the same way that it always does. I can feel the dampness from the uncut field soaking through my school shoes, but it doesn't matter. Our tree looms invitingly in front of us. If I'd slowed down a little,

I might have seen the rope before we got there, or I might even have heard them, but I don't. All I can think about is helping Hardly up that first branch, and then hoisting myself up behind him.

He's up and on his way, and I've just reached the first branch, when I hear it. First, there's the cry of, "Fire," from a voice up somewhere in the tree. Then, the steady stream of liquid comes at us from different directions. I make the fatal mistake of looking up only to be met with a mouthful of warm piss.

The laughter is unmistakable. McGregor and Douglas and whoever is tagging along with them are up our tree, cocks hanging out, pissing all over us.

I slide down as fast as I can, falling to the ground, covered in their piss, but Hardly stays. I look back up, wiping my forehead and rubbing my stinging eyes, but still he doesn't move. He just sits there on the tree branch, letting them aim at him, laugh at him.

"Hardly...Gerald. Fuck...Hardly, come down. Come down." I can't reach him. I just stand at the bottom, listening to the sounds of their piss bouncing off of him, too disgusted and scared to climb back up.

Finally, when they exhaust their supply and the sounds of their laughter is almost unbearable, he looks back up at them, then climbs down the tree with purpose, jumping to the ground and gaining his balance without any help from me. It's then that I notice the rope hanging from the branch at the back of the tree. The planning for this venture has obviously been in the works for some time.

We know we can't return to the school, smelly and wet, so we cross the road as quickly as we can, trying to ignore the maniacal sounds of the boys who are still sitting up our tree, and make our way home. Hardly doesn't talk, and when we reach the street that leads to his house, he just keeps walking as though he's been alone all along.

"I'll see you in the morning, then. Hardly, don't worry about it. They're assholes, just a bunch of assholes."

When you're 13, almost 14, everything lasts forever. You have no concept of things ending or changing. You're trapped in a monotony of bleak days at school and silent night-time suppers. Then, a tree presents itself, and becomes a bit of light in the darkness and you grab onto it and use it as hope and promise and optimism. And then, just as suddenly as it appears, it's taken away. We'll never be up our tree again. I know that, and Hardly probably knows it too. What I don't know is how we're going to cope without it. The one place in our lives that we can hide just disappeared.

It isn't unusual for my father to be home during the day. He takes work when he can get it, and that sometimes means working on weekends, and often having no work at all during the week. He's working in the yard in front of our house when he first sees me, and stares, stares as though I've just wandered in from another planet. I try to ignore his expressionless look and just keep walking sluggishly towards our front door, hoping for once, for the familiarity of his silences.

"Is there no school? Are you no well?"

I'm almost past him, when he must have caught a whiff of my clothes, and he grabs me as roughly as I can ever remember him touching me.

"What is that? What's the smell, Malcolm?"

I've had enough. I've had enough of waiting for phone calls from Canada that never come and nightly silent treatments. I've had enough of trying to fit in where I know I never will. I pull away from his strong grip, and stand my ground, almost gagging on the stink that is coming from me.

"It's piss. They pissed all over us. We had our tree, and they took it, and then they pissed on us. They had a rope to get up there, and now we don't have a tree. It's piss, just piss." I don't remember ever yelling at him before, but still he doesn't flinch. He doesn't look away. I can't tell if he's angry or concerned or even hurt. He just keeps staring at me.

"Go, get cleaned up Malcolm. Then, get back out here. Get that stuff off of you."

I've never been afraid of my father. Previous to my mother leaving him, he'd been a good, kind, attentive Dad to me, rarely raising his voice. The man that I met when I got off the plane in

24

Scotland this time is different though. This Dad doesn't show emotions. He just seems to exist, working when there's work, and doing the bare minimum to live in a house with a son that he hasn't asked for.

When I come back outside, he's leaning against the side wall of our house, watching me, waiting.

"Come over here Malcolm. I want to show you something. Come on, it's okay." His words aren't menacing, and as I approach him he backs himself against the wall and lowers his stance, so that I'm looking straight into his eyes. His tattered work-shirt is turned up at the sleeves and his muscles are pushing out as though they need a shirt of their own.

"I want you to do something. Look at the wall behind my head. Pretend that you can see right through my head and then punch the wall behind it. Don't concentrate on my head, just on the wall. Hit that wall as hard as you want to hit whoever pissed on you."

I have to stifle my laughter. I won't hit him. I can't hit him.

"I don't want to hit you. I can't hit you."

"Malcolm, hit me. Go on, hit me. It'll be okay. I don't mind."

We go back and forth a couple of times, before he finally raises his voice one last time, and tells me to hit him. And, I do. I hit my Dad.

I draw my bony little fist back and swing it as hard as I can at his head, concentrating on the wall behind him, just as he told me.

"That's good, now harder Malcolm. Aim for the wall and hit my face. Hit it as hard as you can. Think of them. Use the hate. Use yer hate."

His head doesn't move at first, but as I realize that he isn't going to dodge out of the way and let my hand hit the wall, or even worse hit me back, I strike him with increased ferocity, until finally, he tells me to stop. His face is red, and there's puffiness under his right eye, but it doesn't seem to bother him. He just raises himself back up to his normal height, and tells me that I've done well.

We spend the rest of the afternoon punching things. He finds an old cloth bag under the stairs and fills it with wet leaves. We hang it from the railing that leads to our neighbour's upstairs, and he shows me the correct way to punch it.

I tell him about the hair clutching and the head kicking, but it doesn't faze him. He says that the secret is to just keep punching. The secret is to not stop, to not care. Find the target and pound it relentlessly, until you're either too tired to continue, or your opponent has stopped fighting back.

"Ignore the hits you take, Malcolm. You can deal with the pain later. Just keep going forward and don't think about how much he's hurting you."

By supper time that night, I'm sore in places that I didn't realize I had, even though a blow hasn't landed on me all day. As we sit across from each other, slurping down our soup, I try not to laugh as the bruises on my father's face start to show. I make my way to bed shortly after that, and to my surprise he calls me a name that he hasn't in a long time.

"Goodnight, Son. I'll see you in the morning."

I don't turn. I just mumble back at him, and walk blindly to my room. It takes several minutes of sitting on the edge of my bed, before his words have an effect on me, and I realize that my usually silent uncommunicative father may indeed realize that he does actually have a son.

CHAPTER 4

I spot him before I see my mother, and I know that he's the one. His t-shirt has a man playing a guitar on it, and his bulging belly is bouncing around as he waves his arms, gesturing for me to come to him, and laughing, all at the same time. He's tall and chunky and seems to have hair growing out of his hair. When I get closer, and let him squeeze my hand in his, I see only small patches of skin, on a face covered by a beard and moustache, plus two mountainous tufts of hair, one sprouting from each of his ears.

"Say hello to George, Malcolm, *Uncle* George." My mother giggles like a school girl as she slips one arm around his waist, and rubs my hair with her free hand, welcoming me back to Canada.

"Say this for me in your Scawttish accent, Mal, say, 'No Problem, Uncle George, no problem.' That's what we say in Canada, Mal, no problem, nothing's ever a problem here." He has a big friendly grin on his face when he says it, and I find it very hard not to smile back at him.

There have been others of course. My mother doesn't like to be alone and seems to have no trouble finding male company. I call them my one visit uncles. I meet them at the beginning of the summer and the next year I meet their replacement. She calls each of them the man of her dreams, the man she's been waiting for her whole life. And each one of them seems to worship her. We live in their homes and eat at their tables and of course sleep in their beds, and my mother makes it seem as though it's the most natural thing in the world. We do family type things from time to time, and are all very polite as we try to pretend that we're all exactly where we want to be.

I remember the uncle from two summers before George. My mother called him Richard, but everyone else called him Dick, just plain Dick. Dick was cold and aloof and only seemed to come to life after drinking some of the stubby, little, brown bottles of beer that he kept in his fridge. I spotted a calendar one day, high on the wall in the back laundry room. It had my arrival date circled and then every day that I'd stayed with them had a hard, red 'X' drawn through it. When I turned the calendar over to the next month there was a smiley face drawn across my departure date. It was in Dick's writing. I'm sure of that.

28

It's hard not to like George though. He's loud and boisterous and seems to be genuinely pleased to see me. By the time we've driven from Vancouver airport to his house, I've heard his life story. He's a long-time bachelor, works as a mechanic at the local car dealership, and is tired of playing the field. He doesn't have to tell me that he's totally enamoured with my mother, but he does anyways. As he's driving, he reaches over and pulls a small blue bottle from the glove compartment and, with one hand on the wheel; he removes the lid and pours the liquid from it onto his hands. Then, to my surprise, he rubs it between both hands and loudly smacks it onto his face.

"That airport always makes me feel sticky, need to freshen up," he says, winking at my mother. "A man's gotta smell good, Mal. Ain't that right, gotta smell good for the ladies." He's laughing a warm, hearty laugh as he says it, and it's impossible not to laugh with him. "Here, Mal, you try it. You're gonna need it for those young Canadian girls that you're gonna meet this summer."

The bottle flies through the air and lands in the back seat on my lap, and I wonder how he managed to throw it so expertly without adjusting his eyes from the road. It smells medicinal and I wonder why anyone would want to smell that way, but out of politeness I pour some onto my hand and then smack it on my cheeks, just the way he did. I learn later, when I see the shelves in his bathroom that he has lots of similar bottles that say, Hai Karate, and Brut for Men, and the one that he carries in his car, Aqua Velva. I wince in pain at the self imposed smack, and my mother

29

laughs; George laughs; we all laugh. It's a good moment. It feels right and I realize that I haven't thought about Hardly or my father or Scotland since I've landed.

I'm tired when we reach his house, but I'm an experienced traveller and have learned the tricks to beat jet lag by now. The secret is to eat and to stay awake for as long as you can. It helps you adjust to the time change. My mother stands over the electric stove, scrambling eggs and toasting bread, while I sit at the kitchen table with my head held up by my hands, forcing myself to stay awake. George has moved to the other room. There is a television on and I can hear him talking to it, telling the players to move faster or hit harder. Once in a while he calls out to my mother or to me, relaying an incident that just happened, asking us if we can believe it, telling us what he would do if he were playing.

"See, Malcolm, he has a television set too. He's watching football, but he likes his hockey, too. You'll see. You can watch it with him, tomorrow of course, after you've slept. He's a good man, Malcolm, the right man. This time I've found the right man."

She's staring hard at me when she says it, and her eyes seem to be asking me to believe her, to trust her, but it's late and I'm tired, and I've forgotten the unwritten rules that have been established on previous visits.

"My dad knows hockey, too. We talked about it at the airport before coming here, just earlier, while he waited with me." I can still hear the television playing after I've said it, and George is still making his noises, but the sound of the eggs being scraped

30

on the frying pan has stopped and I know that she's watching me. I only realize that my eyes have closed when the toast jumps out of the toaster, and I remember where I am and what I just said.

"Tell me then, Malcolm. Tell me about your hockey conversation with your father. I'm very interested." The pleading in her eyes is gone now, and she's turned away from the stove and has one hand on her hip, while the other holds the spatula as though it were a weapon.

We had listened to a football, or fitba, game on the transistor radio, the night before I left, and he talked to me about it as we sat waiting for my plane at Glasgow airport. Celtic and Rangers were the local rivalry, although rivalry isn't a strong enough word. It was more of a battle, and sometimes, even a war.

"Ye wullnae see games like that where you're going. I'll have to bring you up tae speed when I phone or when you come back. Canada doesnae have matches like that, dae they?"

"No, they have hockey though. They like hockey."

"Aye, I know hockey. The lassies play it here."

"No, Dad, it's on ice. It's a different type of hockey."

He thinks for a moment before answering, visualizing I suppose players skating around on ice, with their skirts flapping, playing hockey.

"It's just a game to them though, is it no? I mean, it's no like our fitba, is it?"

I stifle a smile and come back to the present, as I see my mother raise the spatula and point it towards me.

31

"George, honey, can you come in here?" She doesn't take her eyes from me as she calls into the other room, but to my relief she does put the spatula on the counter and moves the frying pan off the hot burner.

"George, sorry, Uncle George," she corrects herself, "as we told you, is an automobile mechanic, Malcolm."

"I'm a grease monkey, Mal, don't listen to her. I fix cars at the dealership, that's all."

He's leaning in the doorway with one eye on us, and the other still on the game in the other room.

"Go on honey, tell him. Tell Malcolm what you've got for him."

George straightens his back and smiles at my mother, then looks at me with an almost pained expression on his face. "I have a job for you, Mal, a summer job. They need a cleanup kid, a Lot Lizard we call them, at the dealership, and, well, the job's yours if you want it."

"No, not if he wants it, not if he wants it at all. The job is his. Malcolm, you have a job and you start tomorrow. Congratulations."

I'm not sure if I'm relieved that she isn't going to strike me with the spatula, or relieved that she doesn't want to hear about my father's theories on hockey, so I just smile and thank George, who offers me a big, goofy grin and goes back to his game.

My mother smiles and turns away, back to preparing my meal, and the rules of our game start to become clear again, even to my jet-lagged head. We don't talk about my father. We don't mention Scotland. And, we pretend that everything is okay. Everything is normal.

That night, as I lie in the small, single bed that they've prepared for me, I toss and turn and think of my father and Hardly and fitba and my mother and George all at the same time. Then, when it seems as though I'll never fall asleep, I have my dream. t's the same dream, the same one that I always have. It's the dream with no beginning and no end.

In the dream, I'm leaving something bad and heading towards something good, or if not good, then at least something better. It's very hard to explain. There really are no specific things happening, it's more about sensations, good and bad sensations. I don't know where I am, although sometimes, I think that I'm on a plane, and I experience this overwhelming sense of dread. I know that something bad is behind me, always just behind me. I never can figure out what I'm running from, or what I'm running towards. The result is always the same and this night is no different. I awaken to my pillowcase soaked in sweat, relieved that I'm whole and alive, but unable to figure out what I've been running from. And on this night, of course, unable to figure out exactly where I am and whose bed it is that I'm sleeping in.

CHAPTER 5

I left Kilmarnock more abruptly than usual. After losing our tree
and being pissed on by McGregor and Douglas, my father decided
that I wouldn't be going back to school. He made the call to my
headmaster from the upstairs neighbour's telephone while I stood
in the doorway, listening to him.

"It's Alex Wilson, here, Malcolm's father. Malcolm will
not be attending school until the autumn of this year."

His expression doesn't change as he listens to the
response on the other end of the phone.

"I will repeat for you," he says in a slightly louder, yet
still not agitated voice, "Malcolm will not be attending school
again until the autumn of this year. Now Cheerio, sir."

And with that I had two weeks of punching cement bags
filled with leaves, and readying myself for Canada. I thought of
Hardly from time to time, even walking towards his house at one
point, but halfway there I decide to turn back, once again letting
him fight his own fight.

I think of these things but then remember that I'm in
Canada, Vancouver, Canada, in George's house, staring up at a
poster on the wall of a creature covered in black and white
makeup, breathing fire into the air, and singing into a microphone.

"It's a band, Malcolm. They're a band, a rock n' roll
band. George thought you'd like it. I told him that you wouldn't

know who they were, but he insisted, so humour him please, Malcolm. Tell him that you like it."

She's standing at the doorway to the bedroom, not looking at me but looking at the poster, just as I was.

"I do. I do like it. It's great, Mum."

Still she stares at the wall, arms folded in front of her, wearing her nightdress. Shivering a little, she doesn't look like my mother. There are lines under her eyes that I haven't noticed before, and her shiny blonde hair looks duller, less blonde, less vibrant, somehow. I look for her confidence, her cockiness but this morning it just doesn't seem to be there.

"Listen, I know this isn't *great*, Malcolm, none of it, but just try, okay, try to get along."

I want to touch her, to hold her, to let her hold me. I pull the covers around me and sit upright as I answer. "I will Mum, I always do. I'll try my best."

She's gone though, and I'm sitting holding my knees, with the covers falling away from me, and it feels like she was never really there at all. All I hear is her voice coming from the hallway, telling me to get up, and that I'll be riding with George, to my new job.

The ride is loud and lively. George is able to turn the big steering wheel with one hand while watching the road, talking to me, and sipping from a huge coffee cup that fits into a special holder on the dash, all at the same time. I thank him for the poster, and with his free hand he pulls out a box filled with cassette tapes.

"Mostly my stuff, Mal, but some of it's your mother's, some of it I keep here for her."

I think of the two of them riding in the car with the music playing on the stereo, my mother probably touching George's shoulder just as she was at the airport, and holding her face high and proud, for all the world to see.

"You see this one, Mal. This is what I'm trying to explain to you. This is crap. It's sentimental bullshit, sorry Mal, crap. It's three basic chords, a catchy chorus, and a week and a half in the top twenty. It does nothing for me, nothing at all."

I nod as he speaks and before long, I'm smiling back at him, enjoying the animated way that he explains things to me.

"You need to feel it. You need to feel it down here, Mal," he tells me, gesturing somewhere below his ample belly. "For me to buy into it, for me to accept it as being real, and I mean real now, Mal, it has to move me down here."

I keep nodding as he points down, while his eyes stay on the road, and he plays with the dials on his stereo.

"I'll show you. Listen to this. You tell me which one gets to you. Tell me the one that you can't describe in words."

I'm smiling so much that I find myself breaking into a laugh as he pops in tape after tape, letting me listen to a minute or two of each.

"It's fine, you laugh at me," he chuckles back, "but I guarantee you, we'll find one of them that floats your boat. No problem there, Mal, no problem at all."

I listen to the sounds of guitars and pianos and other noises that I can't associate with any instrument that I've ever heard. The singers sing of a *highway to hell*, and a man who seems to have a stutter shouts, *my my my my generation*, and another sings that, *we are the champions.* George never tires of putting in tape after tape, laughing while watching my reaction out of the corner of his eye. I smile and nod at all of them, enjoying the beat, the sound, but still not understanding what he means.

"Listen to this Mal. This one reminds me of your mother."

The song is slower and the words are easier to understand as the singer sings about, *her golden blonde hair shining in the sun.*

"Crazy, I know, but it makes me think of her every time. Man, that blonde hair sure turns heads, Mal, that golden blonde hair." He's smiling as he says it and obviously thinking about my mother, but the laughter is gone now and he doesn't look at me. His gaze is firmly on the road ahead of us as he puts another tape into the stereo.

Then, I hear it and I don't have to tell him. I know that somehow, he knows. He just seems to know.

"Aha, you little bugger. You little Scottish bugger," he laughs. "I knew that you'd get it. You can feel it can't you? You know what I'm talking about, don't you?"

All of the other sounds in the world have stopped. I know that the car is running and I can see George laughing and hear his words, but nothing else can dampen the music coming from the stereo. It seems to move effortlessly from a thunderous blast of guitars and piano with the singer not singing but yelling, pleading almost, to a softer melody where he's talking, whispering the story of the song, while the piano plays beautifully in the background. It makes me feel something inside that I've never felt before. I feel happy and angry at the same time. There really is no other way to describe it other than that, just happy and angry, all at the same time.

I'm smiling as the song ends and George turns the volume down. Looking at me, then looking at the road, he's hardly able to contain himself.

"You see kid, that's what I mean. That's the music that you can't describe with words."

He's right. I've never heard anything that made me feel that way before. "How did you know, George? How did you know that was the one for me?"

"You stopped nodding, Mal. You stopped nodding and you got a real serious look on your face, as though something important just happened."

"Maybe it did," I laugh, pleased with myself, "maybe something important did just happen, George."

"Yeah, kid, no maybes about it. Something important did just happen."

We reach our destination and George pulls into the entranceway of a large lot filled with cars of all different shapes and sizes. I wince at the glare coming from the windows on the building in front of us. The windows are huge and behind them, inside the building, there are even more cars. As he turns the vehicle off and parks, in my head I can still hear Bruce Springsteen singing about fast cars and pretty girls, and running away from everything. I smile and think about how the music makes me feel, and when I look over at George, he ruffles my hair and grins back as though he knows exactly what I'm thinking.

CHAPTER 6

The basics of car washing are easy to learn. One-and-a-half scoops of the green powdered soap are mixed with one full bucket of water. This leaves the soap strong enough to take any grime off the cars without wasting any of the expensive green powder. The hoses and soap powder are kept in our shed that is at the rear of the lot, and the shed door must be kept locked at all times. The hose is to be coiled and uncoiled very carefully from the steel spool that holds it. By doing this, there is little chance that the end of the hose

could fly up and scratch one of Mr Allister's cars. They are all Mr
Allister, or Bill Allister's cars. He owns the dealership. I work with
Terry. Terry is Bill's son, and he calls him Dad. I decide to call
him Mr Allister, and thank him for giving me a job.

"You're very welcome, Malcolm. Terry will show you the
ropes. Just listen to Terry and you'll be fine, and don't worry if the
salesmen squawk at you; they're all vermin anyway. They just like
to show what assholes they are once in a while." He smiles at
Terry in a way that seems to say that they've had this conversation
before. Terry grins and hands me a brush, nodding and smirking,
while leading me towards the little shed at the back where we keep
the cherished green soap.

Terry fills me in on what it means to be a *Lot Lizard*. The
main part of the job is washing. We're always washing cars. The
important thing is to start from the top down and rinse more than
you scrub, and always remember to rinse thoroughly. We unload
any deliveries that arrive also. They have to be unloaded at the
back door, then, you knock and wait for someone in the office to
let you in. Never, ever, ever go in the front part of the office or
showroom. We are lot staff, and can only enter the building from
the back shop, or the door at the rear. Always listen to the
salesmen or the mechanics, but if there's something that they ask
you to do, and you're not sure that it should be done, then ask Mr
Allister whether *he'd* like it done.

The washing part is easy and I catch on quickly. It takes the
rest of my first day for Terry to show me around the dealership and

train me on the additional duties that we have, but it only takes an hour before he fills me in on all the different personalities that make up the dealership.

"He's Marvin, Starvin' Marvin. That's what we call him. Don't look; just keep pulling the hose out towards the centre of the lot." Terry stifles a laugh as we both glance at a tall skinny man, wearing a suit that seems to be several sizes too large for him.

"I'm watching you, both of you. That blue Chevy looked like shit when I test-drove it last night. Try a little elbow grease, boys, a little hard work never hurt nobody. You got Snottish Boy to help you now, Terrance, so no excuses, elbow grease, lots of elbow grease." Marvin is waving his arms as he yells at us, the sleeve of his suit jacket flapping in the wind almost in time with the wide flaps at the bottoms of his pants.

Terry ignores the name that I've been called, and just laughs, as Marvin turns and walks away. He doesn't have to tell me that this is one of the assholes his father warned me about.

"He bangs his customers, the women ones anyways. He's our top producer, but he's always got a jealous husband or two trying to find him. Once he came in all bruised and battered after a close call."

"A jealous husband caught him?"

"No, but it was close. He had to jump out of a bathroom window when he heard the front door opening, and then he fell two stories into a dumpster. True story, true story." Terry's eyes light up in a way that they never lit up when he explained to me how to mix the soap.

"And they call him Starvin' because he's so skinny?" I realize that it's an obvious question right after I ask it, but Terry has no interest in mocking me, none at all.

"Yep, they call him that because he's so skinny. He only eats once a day and the rest of the time he sells cars or talks about women. I think he's banging Sylvia. I almost caught him once, coming out of our shed, dirty old man, still pulling his pants up. I know he's got a key; I just haven't caught him with it yet. He tried to look all innocent and kept walking towards me with his arms out so that I couldn't see behind him, but I know I saw someone and I know Marvin. I know what he's up to."

"Sylvia is someone else's wife? She has a husband?"

Terry lets his brush drop to the ground and stares at me for a moment before answering, his face almost bursting open with a childish look of delight. "That's right, you haven't met Sylvia yet. Well buddy, you're in for a treat. Sylvia works in the office. Sylvia and Gloria work together. Gloria does all of the work but Sylvia, well Sylvia has *assets*." He cups his hands in front of his chest, as he says the word and gives me a devilish look. Immediately, I can't wait to find out more about Sylvia's assets.

We spend our coffee and lunch breaks sitting on buckets in front of our little shed, watching the rest of the dealership at work, everyone doing their part to try and sell cars. Sometimes Mr Allister comes and stands beside us, visiting. He carefully eats his orange or peach, while slightly leaning forward to avoid spilling any juice on his shirt and tie. It amuses me to see the two of them, father and son, interacting, one a smaller younger version of the other, both of them so similar. While both are short, Mr Allister is wide and stocky where Terry is narrow and lean. Both are strong people. You can see it in the way that they touch things or lift items with little or no effort.

Terry and his Dad speak almost in code about a secret project that Terry has been working on. Every time he visits us, Mr Allister asks his son the same question, with the same smirk on his face. "Is it ready yet? Is it done?"

And every day he gets the same answer, "still some quirks, Dad, still some things that I'm trying to work out. It'll be done soon." Terry gives his father *his* version of the Allister smirk and continues munching on his sandwich while the three of us watch Starvin' Marvin trying to entice a middle aged woman to get into the driver's seat of a shiny red convertible.

"Well," Mr Allister stretches out the *well*, while finishing his fruit and winking at us both before returning to his office in the showroom, "you be sure and let me know when it's done, son. I'm looking forward to seeing it. You boys have a good afternoon."

I never ask what *it* is and they never offer. After hearing the conversation a few times, I begin to wonder if there really is a secret project or if it's just some kind of an inside joke that Canadian fathers play with their sons. I always nod politely and smile when they have their conversation just in case I'm supposed to know what *it* is, and that somehow, with all the new information that I'm learning, I've managed to forget.

We always wait right until the end of our lunch break before resuming work. It's not because we want to maximize our break before getting back to car washing and moving and loading supplies. It's because at three minutes before our break ends, Gloria and Sylvia, with her assets, sneak out the back door of the office and smoke their cigarettes. Gloria wears large, dark rimmed glasses that she's constantly taking off and cleaning. She's small and dark haired and seems to almost cower against the wall as she smokes, while Sylvia is exactly the opposite. Sylvia has large, wild, red hair and cannot talk without excitedly waving her arms in the air. With every movement that she makes, her tremendous assets fly up in the air, before gravity takes them back to their resting place.

"Red, she's wearing red again. Shit. Why does it always have to be red? Red drives me mental. It really does. And look at the cleavage, Malcolm. I'll bet you don't see cleavage like that in Scotland, do you?"

From our spots in front of the shed, peering between the rows of parked cars that await our attention, we watch her, but of course we're not really watching *her* at all. She seems to be almost twirling around, cigarette in one hand, and her free arm waving, while talking to Gloria. "I don't think so, Terry. I can't remember ever seeing cleavage like that in Scotland."

As though she's been listening, she immediately turns, and her bright, make-upped face is staring directly towards us. "Whatcha starin' at, Scottie? You never seen a couple of girls having a smoke before?" When she says the word *Scottie*, she poorly imitates my accent, drawing the word out, mocking me.

I can feel my face redden and my insides shrink all at the same time. I try to move, to speak, to do anything, but I'm glued to the bucket that I'm sitting on. Sylvia shows no mercy as she continues to stare us down across the parking lot, her arms raised, as though she's waiting for an answer. Her assets are still there, and are every bit as prominent, but it's her look and the way she called me *Scottie*, that have rendered me speechless.

Minutes pass in my head, as she continues to stare me down before Terry rescues me. "Just enjoying the day, ladies. Just enjoying the day." He's on his feet, and has his lunch kit inside the shed; before it occurs to me that I can actually stand up and don't have to keep staring at the woman across the parking lot, whose arms are still up in the air as her cigarette smokes from her hand.

"You boys be careful in that shed back there. You never know what's going on in a cute little hiding place like that." I daren't look back, but I hear her laughing and know that she's turned away and is looking at Gloria. I decide that I like Gloria and am sorry that she has to witness my humiliation. I can't imagine that she's laughing too. I can't tell though, as I do everything in my power to ignore my burning face and try to completely concentrate

45

on pouring one and a half scoops of green powdered soap into the full bucket of water that Terry has mercifully placed in front of me.

CHAPTER 7

I've become a master at identifying the differences between the rains of Kilmarnock and the rains of Vancouver. In Kilmarnock, the rain is cold and often horizontal. It comes at you from the strangest of angles and instantly feels as though it's soaked, not just through your clothes, but through you entire body. Vancouver's rain is warmer and friendlier. Both can be constant and aggravating. And although I experience Vancouver's only in the summer, it's still often relentless.

Terry and I wash cars between rainstorms, and in the times in between, we busy ourselves tidying our shed, or helping George and the other mechanics in the shop. I love the physical nature of the work. Even on weekends, when I'm trying to stay out of my mother's way, I think about the feeling of carrying the heavy hose around, or lifting boxes of supplies from the truck to the loading area at the rear of the office.

My body begins to feel different. As I drive home in the evenings, with George singing along to the radio, or as the three of us are eating dinner, I can feel differences in the oddest places. My shoulders go from being stiff and sore to being solid. I run the palm of my hand along my shoulder blades and notice how hard they've become. My hands and forearms and wrists change too. Instead of being firm and functional, they are now solid and strong. Even when I tie my shoelaces, my fingers feel different, bigger, tougher. And of course I am growing. My mother and I were able to stand shoulder to shoulder the previous summer but now I feel taller and certainly broader than her small frame.

We settle into a routine of jovial drives to work and evenings eating my mother's special casserole. Occasionally, she'll have Chinese take-out ready for us, laid out in large styrofoam containers. When George asks her about her day she tells him that she's busy, working on herself. Neither of us understand what this means, but we still gratefully eat her casseroles or take-out food.

Every Friday, on payday, we pay her. George takes some of his money and puts it into the jar on the top of the fridge, then slips some bills into her hands, or when he thinks that I'm not watching, down the front of her blouse. I can't remember my father ever giving her money in quite the same way, but I like George, and I appreciate the fact that he waits until he thinks that I'm not watching before he does it. I wait until he's in the other room, turning on the television, and then sign my own paycheque over to her. It's for room and board and to help pay for my airline flights, she tells me. Then she takes one of the bills that George has given her and hands it over to me for pocket money. It's more money than I ever have in Kilmarnock, and I'm glad to have it, so I don't feel the need to remind her that it's my father's overtime hours that pay for my flights back and forth.

On weekends, it's George's job to cook, and he barbecues hamburgers and hotdogs, or sometimes even salmon in the backyard. The salmon is cooked in a foil and covered in pieces of onion and lemon, then sprinkled with lots of salt and pepper. It's unlike any fish that I've ever tasted, and my appetite for it is almost insatiable.

"If you don't stop eating all that salmon you're going to bust your gut through that tee-shirt, Malcolm. Slow down for heaven's sake." My mother is reclining in a lawn chair, her oversized sunglasses jiggling as she laughs, and scolds me at the same time.

George has placed another piece of fish on the barbecue and the sweet smell mixed with the odour of the charcoal is making me salivate. He's trying to watch the hockey game on the living room television through the patio doors while re-arranging the fish on the grill. "Grab me some of them there briquettes that are in the hallway cupboard, Mal. Hurry, we don't want your fish going cold."

My mother and I share a strange moment as we glance at each other, knowing that George doesn't seem to be in need of briquettes, and that they certainly aren't kept in the hallway cupboard. It isn't until she nods at me with a puzzled look on her face, that I get up from my place at the outdoor table and shuffle my way into the house.

There are no briquettes in the cupboard. In fact, there is very little in there other than a pile of clothing folded and sitting neatly in the middle of the floor. George's voice comes booming from the backyard as I stand motionless in front of the open door, "Pick them up, Mal. Pick them up and bring them out here."

With the exception of my school uniforms I can't remember ever having worn new clothes, but these ones are certainly new. They have labels and pins in them and some of them are covered in plastic wrapping. Twice a year, my father and I scour the local church jumble sale to find the best hardly worn work clothes for him and casual clothes for me. These are different though. They have a smell about them, a smell that says they've never been worn.

I come back to the table with the pile of jeans and t-shirts, and long-sleeved shirts, held in my outstretched arms, afraid to acknowledge that they are indeed meant for me. My mother is sitting up now, her sunglasses in her hands and she too, keeps her eyes fixed on the clothes.

"Thought you might like to freshen up that look of yours, Mal. And besides, you lean over that hose one more time in those ratty old shorts, you're gonna split them wide open. And that isn't something that any of us want to see, Mal, believe me." He's watching me and smiling as he says it, barely paying attention to the fish at all.

I put my hand on top of the pile of clothes and hold them tight. The smell is even better than the smell of the salmon. I want to rub the new fabric against my face but make do with just feeling it touch my hand.

"It's his father's responsibility, George. I told you that. It's the agreement that I have with his father. We should not be buying him clothes. That wasn't agreed to, not at all." She's not really angry with him, I can tell. She has her angry face on, but her voice isn't raised and her expression remains steady as she reclines back into her lawn chair.

For once George ignores her and turning from the grill, he looks straight at me as though she isn't even there. "Go on, go try them on, or you're gonna drop them all over my absolutely perfectly barbecued salmon fillet."

He ruffles my hair and pushes me away when I thank him. It's not until I'm in my room that I hear pieces of their conversation. I can't hear what my mother says but George's response is loud and forceful enough that it can't be missed.

"The boy works hard for the little money that he gets, Agnes. Let him enjoy his new clothes. God knows, he deserves it."

I don't want to hear anymore. I want that to be the last thing said about me and my clothes for the night, so I do what I've learnt to do. I hum. I lay out the clothes on my bed and quietly hum to myself, concentrating on the words from the Bruce Springsteen song that is playing in my head. It works; I can't hear any more of the conversation outside. My imagination takes me to the world that he sings about mixed up with my own world. It's a world of fast cars, and washing cars, and girls, and of course new

50

clothes that smell like they've never been worn. The cars in my mind are always sparkling clean and never really need to be washed, and the girls always look the same. I've tried to change my mental image of them when I've performed this exercise before, but it never works. It's always the same girl. She always has flaming red hair and tremendous assets and she's smoking. She's always smoking that cigarette and waving her arm around while her assets bounce up and down, over and over again.

CHAPTER 8

The weeks turn into months and as July becomes August, summer finally begins to appear. The days of rain and wet change to warm days, and the cars at Mr. Allister's car lot get dusty instead of grimy. The salesmen get grouchier in the heat, and a certain secretary wears less and less clothing. Terry and I continue to monitor Marvin and her whenever we're able, and of course inspect our shed for any signs of illicit activity. Terry is a year older than I am and seems to know what he's looking for as he checks whether our boxes of rags or buckets of chemicals have been disturbed. I only lift things up and put them back down, pretending that I know what would be involved with their secret encounter.

"Try to be careful with that stuff, Malcolm. It's still not done."

It takes me a moment as I hold in my hand a crudely fashioned length of pipe that seems to have pinholes all through it before I realize that I am holding the "it" that Mr Allister asks his son about every day. I place the pipe back on a pile beside the other pieces that have the same holes in them and the same odd shaped fittings attached to their ends, and realize that Terry is almost holding his breath while watching me.

I don't need to ask the question; somehow I know that he'll tell me. We've washed enough cars together and spied on enough salesmen and secretaries for some kind of a bond to have been formed, so I pick the piping back up and hold it carefully, waiting for an answer.

"You can't tell anyone, Malcolm, not George, not Marvin, not any of the asshole salesmen, no one."

"I don't talk to Marvin, Terry, you know that, and if you don't want anyone to know then don't tell me."

"It's not that I don't want you to know. It's just that it's not done yet, Malcolm. I can't get it done by myself."

And with that statement and the famous Allister smirk, Terry enlists me in helping him finish his project.

We work after the office closes in the evening, when there is only Marvin or one of the other salespeople up front, sitting with their feet on their desks. They can't see us from the dealership, as the shed is in the way, and we're in the open area at the far end of the lot. George actually sounds disappointed when I tell him that I'm going to spend some time with Terry after work, and that Mr Allister will give me a ride home. He's quick to recover though, probably glad to be spending some time alone with my mother. Grinning, he tells me that it's okay to get into a little bit of trouble but not too much, and turns the music up, backing his car out onto the road.

It takes two nights of climbing ladders and assembling pipes and fittings and brushes and wires before *it* begins to take shape and I start to see what we're building.

"I can't believe you don't see it, Malcolm. It's pretty obvious to me, and to anyone else that might stumble by here."

I think I know what it is, but I'm enjoying teasing my friend and his 8 foot high by 20 foot long contraption far too much. "Well, if I could see the plan, Terry, then maybe I'd have a clue, but I've yet to see the plan."

"It's all up here, Malcolm," he says pointing at his head with his finger and smiling, "I see things that I want to make but there's never a plan. They're always just in my head."

It isn't until he asks me to get a couple of scoops of the green soap from the shed that I realize I can't keep pretending any longer.

"Oh, Terry. It's brilliant. What a great idea."

I rush back with the soap from the shed, not bothering to close the already open door, and stand back, admiring his creation. We've built an apparatus with pipes and hoses running along the roofline and walls. There are two pumps, one at each end, and a bucket, that is raised to the roof, where we place the soap. There are brushes attached to cables that are in turn attached to an old steering wheel. There's no provision for drying them but if it works the way he says it works in his head, then his unsightly structure will wash and rinse the cars automatically. At the edge of Mr Allister's car lot, tucked behind our shed, we've built a car wash.

Although he isn't old enough to drive on the roads legally, Terry is allowed to drive the cars around the lot, and he pulls a dirty, black station wagon carefully under the rows of suspended pipes and hoses.

"I'll plug it in, Malcolm. I want to wire in a switch and then hard wire it all, but for now I'll just plug it in to test it."

I think of the cartoons that I watch with George on Saturday mornings. The Roadrunner will flip a switch or turn a dial, then wait for mayhem to strike. Something always blows up or catches on fire and it never, ever, works out the way it should. Terry's invention doesn't operate that way. It does everything that it did while it played in his head. The water comes out and completely rinses the car when we turn the fitting to the first position. We pull on a rope and the soap drops from the bucket and suds up the vehicle. He calls for me to wind up the old steering wheel and the brushes firmly scrub the vehicle down. Then, when we turn the fitting once more, the car is rinsed perfectly clean. The whole process takes about ten minutes and the car looks as clean as if we had scrubbed it ourselves.

I'm giddy and can hardly contain myself. I haven't jumped up and down in many years, so I just clap my hands and laugh and congratulate my friend on the perfection of his homemade car wash.

"I don't like the pressure on the final rinse, Malcolm. I think we need to regulate that a bit. If I can get the PSI's up a bit then it'll shorten the wash time."

"You dumb shit, don't you know what you've done here. You've probably invented the world's first homemade car wash and you've done it with old parts that your dad had lying around. You should be happy; this is a very, very good thing that you've done." I'm still laughing, and my frustration at my friend's reluctance to celebrate is only half-hearted.

He stands back and looks at it proudly. "It does look good, doesn't it? You know I have these things in my head and I see them so clearly sometimes that it almost hurts. I just know that I have to get them out; it's the only way for it to stop hurting. So I make them, or I try to anyways. This is the biggest one though, for sure. This is definitely the biggest one."

It occurs to me that we're looking at the car wash as though we're parents fawning over our first-born, or at least a proud master watching his dog give birth to pups. "You should call it something; you should give it a name."

He laughs but it's a Terry laugh, a warm, generous laugh. "You're right, you're right. I was just thinking that. It's Brutus. We're going to call it Brutus."

"That's a good name. That's a very good name for a car wash, Terry. It's a Brutus."

Still smiling his infectious grin, he corrects me. "Nope, it's not a Brutus, Malcolm. It's Brutus, just Brutus."

It's hard to turn away from Brutus but we know that Mr Allister will be sounding the car horn soon and driving around the front of the showroom, waiting to take us home, so we start to clean up the assorted spare parts that are lying around. It isn't until we're within a few feet of the shed, our arms loaded down with parts and tools that we realize that the door is ajar with the padlock lying on the ground.

"You left it open when you went to get the soap. It doesn't matter; I doubt that anyone is going to be back here at night anyways."

As I lay the equipment outside the shed, I try to mentally retrace my steps and remember exactly how the door looked when I had come to get the soap. "Yeah, you're right, I did leave it open but you know what? It was open when I got here. We must have left it that way when we started working tonight. It definitely was open when I got the soap. I would have been too excited to get the lock undone."

It takes a moment before we realize what has happened and Terry is up the little step and into the shed before I am. "Dirty bastard, dirty old bastard. He's been in here. He's been in here with *her*, and we missed it. I can smell the sex. I know I can. I know damn well that I didn't leave that door unlocked. I know that I locked it up. Dammit, he's been in here and we missed the whole thing."

All I can smell are the damp rags hanging from the rafters and the same smell that always seems to be in the old shed, but Terry seems certain as he stomps around without touching anything.

I try to think if there had been anything out of place when I came back earlier, anything that might not have seemed right. I'm sure that I would have noticed, sure that I would have seen another person. The only area that looks different is on the floor where the parts for Brutus had previously sat. "Maybe there, Terry, if anywhere, they might have been there."

"You're right; you're right, look at the bag of rags stacked there, they used that as a pillow, didn't they? There's no way that was there before, no way." He takes a minute and I know that it's not anger on his face, just frustration. It isn't about catching Marvin doing something in his Dad's car lot that he shouldn't be doing. It's about something else. It's about a certain secretary and her assets and perhaps even catching a glimpse of those assets. I know this because it's exactly the way that I'm feeling, and even though we don't admit it to each other; I know that it's a shared feeling.

A strange flicker of excitement flashes across his face, the same flicker that happened when I first saw him talking to his father about his invention. "You know what. I've got an idea. Don't touch a thing. Just leave it all there. Let him think that we don't know. Let him think that he's gotten away with it. You and I are going to come back tomorrow night and the night after that too if we have to. We'll pretend that we are still working on Brutus. I've got a way; I've got a way that'll catch both of them."

He built a car wash from a picture in his head using junk that was just lying around, so there's no doubt in my mind that we're going to catch them. I just don't exactly know how. I imagine a hidden camera with a huge screen set up on the back wall so that we can view it while sitting on our overturned buckets, or a tape recorder hidden in a hollowed out soap bucket. He doesn't seem to be frustrated now; he just looks like he's processing. His eyes come alive as he puts away the leftover parts that Brutus didn't need and he's excited again, excited and alive, probably picturing his next invention in his head.

We make absolutely certain this time that the padlock is in place on the door when we lock it for the night, and by the time we reach the front showroom, Mr Allister is leaning against his car, listening to Marvin as he tells him about his latest conquest. It's difficult to tell from the partial conversation that we overhear whether Marvin is talking about a woman that he's had his way with or a deal that he's closed.

"I'm telling you, Bill, when it's there, it's there. It just takes the right man to push her buttons. And let me tell you, I knew exactly where her buttons were." Marvin is leering and his body bends at the waist in an unnatural manner as he tells his story.

Mr Allister seems relieved to see us as he turns away from Marvin, "Here they come, the two amigos. How was your evening, guys? Interested in stopping for some pizza on the way home?" His smile is different from the one he gave to Marvin while listening to his story. It's friendlier, more genuine.

"Pizza sounds good, Dad. It's hungry work getting this thing up and running. Just another night or two and we're all set. Just a couple more nights of Malcolm and me working and *it* will be all done." He sounds a bit insincere to me, but no one else seems to notice as his father mockingly punches him on the shoulder and grins. Marvin stands back, teetering from one long, skinny leg to the other and sweating, sweating even though the sun disappeared an hour earlier. Even as we climb into the car, he still stands there, sweating and leering. Terry smiles and waves, then flips his middle finger in the salesman's direction but it doesn't faze him one bit. He just keeps watching as we drive away. He's not watching Terry and his rude gesture though. He doesn't seem interested in him at all. He's staring hard, directly at me, only at me, of that I'm certain, absolutely certain.

CHAPTER 9

My father calls every Saturday night. Even though he's thousands of miles away, it's easy for me to picture him, pacing back and forth on the creaky floorboards in the upstairs neighbour's house. His strong Scottish words come through loud and clear. George politely says, hello Alex, to him, then tries to hand the phone to my mother who waves her hands, and mouths the words, *Malcolm, give it to Malcolm.*

He tells me about Celtic's latest fitba game that he's heard on the radio, and then asks if I'm eating enough and getting enough sleep. He's stiff and formal on the telephone as though his conversation is being listened to by many, and in a way it is, as his booming voice reaches everyone in the room. We're in the family room, which is the Canadian room that holds the television and stereo, and George has politely turned the volume down in order for me to speak to my Dad.

"Your voice is changing, Malcolm. It's cracking, you sound different to me. You sound like a Canadian." He's disappointed and bemused at the same time. I know my father. I can hear the emotions in his voice.

"I'm no, Dad. I'm still the same." I easily lapse back into my Scottish accent and leave the newly acquired Canadian one alone for a moment. George smiles, while my mother mocks me by mouthing my words. And then I do something that I've never done. Maybe it's an aftermath of hearing her talk about my new clothes, or maybe it's the way she's trying to ridicule me to George. I hand her the phone, and tell her that my Dad wants to talk to her.

George sits up straighter, but still keeps his eyes on the television set, as my mother hesitates, then angrily pulls the phone from my hand. "Yes, Alex, he's well. All is fine here, nothing to worry about at all. He's such a smart boy, a smart, smart boy." She says the words harshly, while looking at me as though she's trying to expel something distasteful from her mouth.

"It's the discipline that the masters instil in him here, Agnes. They put up with no guff, none at all. He's always top of his class in his studies," I overhear my father saying back to her.

My saving grace has always been my studies. The answers come easily to me. While my classmates struggle, I seem to have this ability to go from problem to solution with little effort. I sometimes feel as though I carry a map, and the rest of them are searching for signposts. Whereas Terry can build things after seeing them in his head, my strength is numbers. I seem to instinctively know how to find the answers, without knowing the precise formulas that have to be learnt in order to get me there. My mother usually takes little interest in my marks or grades, but I know that this time she won't give credit to my father, or Scotland and its schools for that matter. She's out of her chair now, standing upright and very straight, and is quick to respond to his proud boasts.

"I don't know, Alex. I just see a lot of myself in him. I was always a very quick learner. I'm more inclined to believe that it comes directly from me."

The back of George's chair moves as he straightens up yet again, while he listens to her comment, and it looks like the little hairs on the back of his neck are standing up. She cuts my Dad off, and quickly ends the conversation, telling him that he can call again next Saturday if he so desires. It's very quiet all of a sudden, as she hangs up, without giving me the option of talking to him again.

As she sits back down in the large recliner beside George, I wait for the scorn that usually comes. I wait for her usual comment, where she tells me that I sound like 'a common Scot.' There's nothing though. She just smiles a strange smile and keeps watching me, watching me and smiling. I can't hold her gaze. I never have been able to. So, I just stare down at my feet, before quickly excusing myself to go to my room.

It takes three days before it happens, but it does indeed happen. Terry has rigged wires and boxes and gadgets inside our shed. He nods and winks and tells me what I can touch and what I can't touch. There is a large switch that he's installed that we have to turn on and off every time we leave. It's from a train station, he says. They switch it when they need to divert the train from one track to another, and he's wired all of the controls into it. There are three horns hidden just behind the rafters in the ceiling, and he's taken out the light and replaced it with what looks like a very large bell. Our little shed is alarmed as though it were Fort Knox. It won't go off right away when the door is opened though. It's rigged to wait for two minutes, *just long enough for them to start getting comfortable,* Terry tells me. I almost feel sorry for Marvin, almost that is, until he takes his usual daily jabs at us.

"You little perverts finished building your amusement ride yet, or are you gonna stay late whacking off back there every fricking night of the week?" He's wearing the same suit that he wears every day, with the same coffee stains on the lapel, as he stands yelling at us from the back of the showroom.

I keep scrubbing the car in front of me, and Terry keeps hosing it down, as we try to pretend that he's not there. Then in his usual fashion, Terry flips him the bird just as he's about to turn away from us.

"Careful, you little bastard, I'd hate for your father to see you displaying that disgusting kind of behaviour towards his top earner." His leer is so intense, so repulsive that it's impossible to feel sorry for him. Starvin' Marvin is at the lowest end of the food chain. I'd heard both Terry and Mr. Allister describe him that way, and I'm beginning to understand what they mean.

Terry just smiles and keeps hosing down the car. He knows, we both know, that if our guess is correct, soon Marvin won't be leering quite so much. Finally, he gets tired of us ignoring him and slinks back to his office.

It's supposed to happen at night when there are fewer people around. Marvin works almost every evening, and we assume that Sylvia sneaks away and joins him in our shed, while we're in the back of the yard, on top of Brutus. We're not sure where she smokes afterwards, but we know she must smoke somewhere, after rolling around with Marvin and his greasy suit.

Our prediction is close but it isn't perfect. We end up being wrong about two things, two very important things. First, it's not after hours when the alarm goes off, it's 4:15 in the afternoon and everyone is still working at the dealership.

The noise is deafening. The bell that we mounted in place of the light is ringing as though warning us of a train barrelling through the middle of the dealership. All three buzzers are howling simultaneously, and there are people yelling. I don't know who they are or what they're saying, but it's loud, very, very loud.

Our immediate reaction isn't to run to the shed, but to cover our ears. The noise is painful, just painful. It's awkward to run as fast as we can with our hands over our ears, but somehow, staggering in our excited state, we manage it.

Everyone from the dealership is staring at the shed and its open door. Even George and the mechanics have come from the shop, ears covered with their black greasy hands, menacingly surveying the proceedings. Mr Allister is holding his tie and forcing his way past everyone to see what the commotion is. And, to my surprise and dismay, Gloria and Sylvia are standing off to one side. They alternate between covering their ears to drown out the sound, and covering their mouths in shock. I can't stop staring at Sylvia, wondering why she's there, and she keeps staring back at me. They all seem to be staring at me, not at Terry, just at me.

When I do turn and look at our noisy shed, Marvin is backing out the door and pulling up his pants. We were right about him. That part we'd predicted correctly. Unfortunately it's not red hair on white shoulders that I see coming from the shed. It's blonde. It's the familiar blonde hair that I have known all my life. The second thing that we'd been wrong about was the girl. We had the wrong one. Sylvia is standing right there with Gloria, alternately staring at me and then at the shed, along with everyone else.

The noise doesn't seem to bother my mother at all. She just steps daintily from the shed, straightening the skirt that George bought her, and returns everyone's stares. She's dressed up the way she gets sometimes to make herself feel better, and looks as casual as though we've caught her innocently drying the dishes. As she walks past, she doesn't look at me, but her gaze does linger briefly on George, before she makes her way to the front of the dealership. Terry stands closer, supporting me, I suppose, giving them all something else to stare at. My mother just keeps on walking, seemingly oblivious to all of us now, as she weaves her way in between the cars, her high heels clicking on the asphalt.

George drops his hands from his ears and stares a sad, sad look at my mother as she passes by. Marvin is running. I'm not sure where. Maybe he thinks that George will be coming for him. He doesn't have to worry though. George is lost. I know that look. I'm familiar with it. He isn't interested in Marvin at all. He's just lost.

As Mr. Allister yells at Terry to *shut that cotton picking thing off*, I realize that I know very little about life. I'm fourteen years old and I have one Scottish friend and a new Canadian friend. I like the music that George has shown me and the way that it makes me feel. Sometimes there is nothing better than being with my dad. But I know nothing, absolutely nothing, about my mother. I certainly don't know why she did it, or how she managed it without anyone knowing, or even how often. I don't even know how she knows Marvin. There is only one thing I know for sure, and as I look over at my Canadian friend and the rest of the workers as they stare at the poor little Scottish boy, I feel as though they know it too. My Canadian summer has come to an end, and I'll be heading back to Kilmarnock very, very soon.

CHAPTER 10

You can stare out the same window for a long, long time and see nothing. Even if there's something happening out there, it can barely register in your mind. George and I do this. We watch the comings and goings of the street. We see people leaving for work. We see the odd stranger or friend arriving at the same doors later in the day, then leaving afterwards, and we see the same people coming home from work. I'm not watching for any particular reason, other than just to watch. And George, well, he's looking and not seeing. He has this vacant stare in his eyes. He looks as though he's asleep and awake at the same time. Every time the phone rings he tells me to let the machine answer it, and continues to watch the outside world from the safety of his recliner, while the television remains turned off.

"George, it's Bill, listen, you take as much time as you need, Pardner. Sort out things on the home front, make that right first. You come back when you feel like it. No worries at all. You just take your time." I can picture him adjusting his tie with one hand and holding the phone with the other. Then, in what sounds like an afterthought, he adds, "Oh, and tell the kid that everything will be okay. Tell him it's all okay. And oh yeah, Terry says hey, and Brutus too-whoever the hell Brutus is."

I smile at the thought of Terry, probably whispering to his Dad, while Mr Allister leaves the message for us. There is no mention of my returning to work, so I assume that my days as a Lot Lizard are over.

"Georgie, it's Rosie, call me honey. You call me, and stay strong. You just stay strong." Rose is George's sister, and although I've never met her I know that his eyes almost always light up when he talks about her. It doesn't matter who calls; his expression still doesn't change, as the messages accumulate on the machine. He just keeps staring as though he just doesn't care what happens. When we finally hear my mother's voice, he makes no effort to get up, but tells me to take the call if I want to.

"Malcolm. Malcolm." There is a long pause, and I stay in my seat, listening to the frustration in her voice grow as we sit there, ignoring her. "Fine. Malcolm, I want you to get ready to leave, and yes, I have notified your father that you're going home. Make sure you pack everything that's in that house that belongs to you. There'll be a ticket at the airport waiting on Friday. If you have a problem getting there," another pause, "just let me know and I'll make alternative arrangements for you. I will try very hard to be at the airport, but my schedule is very, very hectic right now." Then, there is a longer pause before she comes back and in quite a breezy, carefree voice, gives us the flight numbers and times. And finally, with what sounds to me like the slightest of hesitations, she says goodbye and that she'll be in touch.

It's difficult to describe how her voice sounded. She didn't sound worried or concerned at all, but then again I hadn't expected her to be. I decide that perhaps I know my mother a little better than I thought I did. She's a survivor, I can see that now. And, she'll remake herself into whatever she has to in order to survive. Is she with Marvin, or is there someone else? It doesn't matter to me, and from the look on George's face, it doesn't seem to matter to him either.

I thought he'd fallen asleep, but a few minutes after she leaves the message he tells me that he's going to keep his promise, the promise that he made weeks ago. Although part of me knew that he would, part of me wishes that he wouldn't. Truthfully, I just want to leave. I don't want to think about the look on those people's faces as they watched my mother climb out of that shed. I want to go home, even though it's earlier than usual, and run away from it all.

"We're still going, Mal. We're still going to go, just like I told you we would. A man keeps his promise; a man always keeps his promise."

"George, you don't have to, it doesn't matter. You really don't have to." I want to go, and I don't want to go. It's hard to explain. I want it to be the way it was before, and I want his face to light up the way it did when he first told me that he would be taking me to a concert, a real rock concert. Now things are different. Now it doesn't seem as though he's taking me to show me what the music will feel like. Now it seems as though he's taking me out of a sense of duty. Either way, I can tell by his solemn look that we're going, and I'll have one more new experience on my last night in Vancouver.

They're just local boys, probably not much older than I am, but they play in a band, a real band, and that's something that I've never seen before. George explains to me about festival seating. That means the earlier you get there, the better seating, or standing in this case, you can count on. It doesn't matter though; we don't have to line up for seats. He knows a guy. George always knows a guy. When we arrive, our local park looks as though it has been taken over by some kind of a circus. There are large green tents set up with young women selling beer and pop, and a stage has been erected in the middle of a cluster of trees where crowds of excited young people press up against each other, waiting, waiting for something to happen.

He can see my look of concern and answers before I can even ask. "Don't worry, I told you. I know a guy." He almost smiles, and I try to smile back. It's the best that I've seen him in days, and all of a sudden it almost feels like me and George again, me and George riding to work in his big car, listening to loud music.

With his big hand gently pushing on my back, he leads me to the back of the stage. Then, with a nod to a man who is even larger than George, we slide past generators that are humming and step over large power cords until we are standing directly off to the side. There are a couple of young men pulling on cords and checking wires, but for the most part we are alone. We have the perfect view and our timing is ideal. George pushes me in front of him, and I put my hands on the lip of the stage, just as the boys pick up their instruments and the drummer half stands, half sits, and bangs his sticks together in time.

I don't know if they are good or bad. There are two of them playing electric guitars. One stays towards the back, and then sheepishly ventures out from time to time, before retreating back to his microphone. The other is more flamboyant and winks at the girls, while wandering along the front, tilting his guitar towards the crowd. He sings most of the songs. There is another boy who sports a very fine wispy moustache, playing what looks like an electric piano, and he sings too. And of course the drummer is at the back, in a world of his own, hitting his drums with amazing accuracy and rhythm. The young people in the crowd grow noisier and yell louder when the popular songs of the day are played, but offer only polite applause when the band announces their own, original music. I enjoy it all. I enjoy watching them each contribute in their own way to the sound, and I enjoy feeling George's hand resting on my shoulder from time to time. It isn't until near the end of their show, when they play their last song, that I start to feel it though. I start to feel the way that I felt that first time in George's car.

The lead singer is controlling the music this time. Smiling playfully, he nods to each of his band mates for a moment, before a final definitive nod to the drummer, who's waiting patiently, perched once again, half-standing, half-sitting, on his little stool behind the drums. Then, with his nod, the music begins, but it doesn't sound like it did before. It doesn't sound like four young boys each playing their own instruments. Instead, it sounds like one solid piece of music blasting in waves from the stage right over me and into the whole park. There are no gaps as the sound from the guitars meets the melody of the piano while the rhythm of the drums holds it all together. I don't know the song and it doesn't matter. It's all just music. It just sounds right, and I realize that I'm holding onto the stage as though letting go would cause me to fall. The flamboyant guitar player sings the song, but never seems to forget about the other boys in the band. They're all a part of every word that comes out of his mouth, as he looks almost pleadingly towards them, coaxing the right music from their instruments. He wanders towards the other guitar player, or the keyboard player, and somehow pulls them into the song by smiling a secretive smile at them, or just nodding, nodding as though there's something going on that only they can sense, only they can feel. He's wrong of course because I can feel it too. I feel part of it, part of whatever magical thing is happening up on the stage. Finally at the end he looks over at the drummer, and from our vantage point I can tell what he's doing. I can tell what he's saying to the drummer, even though there are no words exchanged. He's asking him if it's time.

He's asking if it's time to stop, or do they keep going, keep whatever it is that they've just created alive for a moment or two longer. Somehow an agreement is made and with sweeping thumps along every drum that is balanced in front of him, the drummer ends the song while the guitar player looks one last time at each of the other members, before flipping his sweaty head towards the crowd and mock bowing to the applause.

It's not just the music. The music is important, I can see that, but it's more than that. The music is just part of it. It's the relationships. It's the relationship that the music forms between the boys that are playing, and it's what they do with it. They played music all night, but somehow in that last song, for four or five minutes, they created something else, and that was what George had wanted me to experience. That's why he brought me, that part I know for sure.

The crowd edges its way over towards us and there are young people now standing beside me, witnessing the music, calling out for more. I have to almost pry my hands from the stage, as I've been so intent on listening to the band, feeling their music, that I forgot for a moment where I was or what has been happening for the past few days. George's hand is gone from my shoulder and when I look back his face is wet with tears. When he tries to speak the big man has to lean down and press his head against mine so that I can hear him, as the crowd around us keeps cheering for more.

"It's got nothing to do with you and me, Mal. It's got nothing to do with us, remember that. It's her and me, and you and her, but it's not me and you. Me and you is a different thing, a different thing altogether. You and me is here and now, and that last song, and how it makes us feel, and there's nothing, Mal, nothing, that she can do to change that." Tears run down his face as he speaks to me, and I can feel their wetness against my own cheeks. I don't even try to stop from crying. I just let the tears come. And when he puts his arm around me, leading us away from the crowd and back to his car, I let him, wishing that we could just stay that way for a long, long time.

Never underestimate the healing power of a torrential Scottish rainstorm. It really is a wonderful thing to behold. As we ride the bus home from the airport, my Dad is telling me about the changes that he's made since I left, while I watch the rain falling angrily from the magnificent black sky. He's working as a janitor now. The pay is higher and the work is regular. Things are better now, much better. We might be able to move to a bigger place, get our own phone line installed, and perhaps even buy an automobile. He's right of course. Things will be better. I can tell already. He talks about Celtic, our fitba team, and all of the things that have happened in the neighbourhood. He pauses from time to time, and

I expect him to ask me about Canada, or why I've come home early, but he doesn't. Mercifully, he just keeps telling me, in his own way, that he's missed me. I'm too tired from the flight to turn towards him, so I just rest my head against the window and listen.

The rain buckets down, and lashes against the houses that we pass, as though it's trying to wipe the greyness right off them. I'm dressed in clothes that George has bought for me, a pair of shorts that I seem to be outgrowing already and a tee-shirt from the concert the night before. The music is fainter in my head now, and it's not boys jumping up and down on a stage that I see. It's rain, just rain, bleeding its wondrous colours through the mud of the Kilmarnock streets. I know these streets and what happens on them. There are few surprises here, and when I think about Canada and Brutus and George and Terry and Marvin, and of course my mother and all the things that happened, none of it really makes any sense to me. So, I decide that I'm glad to be home. I'm glad to be back in the safety of my black and white world. I'm glad to be back with my Dad.

CHAPTER 11

School Picture Day always seems to come far too early. It should be sometime after Christmas. It should be once we've had time to settle into our classes, once we've realized that the little bit of freedom that summer gave us, is gone. It's not though; it's the same every year. At the beginning of September, we're marched, class by class, into the gymnasium, where a terrified looking photographer waits to take our pictures.

Hextall, with his cane tapping at his side, and Mr McRae, the Physical Education Master, line us up on a shaky old set of bleachers according to our height, tallest to shortest. I've moved this year. Instead of being in the middle row, I've made my way all the way to the back, standing with the tallest boys in my class. So, either everyone else has shrunk, or I really am growing very quickly. Hardly, on the other hand, the shortest boy in our class, is in the same spot he always occupies, right in the middle of the bottom row. I haven't spoken to him since school re-started. I've tried, but when I reach the end of his street, to walk to school with him, he's never there. Then, during class or in the hallways, he turns away, or just nods and keeps on walking. Perhaps he doesn't want to remember the events of last school year, or perhaps he thinks he stands a better chance of getting through Third Form if he's by himself.

The bleachers creak and groan under our weight, and I can't help wonder what Terry would think if he could see me now. While he's studying at his private academy on Vancouver Island, I'm wedged between two of the hard boys in our class, Derek Robertson and Jim Miller. In front of me, one half of the Craven twins, Kev, is trying to touch a scab on the end of his nose with his tongue. His sister, Ang, never far from him, is a row below, glaring at the cameraman, daring him to take her picture.

"Don't point it at me. Don't be pointing that effin' thing at me." She's furiously scratching her head, while yelling at the photographer, and from my vantage point two rows above, I can see red welts where she's dug her nails deep into her scalp.

Hextall hesitates as though he's going to say something to her, but turns away, choosing instead to usher the rest of us into place. "Right, you lot, get yer smiles ready. We want nice smiles for your mithers and faithers, those of you that have mithers and faithers that is."

No, I can't imagine Terry in a place like this. He's more likely to be surrounded by healthy Canadian boys and girls, boys and girls who don't carry knives or pick at scabs, or yell at photographers.

This is an important year. Most of us will turn 15 while in Third Form, and at that point, we no longer have to stay in school. We can join the ranks of the workers who populate the local factories or head to the shipyards of Glasgow. The two knife-carrying boys beside me will have fewer options. Their future likely lies in whatever criminal enterprise their families are involved in. The rest of us, if we maintain our grades, will stay in school, and try to remain at a level that will allow us to qualify for grants, and in turn head to university. My father tells me to keep studying, and if I keep bringing home the marks that I've been getting, there will be many schools that I can qualify for. It's good advice. It sounds like good advice.

Most of the other classes have had their pictures taken, and innocently mill around the outside of the gym, waiting to be dismissed back to their classrooms. Gordon McGregor and Stuart Douglas are amongst them of course, menacingly standing off to the side of the photographer.

"C'moan, gie us a big smile. Smile for yer Mammys and Daddys, those of ye that have Mammys and Daddys that is." Douglas mocks Hextall's words while McGregor confidently goads him on, standing back, laughing at us.

Their words don't bother me and as usual, the whole process is over very quickly anyways. The man says *smile* and *next* almost as though they were one word, with only the glaring light of the camera's flashbulb separating them. Then we're quickly ordered to climb down from the bleachers.

I slowly make my way down from the top level, and can see that Douglas has spotted Hardly, and is leaning into him, waving his hand in front of his mouth, wafting at his breath. Gordon McGregor is still beside him, smiling, with his arms folded, looking every bit like his father, the butcher, as he stands behind his glass counter serving the housewives of our neighbourhood.

All of a sudden, something strange happens. In between trying to keep my balance and not getting shoved off the creaky old bleachers, I smell something. I smell piss. There's no mistaking it. It's piss. I mean, I know it's not there. There's nothing covered in piss, and although our gymnasium has a wide array of semi-unpleasant smells, it's never smelled like piss before, but in my mind I can smell it. It's piss, just piss. The smell and the memory that it brings back infuriates me, and I quicken my pace, actually jumping from the last bleacher, trying to make my way towards Hardly.

It's too late though. By the time I brush past the rest of the kids, the doors of the gymnasium have opened and everyone's crowding out into the hallways. Douglas and McGregor are leading the charge, shoving their way out, and Hardly has somehow disappeared into the crowd himself.

It's strange. Last year I would have cowered behind someone else who was lingering on the bleachers, until Douglas and McGregor had finished with him, but this time I didn't. This time, I made my way towards them. I don't know what I'd intended to do once I got there, or what exactly motivated me to try and reach them. I really don't know. I only know that once I smelled that piss, that same piss smell that I was covered in last year, I couldn't wait to get there. I sit on the bottom bench for a moment where Hardly sat, and realize that the smell is gone and has been replaced by a smell that I know all too well. It's alcohol, stale, foul, alcohol. I recognize it from my time with Hardly last year, and I know that's why Douglas was wafting at his breath, and tormenting him. While I had my own demons to deal with this summer, Hardly has surely had his, and once again, he's back on the booze.

79

My morning walks with Hardly suddenly resume. I don't ask him why he chose to walk without me, or why he's back now. I just enjoy the fact that he's back in his usual spot, standing at the lamppost at the end of his street when I get there. After three or four days, I notice a change in him. The same change that happened before, and I can't stop myself; I have to say something. I just have to acknowledge it.

"You're back to yourself these past few days. It's good. It's good to see." I keep walking with my head down, kicking the rock in front of me, and although he pauses before answering, he does the same, kicking and missing at his rock.

"I stopped, if that's what you mean. Nae booze. Don't need it, doesnae help."

He means it, and he sticks to his commitment. In the mornings he doesn't smell like booze, and at dinnertimes he doesn't sneak away to drink. Life almost becomes normal.

In the evenings, my father and I talk about fitba, and his new job, or we work in the small garden that we share with our neighbours. Second Form is harder than First Form was, but the answers to the lessons still come easily to me, and present few new challenges. I do the mandatory homework of reading and writing and studying, and in between I practice my best smile in the small mirror in our bathroom at home. Bashfully, I try it out on Nan McHendry, as she walks past me in the dinner hall, or from across the school yard if I think she happens to be looking in my direction. Once, she stops, with her two girlfriends hovering beside her, and actually speaks to me while I sit with Hardly, eating my mashed potatoes and mince.

"Hello Malcolm, did you have a nice summer in Canada, then?"

Her voice seems different, different from the way that she talks to the others. It seems as though it's a tone lower, and it's meant just for me. As she speaks, she flicks her dark, silky hair back, peering at me shyly. I quickly try to empty my mouth of potatoes and answer her, but her girlfriend halts my little fantasy, quickly reminding me of who I really am.

"What's wrong with yer teeth, anyways, Malcolm? The way yer always lookin' at Nan, showin' her yer teeth like that. It's no' right. Neither of youse are right in the heed if you ask me." She shakes her head, and looks at the two of us distastefully, trying to pull Nan's arm away.

I don't answer. I just scoop another forkful of potatoes and put them into my mouth, and pretend that I haven't heard anything. Nan leaves of course. She lets her girlfriend pull her away, then turns and admonishes her with a scowl, telling her to leave us alone, and mind her own business. She doesn't laugh at me though, or even smile at her girlfriend's comments; she just walks away, leaving me alone once again, with Hardly.

Hextall is not our Master for any classes this year, but he still patrols the school grounds at dinner time, his trusty cane at his side, preying on the weaker children as they play their harmless games. I watch him as he avoids the bullies of the school, and walks past McGregor and Douglas or any of the young criminals in my class. He speaks to me once and, although it's only a few words they pierce me in a way that's hard to ignore.

"No trees this year, Mr Wilson. No trees for you this year." He's smiling as he says it and taps his cane against the side of his leg as he walks past. I don't detect the smell of piss this time, but it's not far off. I know that it's there somewhere.

Lunch times are either spent walking around the school with Hardly, talking about the masters and our classes, or I run. Mr McRae takes me aside early in the school year and tells me that I'll be running with the track team. He sees my newly acquired long legs and strong arms and I suppose thinks that I'll be a runner for the school. He's right and he's wrong. I enjoy running. In fact, I like it very much. It starts with my legs being stiff and inflexible for the first few minutes as I run around the school yard with the rest of the team, but then after a while they lighten up and I feel no resistance at all. It almost feels like I'm running on air. It doesn't even feel like running. It's more like I've found a way to move and cover distance that I've never known before. So, yes, he is right. I am a runner, but I'm not a runner who will win races for him. I have no interest in whether I can run faster than anyone else on the team. I run to get the feeling-the feeling of weightlessness and levity that comes from running long distances. I settle into the middle of the pack and try to find my pace. Sometimes I pass other runners and sometimes they pass me. I'm never last or even in the last part of the pack, but I also never win. I just have no interest in it, no interest at all.

The only time that I exert any extra effort is if I pass an area on the grounds where Nan might be sitting with her friends. I hunch my body forward a little and push myself harder, trying to get every inch of air to pass by me as quickly as possible. She sees me once or twice, but I don't look over. I pretend to be so intent on running against the others that I don't notice her. I know that she's there, of course, and I know that she isn't just watching us do our regular laps around the school grounds. Her eyes are firmly on me, and once, I'm sure she smiled and spoke. Staring at me, she mouthed my name and smiled that beautiful, sweet smile as I put every bit of effort into cutting between two of my competitors and flying around the course.

Yes, everything can be normal, monotonous and normal, and then your whole life can change in just one day. You can take every single thing that you know, or think you know, and forget about all of them. This is how it happens, you accept the changes that happen to your body and your mind, and tell yourself that you're fourteen, almost fifteen, and you're changing. That's all that it is, just changes. You start out by being someone who's thirteen and scared, then the next minute, you're older and stronger and braver and everything might just be alright; now life might just get better. Just when the girl that you like is starting to smile at you and say your name, and your best friend has stopped drinking, and your Dad is actually whistling to himself and talking to you. All that can change. Because just around the corner, there is that smell again, that smell that seems to have some kind of control over you, that lingering smell of piss.

Hardly doesn't come to school for two weeks. My morning walks become guessing games of wondering what's happened to him, and when he's going to be back. His desk at school sits empty, and nobody else seems to notice as his name is called, and the response doesn't come. I try not to worry. I try to pretend that everything is normal. He's sick, or is off visiting a relative. He's got some normal, regular reason for not being at school. I'm sure of it.

When he does return, he's leaning against the lamppost, and to my relief, he still looks sober, and clear-eyed. I smile as I reach him, wondering whether or not I'll get a reason for his absence. It only takes a moment for me to realize that the reason is all over his battered face. He has purple bruises on his cheeks, and by his right eye there's a yellow stain with a heavy imprint around it. He's been hit several times by something heavy, by the look of it, and the wounds are healing, healing enough for him to return to school, I suppose.

I walk and he limps, almost the whole way to school, without talking, and it isn't until we reach the grounds that he finally stops and speaks.

"I didn't drink. It wasn't that. He just loses his temper. They both do. I'm a burden, their burden. Five and a half more months to go, then I'm gone. The Army if they'll have me or the shipyards, I don't care. I'll just be gone, and I'll never come back to this, any of this."

We're at the entrance to the school, and just stand there, neither of us looking at the other. We just stare vacantly at the day ahead of us, as he tells me the plans that he has for his fifteenth birthday.

"I have to run this dinner time. I can't get out of it, but wait for me. Wait for me by the dinner hall. I'll be there. Just wait for me." I keep staring ahead and clenching my teeth as I speak, not wanting to look at his bruises, but also not wanting him to think that I don't care. He nods back at me, as he walks ahead into the grounds. It's hard to watch him, as he tries so hard to walk straight, every once in a while favouring his good leg and limping with the other.

The morning is a blur of more assignments and reading and watching the back of Hardly's head as he goes through the day as though it were any other day. When dinner time comes it's lashing with rain, but Mr McRae still makes us run. We do our mandatory laps around the grounds and I lead the pack for once, anxious to finish and meet my friend. As I pass the entrance to the dinner hall I see him there, sitting under the shelter at the entranceway and I signal how many laps I have left. Then, the next time around, he anticipates me coming and holds up his hand telling me the amount of times around remaining. He's smirking through his bruises and the heavy imprint around his eye is shiny from the rain water that's dripping on him. The next time around he's not alone though; Stuart Douglas is standing over him, in front of a group of boys with, of course Gordon McGregor, goading him on. The rain is soaking all of them and Douglas is laughing, and kicking at the air, narrowly missing Hardly's head. Hardly just sits there, holding his hands up and cowering away, as though he's waiting for yet another hit to come.

You don't think about it. You just do it. That's how it happens. You just do it.

I veer away from my running route, and can hear McGregor yelling something at Douglas, then Douglas turning and smiling, as I come charging towards him.

He doesn't move. He just steps back, sideways almost, and lifts his hands in the air, waiting for my challenge. He seems to be bouncing on his feet, up and down, up and down. He's not scared at all. In fact, he looks happy, happy that I'm coming towards him.

He doesn't have a chance, of course. I have the advantage of my rage and the overwhelming memory of the scent of piss almost choking my lungs. I can't make out all of the voices, as the other kids form a circle around us. Mr McRae, or maybe it's Hextall, is yelling at me, telling me to stop, but it's too late. I land the first blow and my fist is striking Douglas on his face, harder than I've ever struck any bag of wet leaves. He hits me back solidly enough to hurt but I can't feel anything right now, especially not pain. My blows are relentless and persistent. I keep aiming at the spot behind his head, just as my Dad taught me, and I know that nothing will stop me from hitting the boy. He goes down from one of my punches, crumples almost, and I have no control over my hand anymore. I crouch over him and keep striking his head and his face over and over. When I feel the arm trying to pull me off, I know that it must be McGregor, the laughing son of the butcher. I don't look back. I keep my attention on Douglas. I just fire my elbow back to shake McGregor off of me. I elbow him so hard that I can feel the bony part solidly striking his chest, sending him flying backwards.

Douglas is done. His face is a bloody mess. He lays there, rain pouring down on him, crying, asking me to stop. When I look back, McGregor isn't on the ground but is actually standing away from the two of us beside Nan. Their faces are white with shock, and lying behind me is Hextall, holding his chest, with his cane at his side. Mr McRae is standing over him and looks at me with the same look of disgust that Nan now has, as she lets McGregor lead her away.

My knees are weak and my hands are sore, but I lift myself up and make my way over to sit beside Hardly, who's still on the step. I try not to look at Hextall, as he attempts to sit up, grabbing the ground beside him, searching for his cane. I don't want him to be lying there. I want it to be McGregor. It should be McGregor. In my mind I knew it had to be him. It had to be him, backing up Douglas. It isn't though; he's long gone, with Nan by his side.

Hardly is giggling and nudging me with his elbow. He's drunk. I can smell it. The piss smell is gone and now all I can smell is the liquor on his breath. Somehow between morning and dinner time, he drank and he's back on the booze.

Through slurred words and tears, he points to the imprint around his eye. "It was the iron. They hit me with the fucking iron. That's why there's lines there. I can't get rid of the lines, Malcolm. The fucking lines won't go away."

I can't look at my friend. The smell coming from him and the mess that I've caused is just too much to bear. I'm cold and sore, and as I start to think about the consequences of what I have just done, I can't bear to look at it anymore, none of it. I turn my head to the side, away from Hardly, away from all of it, and throw up whatever is in my stomach, letting the pounding rain wash it all away.

CHAPTER 12

My Dad and I call all the schools in the area. There are three secondary schools in Kilmarnock, one in Stewarton, one in Dundonald, and one in Galston. We call Ayr and Troon and even try a couple in Glasgow, but they all tell us the same thing. A pupil can bully and beat other pupils senseless. He can carry a knife to school concealed in his duffle bag. He can climb up a tree and piss on his classmates, but under absolutely no circumstances can he hit one of the masters. And if you do happen to strike one of them, even in error, and you are a few months away from being able to leave school, then the Ayrshire school district will simply wait it out until they are no longer obliged to offer you an education.

The fact that Hextall recovered quickly and was probably back swinging his cane within a day or two is irrelevant. We're told over and over again that I'm not welcome back at Kilmarnock Secondary. The headmaster wryly adds that a decision on my future will be made as quickly as possible, hopefully within a few months.

They're stalling, that much is obvious. My Dad tries explaining in his calm, reasonable manner, but it's useless; they've already made up their mind. I'm six months short of turning 15, and I have precious few options.

I tell my Dad everything. I tell him about Hextall and his cane, and Douglas and McGregor, and I watch as his teeth clench together when I tell him about Hardly and the iron. He takes time off work to contact the other schools, and then calls me to the phone when he finds a sympathetic ear that will listen to my side of the story. He's tireless going up and down the stairs to the neighbours' house, with his two pence pieces in his hand, to drop beside the phone as payment. After a while I can't do it anymore. I can't stand beside him listening to the same story over and over again, of my misfortunate elbow to the chest of Master Hextall. I stay downstairs, in our house, and sit rubbing my knuckles, enjoying the fact that my own pain is some kind of a punishment for what I've done.

It's two days of phone calls and climbing stairs, before he comes into the living room and sits with me, looking as though he's given up. At first I think that perhaps he's angry with me but it's not that. He's just tired, very tired, and scratching his head, he slumps into the big armchair, facing me.

"I have some news, Malcolm. There is a school, not here, but there is a school and I have it sorted out, temporarily, only temporarily." He's facing me as I sit on the couch and looks about as glum as I've ever seen him. He keeps looking at me, and then looking away as though he's not quite sure what to say. I just wait. I know my Dad. The words will come.

"I've spoken to George." The silence that comes after George's name hangs in the air between us. "He's arranged your admission into a school in Canada. He's very fond of you, Malcolm. He wants to help you." My Dad pauses, and draws air into his mouth before continuing. "He wants to help us."

Before I can ask the question, he anticipates me, and answers it himself. "Your mother is not involved in this, and will not be involved in any of it. George, and I have sorted out the financial details, and he's looking forward to seeing you. He'll make all the arrangements, on a temporary basis, Malcolm, only temporary." He's staring at the worn-out pattern on the carpet that lies between us, looking up from time to time to make sure that I'm still listening. I can hear the clock ticking in the background, although I don't remember ever hearing it before. The lines in his forehead crinkle and he's holding tight to the seat cushion and nodding as though he's convincing himself that it's the right thing to do.

It's not until he looks up and stares at me, that I realize he's crying. He has a glassy look in his eyes and he keeps blinking, trying not to acknowledge the tears, while I hold my face hard, trying not to breathe, trying not to cry.

"Dad, I could go to work. I could go to work with you or wait it out and then try next year. I could..." I have to stop talking or I'll sob. I hold my head in my hands, and try to breathe, try to think. I just need to think.

"You have this," he points to his head as he talks to me. "You have this gift, Malcolm. You're no like us. You think. You know things. You have to use that. It's a gift, Malcolm, it's a gift." I know this look, the look on his face. It's the same look he had when my mother left us years ago. He's somewhere between pain and anger right now. He raises his voice slightly and I know what he's doing. I know that he thinks it's the best thing to do. "We're no gonna waste it. We will not squander that gift."

Although there are things I like about Canada, it's still not home. It's just a place that I go to in the summer. It's the place that I go to because of the divorce agreement.

"And, you'll come here for your university. They have no choice but to take you to the school of your choice then. You keep getting good marks and they have to let you in. Glasgow,

Edinburgh, Aberdeen, we'll look at all of them and then you can decide. Then you'll come back. And in between you'll be here for Christmases and summers and whatever else we can afford. With the new job it'll be easier, much easier to get you home."

He's right. Scotland will have to take me back for my university schooling and of course they'll have to pay for it too. Terry has told me how expensive university is in Canada and was amazed when I explained to him that in Scotland anyone who maintains a certain grade level attends university at no cost. For a brief moment I think about the private academy that Terry attends but I know that it isn't an option. My Dad's new job may have changed our financial position but it still doesn't put us in the same league as Bill and Terry Allister.

Before I can ask him when I'll be leaving, he answers me. "Soon, son, next week, next week, as long as I can get you on a flight."

I have my head hung down, not wanting to look at him or anything else right now, and when I look up; he has moved over and is sitting beside me on the couch. He pulls my head to his chest, holding us both tight. His tears and my frustration are gone now, and it feels as though we've resolved to doing whatever it is that we have to do. I can hear his breathing and take comfort in it. I remember as a young child, sitting on his lap, trying to match my breaths with his, never being able to match his rhythm. I dread the thought of another plane, another place to live, a different school, and more awkward places to try and fit in. I just sit there and listen to the two of us breathing, thinking about how difficult it must have been for my Dad to make that call to George.

I think about the movie of my life that plays in my head and I realize that there is one last thing that I have to do before I leave, one last thing that's been heavy on my mind since that last day at school. "I want to see Hardly. I want to see him before I go, Dad."

As he straightens up, he has just the trace of a little smile, the same kind of little smile that I had when I was jumping down the bleachers, trying to make my way to Stuart Douglas. My Dad has two voices. There is the voice that he uses to talk to the Masters and Headmasters on the telephone, and then there's his street voice. This is the one he uses when he answers me and talks about visiting Hardly's house. "That's a good idea son, I'll come too. We'll go the night and I'll come ower there with ye. It's been a long time since I've seen Rab."

Growing up, before my Mother left, my parents would take me for walks through the streets of Kilmarnock, through our neighbourhood. We'd pass Taylor Avenue, Craigmore Avenue, Longpark Avenue, and they'd tell me who lived in the houses that we'd pass. They'd tell me about the boys and girls, who later became men and women, that they went to school with, and show me their houses. They'd tell me which ones they liked, and which ones that I should avoid. They'd tell me about the women who married young, and the women who were left alone when their husbands ran away in the middle of the night. We'd pass the houses where the boys lived who stole things that they later claimed, 'fell off the back of a truck'. And, they'd tell me stories about girls setting fire to their homes, sometimes by mistake, or sometimes desperately trying to get some attention. None of the stories are unique. It's just a poor neighbourhood, and it's just the way that it is. We all know each other, and the common feelings of hate and indifference and I suppose, sometimes love, linger between the relationships that hold all our houses together.

My Dad knows Rab, Hardly's father. I don't know how and I don't ask. I assume that it's through their school days, or from playing fitba in the streets as children, or it might even be from work. When he chaps on the door of Hardly's house, it isn't a friendly tap, but more of the type of knock that you would make if you were trying to break a door down. An older, larger, version of Hardly immediately comes to the door, and he looks every bit as angry as I'd imagined him to look.

"Rab."

"Alex."

We stand that way for a moment with the two men looking at each other, and I stare at their expressions while trying to pretend that I'm not actually staring at their expressions. My Dad looks steadfast and firm with the same little smile that I recognize from earlier, while Hardly's father's goes from anger to curiosity before he finally says something.

"These two lads, Alex, getting up to too much bloody trouble, too much trouble. We'll have the polis roond here next. You mind, it'll be the polis next."

"I huv tae apologize tae ye Rab. I really dae. I really have no been a very guid neighbour at all. Here oor two boys are friends, and I havenae been by to see you at all." My Dad's street voice is in full force, and his Scots accent is as thick as I've ever heard it. His expression doesn't change. He just keeps standing there and smiling, waiting.

"Oh, that isnae necessary, Alex. They're just lads, just wee lads. I'll get him the noo." He turns his head and yells into the hallway behind him, "Boy, oot here, company's here, get yerself oot here."

Hardly squeezes through the narrow space between his father and the door opening, and when he sees me, he nods, and we leave the two men, and walk to the edge of the street.

My father's voice is loud and firm as he keeps apologizing to Rab. "I mean it, Rab, I'm gonna change my ways. I'm here to tell you that even though my son is leaving for Canada next week, I'm no gonna neglect yours. In fact, I'm gonna come and see him once a week, every week."

Hardly and I leave the two men and walk to the edge of the pavement, and sit on the kerb. When we look back, we see that my Dad has his finger tapping solidly into Rab's chest, emphasizing his point.

"You dae understand what I'm saying to you, don't you, Rab? I'm gonna be here every week, just making sure that your lad is happy enough and doing okay."

The door slams, and as my Dad passes us, his eyes flicker for a moment when he sees Hardly's battered face. He tells him that he'll see him next week, and that he'll see me back at the house. I want to smile or even laugh. I know what my Dad is doing. It's like sweeping out the area under the stairs, or making our lunches for the week, days in advance. It's one more duty that he'll fulfill. He's a creature of habit, and when he says that he'll do something, he does it. I know without a doubt that one week from now, and every week until Hardly leaves, on his fifteenth birthday, he'll be knocking on Rab's door, asking to see his son. I don't know if it'll make any difference or not, but I want to pretend that it will. I want it to be easy. I want it to be fixed. I just want the problem to go away.

I know that Hardly wanted to speak as soon as he heard my Dad mention that I was leaving for Canada, but he doesn't. He waits until he's gone and we're alone, still sitting on the kerb, in front of his house. "Canada, again, then? It's Canada for ever now, is it? They really arenae gonna let you back in tae the school?" He's grimacing and smiling at me at the same time, leaning forward then back, bobbing up and down to his own secret rhythm.

"It might just be temporary. My Dad says that it might be just for a while." I know it's a lie, and I'm sure he does too, but I say it anyways, as much for my sake as for his.

96

There's a boy throwing stones down the street, one by one, watching them skite down the road and bounce against the kerb. We watch him for a while, and I wonder how many of the broken windows in the houses that surrounds us were caused by him.

"We could write. I could write to you, and you could write back. My Dad would pick up the letters when he comes to see you."

Hardly looks at me and smiles, his face breaking into a broad grin. "You don't write letters, Malcolm, and neither do I, so let's no talk about any letters."

The boy with the stones is moving on now. He's yelling to a couple of other boys who are farther down the road. He doesn't swear, but the coarseness in his words is enough to make us sit up straight and take notice. They move in gangs, these poor boys of the streets. They recognize the desperation in each other and the need to keep moving, the need to keep throwing stones and breaking windows and stealing from houses.

I need to give him something, even if it's another lie. I need to give him something that will take away that look of fear and dread from his face. "Well, there's the army or wherever you end up. Once you get settled you can always try and come for a visit. You could come out to see me in Canada."

He pauses for a minute and we hear the smashing of a window farther down the street, then the laughter from the boy who was throwing stones in front of us earlier, and his cohorts. I don't want his usual depressing response. I want him to buy into it. I want him to at least pretend for a moment or two, and, to my surprise, he does. "Aye, Malcolm, I'll come and see you. Once I get settled in the Army, I'll come ower to Canada and give you a visit. I'll look forward to that."

He holds his little hand out for me to shake, and I take it and squeeze back. I have an overwhelming urge to tell him to stay off the booze, but I don't. I just let him walk back to his door, and watch as it opens, and then closes solidly behind him.

CHAPTER 13

I remember hearing a man speaking on one of my Dad's radio programs about the pulse of the city. I can't remember the city that he was referring to, but I do remember his words. He said that different cities have different pulses, different energies coming from them. He spoke about how the city's pulse resonates through its inhabitants. I remember those words clearly. The pulse of the city *resonates through its inhabitants.* I only really know two cities; Kilmarnock and Vancouver, and if the man on the radio was right, then they both have very, different pulses.

Kilmarnock's pulse has a slow steady rhythm to it. It never gets too excited. It just remains as it is. You break your neighbours' windows or steal their milk bottles and the pulse barely changes. The information just seems to get stored away for another day, and everything just keeps beating along. As my Dad and I ride the bus to the airport, I can feel Kilmarnock's steady pulse coming from all the familiar buildings as they pass us by. I can feel it when he's waiting with me, his hand on my shoulder, giving me advice on everything from the types of food to eat to how to dress for the Canadian winter. At some point between staring at the overhead monitors and waiting for the call to board, he slips his watch into my hand and squeezes it shut. "For your running, Malcolm, it'll keep your timing honest. It'll show you just how fast you can go, and, how far, son; it'll show you how far you're able to go."

I hold onto the watch for as long as I can, not wanting to look at it, just enjoying the feeling of having it in my hands. It's long into the flight before I slip it in my pocket and close my eyes.

Vancouver's pulse is more erratic. It has more extreme highs and lows. I feel it as soon as I land at the airport and George is slapping me on the shoulders, telling me how much taller I've become. By the time we reach his house, and he's thrown my suitcases onto the bed in the spare room, I've heard everything that's happened in the past six months. Rose, his sister, has moved in and taken up residence in the other bedroom. She's a great cook and makes the best fried cabbage that I'll ever taste. Since I've never tasted fried cabbage, I'm sure that he's right. He's taken his job back at the car lot, and although it took some time, Marvin has finally been dismissed.

I never asked for any special treatment, Mal, but Bill Allister one day just came in the shop, and told me. He said, "He's gone, he's gone and the *incident* will not be talked about again." And, it hasn't. Nobody's mentioned it and nobody's even mentioned Marvin.

I think about my mother and all the trouble that she caused, all the people that she hurt. I don't want to ask George about her, but he knows, he just knows.

"They're still together from what I hear, Mal. She's living in his house, and she knows that you're here. She's been told that you're moving here." Then, almost as an afterthought, he adds, "I'm sure you'll see her. I'm sure she'll contact you at some point, Mal."

I jog in the streets around George's house. In Scotland we call it running but here in Canada it's jogging. It's just a word; it certainly doesn't make my legs feel any different. I time myself on my Dad's watch. The second hand ticks precisely, never missing a beat, never slowing down. I increase my speed, trying to find the exact rate that will help me to clear my head. I know that if I can get to the point where my legs work naturally, instinctively, then all the pictures in my head will go away. The watch is a heavy old timepiece that is just a little too large for my wrist but I like the feel of it. I like the way it's supposed to keep me honest.

George is right; Rose looks after both of us and is an incredible cook. It seems as though she grabs me and squeezes me against her chest every time I walk into a room. Where George is built like a big barrel, Rose is more top heavy and curvy. She's a tall woman with dark hair that is just starting to grey and is always pinned in a bun on top of her head. She swings her wide hips around the kitchen and sings in a strange rhythm that only she seems to understand while filling jars with jams and vegetables that I'm sure could feed us for years to come.

"It's canning, Malcolm. Don't they do no canning in Scotland?" She has this delightful habit of waiting only a second for your answer, and when it doesn't come, just keeps on talking. "Well let me tell you something, Mr. Malcolm, we're gonna have enough food in that pantry that nobody in this house will ever go hungry. I guarantee you that." She laughs at the end of most pronouncements, and it's the same warm, hearty laugh that her brother has. I give up trying to avoid her hugs after a while and just let her latch on and hold me. It's all part of the same pulse of the city, the same excitable energy that comes from being in Vancouver.

I won't begin my new school for a week so I run to it during the days, timing myself so that the kids are just at the end of their break and heading back to classes. I see them as they nudge each other and playfully call out on their way back to the building. The expressions on the faces are the same as the kids at my Scottish school, but these kids are fatter, healthier, and their clothes are cleaner and newer. George tells me that their dungarees, as we call them in Kilmarnock, are called blue jeans and some of them even wear designer blue jeans. My Dad calls every day and when I tell him that dungarees with little flags on the back of them are called designer blue jeans, there's a long silence on the other end of the phone. It's very, very difficult not to laugh as I imagine his reactions.

"Designer blue jeans? What exactly is a designer blue jean when it's at home?" The words that sounded so Canadian when George said them are different now when said with my Dad's strong Scottish brogue.

"I don't know, Dad. I'll find out at school I suppose. Some of them have little French flags on the back of them, tiny little French flags."

There's no silence this time. His response is immediate. "A French flag on their arse? Why the hell would you have a French flag on your arse and go to a Canadian school?" I'm holding the phone away from my face now because I have to laugh, and I'm not laughing at my Dad. I love my Dad. I'm laughing at the differences. I'm laughing at the differences between dungarees and blue jeans with little French flags on them. "Malcolm, I want you to watch this. I want you to watch for any of this type of thing and report back to me." He's shaking his head now, I can tell. I know he is. "You let me know, son. You keep your eyes open for any of this type of carrying on."

He's only half serious, I'm sure, but he is intrigued by it and there's nothing or nobody in the streets of Kilmarnock that will be able to explain it to him. Whether he means for me to keep my eyes on the arses of the kids who wear these jeans, or just to watch out for anything French in general, I'm not sure, but I will report back on the differences. I know that he's amused by the differences. I think that our call is over when he asks me to hold on and I hear the phone being handed to someone else.

"Well, are you getting along all right in Canada then, Malcolm? Are you still running, then?" His voice is different, but I know that it's Hardly. He just doesn't sound like the boy who shuffled his feet and hid his face as we walked to school together. He sounds stronger, more confident somehow.

"I am, mate. I'm running every day, even in the rain. I start school on Monday, brand new school."

"Watch out for trees, Malcolm. Don't walk under any trees ower there, mind ye." He's laughing as he says it. Hardly is laughing, not giggling in the drunken fashion, but laughing like a man, laughing like a grown up.

"You're funny, Hardly, very funny. What are you doing there anyways? Are you visiting my Dad?"

"I'm staying here, Malcolm. I've moved in. I'm staying with your Dad until I'm old enough to enlist. I'm back at school and putting in my time till then." He's not laughing now, but he sounds okay. He sounds good, relieved even.

I wish it was me, back in Kilmarnock living with my Dad, or living with my Dad and Hardly. It makes sense for Hardly of course, and it even makes sense for my Dad. I don't ask what happened, and I don't really want to know. I just accept the fact that this is the way that it has to be, for now, and smile and grip the phone as tightly as I can, trying to be happy for both of them.

"That's good, mate. That's really good. Ask him to show you how to punch the bags of wet leaves. That'll get you in shape for the army. That'll set you right."

"Aye, Malcolm, I will. We'll start punching bags of wet leaves today. We'll get on it as soon as I hang up the phone. I promise you." He's mocking me now but I don't care. I'm glad that he's away from his parents. I'm glad that he's safe. My Dad and Hardly, living together, and me in Canada thousands of miles away, temporarily, only temporarily.

104

CHAPTER 14

I can hear their voices even though it feels as though I'm still dreaming. I sleep so soundly at night in the spare bedroom in Georges' house. I suppose it's a combination of the remnants of jet lag, and the fact that I run so much every day.

George is talking to Rose and even though he's trying to be quiet his voice is excited, maybe even angry. "She's got nobody else, Rosie. She called. I'm going. It's as simple as that. I'll bring her back here if I have to."

"I just don't know why you have to get involved. It isn't our business."

I climb out of bed and I'm standing at the doorway, watching as George is pulling on his jacket and Rose is talking to him with her hands on her hips.

"We are involved, Rose. We're all involved." He's noticed me now and is motioning towards me when he says it and of course I know exactly who they're talking about.

"It's my mother isn't it? Something's happened?" I know. It's my mother. It has to be.

Rose takes her hands from her hips and comes over to rub my shoulder and stroke the back of my head but it's George who answers me. "She called, Malcolm. She needs a bit of help. I'm going to go and see what's going on." He waits before adding, "It'll be fine. It'll be okay." There's very little conviction in his voice as he says it. I don't know what has happened but something's different. Something's different in the way he's talking and he's never, ever called me Malcolm before.

"I'm coming, George. It's my mum. I'm coming."

He pauses for only a moment and starts to speak, but I'm back in my room grabbing my dad's watch and pulling on some clothes, before he can say no.

"Are you sure you want him to go, Georgie? Are you sure that he should?" Rose is turning to her brother, and for once she seems to be waiting for an answer, instead of just talking over him.

He's standing at the front door as though he's hesitating or convincing himself. The poor man doesn't know what to say, so I just squeeze past them and stand out on the front porch, waiting. It's cold and dark and I hold onto my dad's watch with my hands in my pockets. I pull out the watch and it says 2:15 am. I never knew that it was this quiet at 2:15 am but it is. The only noise that I can hear is the buzzing of the streetlights that are lit up all along the side of the street. It's a calm, dark night and there's a little bit of wind blowing and the top of the lights gently sway as the wind hits them.

I don't know where we're going or exactly what's happened, but I know by the look on George's face that it's not good. I'm sitting between the two of them, in the front seat of George's big car. I want to know more, but they're not talking, so I just stare forward at the darkness, while stealing the odd glance at how tightly George is gripping the steering wheel.

106

I'm not familiar with any of the streets that we pass and in the darkness it's hard to make out exactly where we are so I just rub the sleep from my eyes, and think about how warm my bed felt just a few minutes earlier. Finally, I can't take it any longer, and I have to ask.

"What is it that happened, George? Where are we going?"

"We're going to sort something out, Malcolm. We got a call for help, and we're going to go sort something out. That's all, son, that's all."

His answer doesn't make sense to me. It doesn't make sense that he looks angry, and that Rose keeps holding my hands in hers, telling me that everything is going to be alright. And, it doesn't make sense that he called me Malcolm, and not Mal. He's never done that before. Nothing makes sense, right up until we pull up to an old house, and I see my mother sitting out on the front steps, doubled over, holding herself.

The only light is from the streetlamp, and a porch light that keeps flickering on and off, but it's enough. It's enough for me to see that her face has blood on it, and she's holding her side in pain. Rose and I are beside her as soon as the car pulls over, and when she sees me, there is just a hint of her usual cockiness, her usual confidence. "Malcolm, well I'm sorry that you have to see your mother in this state. I truly am sorry for that." She tries to sit up straight, trying to show me that it's still her, that she's still in control. "There, there we go, now I can sit up and see you properly." When she begins teetering again, Rose is at one side and I'm at the other, and I barely notice as George quietly makes his way past us, through the front door and into the house.

Rose takes control of my mother right away. "Help me up with her, Malcolm. We'll get her into the car. We'll get her fixed up, don't worry, son."

It's not until we've placed her in the back seat that I realize my teeth are clenched together in anger, and that my hands are shaking. "I don't understand, Rose. Did he hit her? Did he do this? Did he do this to her?"

My mother has her head resting on the back of the seat and is turned away from us. Rose's mouth opens and is about to speak when a noise from the house gives me my answer. There is a crashing sound that is instantly followed by a very unmanly sounding scream. I know the voice of the screamer, of course. It's Marvin. It's the same Marvin who bullied and bothered Terry and me every day of the summer. It's the same Marvin who was pulling up his pants and coming out of our shed while leaving my mother partially dressed inside. The same Marvin who ran from George the day of the incident while George just stood there, enduring the pain.

A scream is a terrible sound to hear, but there are worse sounds. There is the sound of the silence that comes after the scream. Rose is holding me, trying to stop my body shaking with anger, as we stand looking at the open front door of the house, waiting for another noise to come, hating the sound of the silence. The seconds hang in the air as I look back at my mother's battered body hunched over in the back seat, then at Rose as she holds her breath and stares at the front door. I want to take the watch out of my pocket. I want to see the seconds ticking by and not feel as though we're standing still, caught in a time that doesn't move. I can hear my mother's breathing from the back seat. I can feel Rose's heartbeat racing fast against me, while she holds onto me. I just can't stand still any longer. I have to move. I have to do something, anything. I break away from Rose's hold, and ignoring her pleas, move towards the front door. I'm moving fast, just as fast as I did when I moved towards Stuart Douglas only weeks before.

I'm almost at the door when George walks out. He keeps walking and doesn't say anything. He doesn't look at any of us. He just goes to the car and swings his big body into the driver's seat. He sits patiently, looking ahead, doing up his seatbelt, while Rose climbs in the front. I stare at the front door of Marvin's house for a moment before following George, and by the time I jump in beside my mother, he's already started the engine and is pulling the big car out onto the street.

I don't know what to do. I'm still shaking, and I'm not sure why. I need to hold onto something. I need to feel something. My mother is turned away from me, and sways back and forth, bumping into me in the darkness, as the car gently turns the corners. I put my arm around her small, weak body to steady her, to steady both of us. I can see George quickly glancing in the rear view mirror. His knuckles are bloody and his grip on the steering

109

wheel isn't as firm now. I know what bloody knuckles feel like, and I know what goes on in your head after you've hit someone, so I wait. We all wait until he's coasted the car back through the nighttime streets, far from Marvin's house, before we speak.

Rose is looking at her brother's hands, then back at his face with a questioning look. "Georgie, is he? Georgie is…?"

George's voice is steady and has a tone of finality to it as he cuts his sister off. "It's sorted, Rose. It's all sorted. He won't be bothering nobody, not for a while anyways, not for a while."

Rose looks at the road behind us, imagining I suppose what Marvin looks like back there. George takes his bloody hand off the steering wheel for a moment and strokes her shoulder before answering. "It's fine, Rose. I dialed the phone. I gave him the phone before I left, somebody'll come help him. He's going to be okay. He'll be okay.

We hear the siren from the ambulance before it passes us. George is the only one who doesn't watch it as it speeds by. My mother raises her head for a moment and watches it too.   When she speaks she spits out the words, angrier than I've ever heard her. "Bastard, he's a bastard, deserves everything he gets. Bastard." I try to keep holding her, try to put my arms around her, but she just slumps her body away from me. Her momentary strength seems to be gone now, and she clings onto her end of the back seat, trying to support herself without my help.

The rest of the drive home and even the next few days go by in uncomfortable silence as my mother is there, in George and

Rose's home, but then again she really isn't there. All I see of her is the closed bedroom door and her occasional trips to the kitchen, or bathroom at night, while I sleep on the living room sofa. She doesn't stay very long at of course. Within a couple of days her cockiness is almost restored, and she's off staying at a friend's home, ready to start the next part of her life. She does hold me and hug me once before leaving. Then, just as abruptly and strangely, she releases and almost pushes me away, before turning and picking up her things and heading out the door. I'm not hurt by her coldness. I'm used to it now, but I will worry about her. I know now that she's not invincible. I know now that she can be hurt too.

The call comes to George's house a couple of days after she leaves. It's the day before I'm due to start my new school, and George hands me the phone, smiling with his mouth still hanging half open.

It's been a while since I've heard Mr. Allister's voice. "Malcolm, it's Bill-Bill Allister here. I want to talk to you, son. I want to, well, I want to make you an offer."

The Allister Motors Scholarship was probably conceived a couple of days after our trip to Marvin's house. I can imagine Terry and his Dad hearing about Marvin and my mother, and deciding that they were going to do something to help me. I don't know how long it took Terry to convince his Dad, or whether it might have been Bill's idea to begin with. I only know that I only thanked his father once. That was part of the deal. There weren't many conditions that had to be met, but that was one thing that Bill Allister was definite about. I was only allowed to thank him one time.

As I listen to the man on the other end of the line I realize that my mouth is slowly opening, larger, and larger. "We've established a scholarship fund here at the dealership. It'll enable you to go to school with Terry. You'll attend the same school. It's a damn fine institution, son. It's on Vancouver Island. You're going to learn lots. It's going to be so good for you."

I'm not sure what to say, so I stammer. I'm thanking him and asking questions at the same time. It's words that are coming out of my mouth, but I'm not sure that they're making sense to anyone. Rose and George are looking at me with a bemused look on their faces as though I've lapsed into another language.

"Hold on, there just a second, cowboy." Mr Allister is laughing on the other end of the phone, giggling almost, as he tries to explain to me. "There are some stipulations. First of all, you need to maintain good grades for the scholarship to be renewed. You need to have a B average." There's a pause as though he's thinking to himself. "Or at least a C+. Yes a C+ would be good too. Damn it, as long as you're trying, as long as you're learning and doing well then I'll renew it every year until you graduate three years from now. And you'll need to work during the summer. You'll work here of course at the dealership with Terry, with my son, if that's okay. Are you with me so far, Malcolm?"

I didn't cry when I sat beside my Dad on the couch while he told me that I'd have to move to Canada. I held it in. I didn't cry when I heard Hardly's voice on the phone, and knew that he was going to be okay. And, I didn't cry when I wanted to punch Marvin with all the might that I could gather. But, now I cry. The tears come streaming down my face as Mr Allister speaks. I don't think they're tears of happiness. They're tears of relief. I quickly mumble that it's okay. I tell him that I want to work for him anyways. I just don't want him to stop talking. I want him to be explaining it to me all day, giving me all the details, telling me that everything is going to be okay now.

"There's only one more thing, Malcolm. If you agree to this, if you want to take advantage of this scholarship, you should thank me, of course, but only once. I mean it too. I don't want you to feel indebted to me or that you owe me something or any of that bullshit. If you want this, then you just go ahead and thank me now and get it over with. What do you want to do, Malcolm? What are you going to do?"

He's stopped giggling and sounds serious now. It sounds as though his voice is breaking too. I think of him sitting in his office, holding the phone in one hand and nervously playing with his tie with the other.

"I want it, of course I want it. I can't thank you enough. I don't know what to..." I want to tell him how much it means to me, how much it'll mean to my Dad, to George, to Rose.

His voice cuts me off and is kind but firm. "One time, Malcolm, just one time. I'm delighted, absolutely flippin' delighted that you're going to take it, so now just get it over with because you're only gonna get to do it once."

Nothing comes out for a moment, so I just do it in the way that my Dad has taught me ever since I was a little boy. "Thank you, Mr Allister. Thank you very much."

"Right, I'll make the arrangements and we'll get you on a ferry over to the island right away. Congratulations, son, you're going to do fine. You'll make us all proud."

George and Rose each grab for me as I hang up the phone. They know. I can tell that they know. Mr. Allister must have spoken to them before he spoke to me. They hold onto me tight, one on each side, congratulating me. Rose has been cooking, and the smells of our dinner are coming from the kitchen. I look around the living room and can see the pile of LP records stacked in the corner, the big console TV sitting over by the front window. I'll miss the sounds and smells of their house, our house. But, I think that everything might be okay now. It really does feel like everything is going to be okay, or at least it might be for a little while. Nothing in my life has ever been forever anyways. Everything is always just temporary, always temporary.

CHAPTER 15

VANCOUVER, CANADA 1996

Terry and I have a game that we play sometimes. We try to find Brutus.

We drive to an area that we're unfamiliar with and look for a car wash. If it's a newer one, we know that it isn't Brutus, but if there's an older service station, we seek it out, and if it has a car wash then sometimes, just sometimes, it's a Brutus. Terry still gets a look of satisfaction on his face when we drive through the rinsing rack and hanging over the drying blaster we see a plaque that says, very simply, 'Brutus, built by Allister Enterprises'.

Terry, of course, left car washes far behind years ago, but it all started with the contraption that he made out of old parts in the back of his Dad's car lot, the machine that we called, Brutus.

Bill Allister had been right. The Provincial Academy on Vancouver Island was a good school. It was a safe, conservative school, and Terry and I put in our time there without ever really standing out. After my tumultuous childhood, I welcomed the chance to have some kind of normal, some kind of typical life. When I left the academy, I disappointed my father by not returning to university in Scotland, and instead, enrolled at a community college in Vancouver. Terry decided that he'd had enough of teachers telling him what to do, and opened a small manufacturing plant adjacent to his dad's car lot, building portable car wash machines. He called them Brutuses of course, and sold them to service stations all over Canada and the United States.

From there Allister Enterprises grew and grew, and Terry diversified. Today, he manufactures and sells novelty electronic equipment. You've seen them; you may even own one or two of them. There is everything from portable polygraph machines (78 percent accurate), to an electronic best friend. For three hundred and ninety dollars you can have a machine that will know you as well as any best friend should. You program all of your personal likes and dislikes into it and carry it with you all day long. Throughout the day it will make comments such as, "Sushi for lunch today? You know it's your favourite." Or, "Let's watch that show on TV tonight. You know, the one that only you and I enjoy."

Terry is driving, and I'm lying back in the passenger seat, enjoying the ride. We've ventured almost a hundred miles from home playing our game, to a small town that has the unlikely name of Hope, but unfortunately, it's been a futile trip. Hope's small service station does have an operational car wash, but it isn't a Brutus. It isn't even close to a Brutus. It's shinier and newer than Brutus ever looked, even on his best days. So, after driving every gravel road that we could find, in order to dirty Terry's car, we've turned around, preferring instead to drive the dusty vehicle home.

Terry has his Dad's friendly grimace on his face when he speaks, and is trying to pretend that he's frustrated. "On the phone

116

the kid told me. He told me that they'd had the same car wash for the last ten years. That sucker's barely three years old. Why'd we drive out here all this way if it wasn't Brutus? Why'd we come this far?"

"I don't know, Terry, maybe he just needed your three bucks. Maybe it's as simple as that." He squirms a little in his seat as I let him pretend that we've come all this way just to see a car wash.

"Malcolm, you can't trust a kid. I should have asked for the owner of the place, when I called. I shouldn't have listened to that kid on the phone. I mean how old was he? Fifteen? Sixteen? What the hell do you know about car washes when you're fifteen years old? What the hell do you know about anything when you're fifteen years old?" His question lingers for only a moment before he realizes what he's said, and he can't help but smile at his remark, thinking back to when we were that age, building our own car wash.

"I know what you're thinking, Malcolm Wilson. I know exactly what you're thinking, but it's different now. It's different today. We had something that they never had. We had vision. We always had vision."

He's half right. He had vision, still does in fact. I, on the other hand, was just trying to survive, flying back and forth between countries, never knowing how long it would be before I left again. When I did get the opportunity to stay in one place, I took it. I only visited Scotland a few times after leaving to attend

117

school on Vancouver Island, and each time my Dad always looked as though he was going to ask me when I was coming home. He'd stand at the airport and the question would hang in the air between us, waiting to be asked. I never gave him the opportunity though, always rushing to get onto the plane, making plans, telling him that I loved him and that I'd see him soon.

I sometimes wonder where the young boy who was so lost, who wanted so badly for things to stop changing, went. My life since school in Canada has been so calm, so uneventful that I don't really know who I am anymore. I'm certainly not the young man who punched Stuart Douglas in the face while he lay on a rainy Kilmarnock schoolyard. But I'm not the boy who was pissed on from the tree either. I suppose I'm somewhere in between, somewhere calmer, safer.

We're passing another little town, both lost in thought, enjoying spending time together, before he broaches the real reason that we took our trip to Hope. "So, you're coming. With or without Marsha, you're still going to come. Don't disappoint us, Malcolm. You have to come. You always come."

I've just endured another relationship implosion, and on the phone, when I told Terry that my girlfriend of eighteen months had left, and that I would not be attending his annual beginning of summer party, he immediately decided that we should play our game. So, we took our road trip, our road trip to find Brutus. It's just an excuse, of course, just a reason for him to talk to me, and to see how I am.

"Her name is Natasha, Terry, and you know that very well. Besides, I came to your party when I worked for you. Then it was different..."

He cuts me off before I can continue. "Natasha, Marsha, it doesn't matter. There'll always be another one. There'll always be another girl. And, remember, you never worked for me, Malcolm. We worked together, just like always, working together."

He's right; we did work together. At first I worked solely for Terry and his Dad, Bill, but soon, with their encouragement, I opened my own small firm. Now Terry's company has grown so large that I'm only a consultant to him, but because of my connection to Allister Enterprises, and my safe, fastidious approach to my work, my small company is modestly successful.

In college, I took the brilliant mind of my childhood that solved problems and equations so effortlessly, and settled. I stuck with my safe, dependable numbers. They're my specialty-numbers, formulas, and my beloved equations. I love how they come together, fall into place and work in perfect conjunction with each other. Numbers don't vary. They don't stray. If a series of numbers add, or multiply, or subtract a certain way today, they'll do that over and over again tomorrow, without fail. I try to live my life the same way. I enjoy order. I love the solace that I get from my numbers.

I am an accountant.

We come over the crest of a hill and the full force of the early June sunshine hits the dirty windshield, and we reach for our sun visors at the same time. "You're right, Terry. We worked together, and that's when I came to your company barbecue. It's a company barbecue, for your employees." I stretch out the word 'company', trying to remind him of why he started his annual party in the first place. "I'm just not in the mood to go this year, Terry. I'm just not there, buddy."

Terry has always had this way of drawing me in, of speaking as though he's sharing a great secret that only I'm able to hear. He can haul his short, stocky, muscular frame into a room, and instantly make you feel his presence. He has personality; this way of instantly making you feel at ease. I can stand beside him with my six foot two lanky frame, and my unkempt hair, and he'll curl his finger up, bringing me in closer, speaking as though he doesn't want anyone else to know what he's about to say.

I know what's coming next. I can anticipate it. Every time I have relationship issues, Terry gives me his theories. I have to listen to them. I have no choice, I'm trapped in the passenger seat, so I recline back and try to smile, enjoying the sunshine that's beaming through the windshield.

"I have an idea, Malcolm. I want you to think about something. I want you to think about this. Forget about work. Forget about Marsha, Natasha, whatever. For you, this summer should be about sex, nothing else, just sex, and the procurement, thereof." He likes to use words that he isn't quite sure of their meaning, and then watch my reaction to see if I'm going to correct him. I never do. I just close my eyes, and let him continue.

"This girl, and the one before her, and the one before that, they're all gone now. You need to look forward. You need to have some fun, and not fall in love with every girl who lets you get your feet under her table." He's smiling when he says it, liking the fact that he's mixing Scottish metaphors with his Canadian theories.

"Where the hell did you hear that, Terry Allister? That's my father talking. 'My feet under her table.' That's hilarious, Terry. It really is." I can't help but laugh, thinking how my Dad's sayings have worn off on Terry.

"Yes, I did hear your Dad saying that. And it's exactly what he'd say to you. When did you talk to him last anyways? Are you still calling him every week? Tell him I said, hello. Tell him that I was asking for him."

Terry met my father when he came from Scotland to see me graduate from college, and instantly liked him. My dad liked Terry too. At first he called him 'a bit of a lad', but soon, like the rest of us, he fell for Terry's charm. As the years went by, and Terry became more and more successful, he'd ask me if I was still counting the bags of money for 'that daft wag'.

"I don't know if that would be my dad's advice, Terry, but, yes, I spoke to him the other day. He's doing well, tells me that he's going to retire, take it easy. I'll believe it when I see it. I can't imagine my dad not working. I don't know what he'd do with himself."

"Maybe, he'll get a woman; find himself a Scottish lady. You know there's lots of fun to be had out there. Do you remember what I was like, before I met Jo? It was about fun, Malcolm. It was always about fun." We leave the side roads, and enter the main highway just as Terry starts to reminisce about his single days, the days before he married Jo, and the car, appropriately enough, begins speeding up.

"That's how it was, Malcolm. You remember. You have to. And that's how you have to think, this summer. Think about the fun. Don't think about falling in love with one girl. Think about chasing girls. In fact, just think about the chase. I'll tell you something, my friend, sometimes the chase was the best part of it. The chase is overlooked far too often. It's the foreplay before the foreplay."

He tells me the story about the girl with the long loopy earrings. It's the same story that I've heard for years. It varies sometimes, in little ways, but it's still the same story.

"Hot, hot, smokin' hot day, Malcolm, and our cars end up stuck at the same light. I'm right beside her, looking into her open window, and she's squinting into the sun. She has this little trace of a smile on her face, and those earrings were dangling, the sun shining right off them. You're listening, right, you're getting this?" He has his not-so-serious, serious expression on now, the one that forces you to pay attention to him.

"Yes, Terry. I'm listening. In fact, I'm not sure, but you may even have told me this story once or twice before."

He hears me but doesn't listen. He just keeps right on talking, trying to make his point. "Yeah, yeah, anyways, I look into her eyes, right directly into her eyes, but it's not her eyes that I see. All I can see are her breasts, her glorious, lovely, hot summer breasts. We talk. We talk about the weather, the heat, but all the while I'm thinking about touching her, thinking about how smooth her skin is going to feel. We pull over, have a coffee at a coffee shop, and an hour later, I'm in her bed."

I'm laughing now because I know what comes next. It's the Terry Allister philosophical ending. His story is an interesting story, and it probably did happen just the way that he says it happened, but it's the way that he sums it up that I enjoy listening to. It's the way that he's motivated his employees, and I suppose, himself, all these years. He's an inventor, a salesman, a husband to Jo, and a good friend to me, but like lots of people, he sees himself as something else. Terry sees himself as a philosopher. No, Terry is a philosopher.

"Now, Malcolm, that little encounter all began with a flirt, just a flirt, but it became much more than that. It's not just flirting. It's about finding a maybe. I looked at her, she looked at me. Then, I asked with my eyes, no words, just eyes, and she smiled back a maybe. And let me tell you, my friend, there's lots of satisfaction in a maybe."

He pauses, and taking his eyes off the road for a moment, looks over at me, making sure that I'm listening. I stretch in the comfortable reclined seat and look over at my friend, allowing him to give me his philosophical summary.

123

"Maybes make the world go round, Malcolm. Maybes give us hope. They tuck us into bed at night, and they wake us up in the morning. Maybes help us navigate our way through just about anything. Yeah, that's what you need, my friend. You need a whole summer of maybes."

I'm smiling now, and after a moment he is too. He's remembering the girl, I suppose, and is smiling the way he always does when he has someone who will listen to his theories.

In the movie of my life that plays in my head, I've tried to imagine myself just as Terry suggests. I see a charming, carefree, ladies' man that sneaks out of bathroom windows in the middle of the night, before husbands get home, and then laughs about it afterwards. I imagine myself juggling Brittanys and Courtneys and best of all Sheenas, and being faithful to none of them. In the real world though, the world I really live in, I know that just isn't me. Terry talks about the girl with the loopy earrings, and all of the others that he knew, but all I've ever really wanted was one girl, or even better *the* girl.

We leave the main highway, and enter the city. He starts weaving his car through traffic, changing lanes and overtaking slower drivers. It's our drive to the water. Both of our homes look out at the same water, only my view is from my fifteenth floor apartment and Terry's is from his house in the hills.

"Yeah, the party will do you good. You never know; you might just meet somebody; you might meet a maybe, Malcolm.

Just remember what I told you. Take a break; take a break from serious for a while. Have some fun, for Pete's sake."

My friend is probably right; I need a break from something. I'm not sure if it's from women, or commitment, or work or all three. I've taken a few days off from my accounting practice to try and forget Natasha, and the ones before her. I'm thirty four and I've been in two serious, and two not-so-serious, relationships in my life. All of which seemed to end the same way.

In my twenties there had been Mona, lovely, lovely Mona. She'd wanted children and I'd only wanted Mona, just Mona. We tried to pretend for almost three years before realizing that our paths were too different.

Later there had been Linda and Lori. I could never decide which was the one for me. Linda and Lori lived together. They'd been roommates since college and I tried to build a relationship with each of them, at different times of course. Unfortunately, their own relationship was more important than any type of connection that they might have felt with me. So, one day they asked me to move on and leave them alone. Somewhere they're out there, still living together, still roommates.

Then there was the aforementioned Natasha. Now my relationship with Natasha seems like one long, long, date that should have ended much sooner than it did. We tried to see something in each other that wasn't there, tried to fill in the blanks instead of dealing with reality. Reality can be so boring sometimes, but it will always rear its head and snap at you, telling you that it's just not working, and with Natasha and me, it finally did.

We arrive back at my apartment, and sit for a moment in the parking lot, watching the sun settling on the water. Anyone passing by would see two men, mid thirties, smiling, talking, enjoying the view. The driver, the shorter of the two, is speaking, moving his hands in the air from time to time, gently making his point. The passenger sits taller, stiffer, his serious face crinkling at the edges, as the driver tells story after story.

That's not where we are of course. We're not really there. Our bodies might be, but we're not. We're in the same place that we always are when we spend time together. We're sitting on overturned buckets, outside the shed on his Dad's lot. Terry is planning his next invention, his next success, and I'm just trying to be Malcolm, whatever that is.

CHAPTER 16

Their driveway is crammed full of vehicles. It always is during their parties. Some of the vehicles are Terry's, and others belong to his guests. Terry's cars have names on them that say XL, or SL, or they're just called the S Series, or the M Series. They're the type of cars, that when he says the name, other men nod and smile, as though he's gotten away with something very sinister. To me, they're blue or black, and look much more expensive than my four-year-old Chevy.

Terry, and his wife Jo, have a television set that is as big as the wall. They can walk into the room and say, "TV on," and it comes on. In the back yard there's a pool shaped in the logo of Terry's company, and for the party they have set up two bars, both manned by bartenders. There's a chef standing at the head of a table, carving roast beef, and there are two Mexican balladeers, sauntering around the garden, playing requests and sweating under their heavy Mexican hats. And there are people, lots and lots of people.

His employees are a mixed bunch. They range from the very intelligent technical types, who use the party as a day to let their hair down, to the very creative artsy types, who never really need an excuse to let their hair down. There's the twenty- somethings that have the confident look of being in the right place at the right time. Then, there's the thirty- somethings trying to fit in with the twenty somethings, yet still trying to look superior and not quite managing to pull it off. And there are the forty- somethings that have the lines in their face and the odd grey hair that comes with having children, or going through a divorce, or both.

My timing is usually perfect at his parties. I get there early and use my tall, strong Scottish/Canadian bulk to move some tables out to the pool area or carry out the cases of liquor to the bars. I enjoy the initial laughter and merriment, have a couple of drinks, and then leave. There was one year that I stayed too long, and got involved in a discussion concerning the correct usage of the word, "pompous", then ended up being pushed into the pool, long after the swimming had ended. Apologies had been accepted, and I left, dripping with water, drying myself off with a towel that Jo had given me. It wasn't until the next day that I realized *I'd* been the joke, and I knew then that the angry young man that I used to be had all but disappeared.

I'm on the other side of the pool, close to the safety of the kitchen when I notice the girl, not in the mouth-dropping, knees-shaking, rest-of-the-room-fading-away, type of noticing but more in the "who's the girl with the green hair kind of noticing."

She stands out even amongst the designer, ripped jean crowd. Tall and erect, she seems to have a detached type of confidence. Wearing a skirt that is too long for a pool party on a summer day, knee-high boots, again inappropriate, and a t-shirt that says, "I am the Revolution." She looks like she's in the wrong place and the right place, both at the same time. Taken with her green hair, and her height, on anyone else it wouldn't have looked right, but on her, it somehow seems to fit.

She's standing alone but with everyone else at the same time. I watch as she walks from group to group, joining in different conversations. They politely let her in. Then quietly, she moves on to the next one or off by herself.

The environment in Terry's company is incredibly competitive. The top producers are rewarded and rise to the top quickly. It's cutthroat, and not always the most politically correct workplace. I know this. He's explained his philosophy to me more than once. For a woman, who's probably in her late twenties, dressed the way she's dressed to be accepted and perhaps even respected amongst these people is impressive.

"So, which one is here for me," I playfully ask Jo, Terry's wife, as I help her carry out some bags of ice.

Jo is a classic beauty. She's the type of a woman who probably never really has to work at looking beautiful. She just is. Marrying Jo was the best decision Terry ever made, and they both know it. "None, I couldn't find a willing masochist this year," she replies, probably only half kidding.

I talk to Jo, all the while watching the green-haired woman, moving, almost dancelike, as she enjoys the conversations from three different groups at the same time. I marvel at how someone can be so comfortable with themselves, while wearing heavy boots, and having green hair, on a summer day at her boss's home.

Terry is performing of course. He has a group of serious younger people, and a couple of his other friends around him, and is using words that I don't understand. He's talking about computer speeds, and an aircraft that he wants to buy, and a trip that Jo and he will take later in the year. I'm amazed how some men can have so much knowledge of stuff, just stuff. How they can remember all the model numbers and brand names. I know numbers. I can tell you the phone number of almost anyone I know. I can tell you the social insurance numbers, and net earnings of most of my regular clients, but I can't tell you the brand name of my television or computer.

"You were staring at me earlier. Why was that?" She's behind me. I took my eyes from her for only a moment, and she must have crossed the pool area and come over to where I'm standing. The hairs on the back of my neck stand up, and my face instantly turns red.

"I was wondering if you were warm, standing in the sun, wearing those boots." I turn slowly to her, hoping to blame my red face on the warm sun, trying to look down at her boots and avoid her gaze.

"You're blushing," she giggles, and laughs. The sun excuse isn't going to work. "No, don't look away. It's cute. It's like you're a little boy."

"I'm thirty-four, being a little boy was a long time ago." All of a sudden, I notice her eyes for the first time, "Oh my goodness your eyes are lovely. They're so blue." I say it, but not in a flirtatious manner. They really are blue, really, really blue.

"Don't change the subject. We're talking about your red face, and thank you, they sometimes change colour, depending on the weather. You dress like a banker. Are you a banker?"

"Accountant," I reply.

She laughs again, but not maliciously. When she laughs, her eyes sparkle, and there's a half dimple on her left cheek. Her laugh is warm. I like this girl.

CHAPTER 17

Her name is Heather, and her hair isn't really green. It's brown, or sometimes blonde, but very rarely green. She tries different colours each time we go to dinner or to a movie. When she tries red, I tell her that it makes her look playful, so the red stays for a while.

She tells me she likes my manners and says I'm her rumpled accountant with the wistful look in his eyes. I tell her what I think and then ask if she agrees, and if she says "no," I listen. She likes this about me; I can tell. When we're together, I'm confident and commanding when I need to be, but I always make it seem like it's a temporary job, and that I'm only doing it until the person who's really in charge comes along.

To me, she's a walking contradiction, and I love the fact that I can't figure her out. She dresses to shock, and wants to be involved in everything, yet seems to want me to make the decisions. There's something vulnerable beneath the cockiness, and sometimes in her eyes there's just a hint of sadness that comes for a moment, then with a shake of her head, or a smart remark it's gone. She asks about other relationships that I've been in, other women that I've been with. When I tell her about Natasha, and the others, she laughs, and says that it doesn't matter, and that none of us just got here.

I ask her about old boyfriends, old lovers, and she smiles and says that there haven't been many; she's been too focused on growing, on living, on trying to be happy.

We're new. There's nothing planned, or usual, or regular, about our relationship. I know that her father lives back east, somewhere in Ontario, and that she was in Alberta briefly, and then settled on the west coast, in Vancouver. She loves the water, and didn't see the ocean growing up, so now, she adores being close to it. The details come out over dinners or lunches when she sneaks away from work.

I reach across the table, during dinner number two, and touch the back of her hand then look into her eyes to ask if it's okay.

"If I said no, would you stop?"

I pull my hand away.

"I didn't want you to. I just wondered if you would."

I wait until the smile comes to her face and the half-dimple forms on her cheek, before reaching out, and taking it, again.

"Why haven't you kissed me yet, anyways?" she asks, squeezing my hand back.

"Oh, I don't kiss. Didn't I tell you that? I don't kiss anyone; haven't in years. I fondle and caress and do a lot of heavy petting, but I don't kiss. It's just a thing that I don't do," I lie.

"That'll work well. I've been thinking about giving it up myself," she lies back. "We could just move right into the heavy petting part. I counted the motels on the way to the restaurant. There are seven of them. You pick one."

And, of course, now, I can't wait to kiss her.

We drive to her apartment and for the third time ever, I walk the girl with the previously green hair, to her front door. Then, with the confidence of a man falling in like, I smile, lean in and kiss her.

"I thought you quit."

"I couldn't resist you," I answer truthfully.

"I'm glad. I liked it." She turns and walks into her apartment building. She doesn't have to look back. I'm sure she knows that I'm still watching her, as the door closes behind her.

When it comes time to introduce her to more of my life, more than just Terry and Jo, I do what I always do when I'm with someone new, I take her to meet George and Rose. My mother is on yet another cruise, with yet another gentleman friend, and my father, of course, is far away, in Scotland. George and Rose became my surrogate parents, after living with them for countless summers, and working with George, at Bill Allister's car lot.

When I introduce them, George holds Heather's hand a moment too long, in the way that is tolerated in an older man, yet can be a slappable offence in a younger one. "Mal was right, you are lovely."

"Mal, oh, I'm not sure I like that," she replies, allowing her hand to be held for the extra moment, and smiling.

"Well, we'll stay with Mal until you can find a pet name for him," Rose interjects, coming out onto the porch and pulling their hands apart, acting more like a wife than a sister, before clutching Heather and giving her one of her trademark hugs.

"I already have one, I just haven't used it on him yet," Heather whispers, looking at me, mischievously.

"Go on and talk as though I'm not here. It's fine really," I mumble, loving the attention.

"Come and help me with dinner, Heather. I can't interrogate you properly out here." Rose takes my newest girl's arm, and gently leads her into the kitchen of their old house, while George and I sit on the porch, listening to the muffled talk and laughter, as the two women got to know each other.

"She's young, Mal. She's young. She doesn't seem young, but she looks young. Do you know what I mean?" His face is kind and he has his warm smile on, as he says it, the same smile that he's given me ever since I was a little boy.

"You don't like her? Is that what you mean, George? Already, you're deciding? And she's twenty-eight. She's six years younger than me, just six years."

When I left my Scottish home of solid, grey, brick buildings and scenic castles, and moved to Canada with its wooden decked houses, flanked by majestic mountains, I was always looking for something. I just didn't know it at the time. I was looking for safety, for a safe place. My mother was always busy trying to find a new husband, and she never did have time for a son, so George and I spent many nights out on his porch, my safe place.

"Oh, I'm not saying that I don't like her, Mal. In fact, I'm pretty sure that I am going to like her. I'm just saying that she's young, even though she seems older. There's something, something that I just can't put my finger on, but yeah, I'm sure I'll like her son. She makes you happy, I'll like her. It's as simple as that."

By the time Rose and Heather join us, I have my legs draped over the railing, and can feel the sun on them. I can almost see new, little clusters of freckles popping up. I never really do tan, I just go red, and then my pale Scottish skin peels, and itches. I love the sun, but always forget to protect myself against it.

"Malcolm, Rose is going to make me eat cabbage. Please make her stop. And, oh my goodness, your legs are turning red," says my new girlfriend in mock terror.

"You'll like it. She fries it in brown sugar, and adds weeds that she grows in the garden. I've been eating it since I was a kid," I answer, pushing against the redness on my legs with my finger.

"They're not weeds, Scottish boy, and if she doesn't like the vegetables cooked the way my Newfoundland mother and grandmother taught me to make them, she can just have a pork chop," Rose answers, pretending to be hurt.

Rose has that old time belief that you decide whether or not you are going to like someone within the first couple of minutes, and from the sideways smiles she's exchanging with Heather, I know that they're already fond of each other.

"Why do you call him Scottish boy? I've gotten so used to it now, that I can barely hear his accent." Heather is helping Rose dish the food onto plates on the small plastic table.

"It comes and goes. When he first got here, or after talking to his Dad on the phone, it was real strong. We spent a week, just asking him to repeat things to us, till we got him retrained." George says, smiling at the memory. "I don't know if you're more Scottish now, or you were more then, Mal. I remember how you'd tell me about the rains, the great rains of Scotland that would come at you sideways and instantly soak you."

Sometimes, it's good to be the centre of attention. Sometimes, having your adolescent life dissected isn't so bad, especially when it's being done by the people that you love and trust.

"When I first met you, you were my little Scottish gentleman, running all over the streets, with that big old watch in your hand. My little Scottish gentleman, look at you now, lounging over that railing, with your sunburnt legs." Rose's laughter is so infectious that we can't help but laugh along with her.

My new girlfriend shifts in her seat, laughing with the rest of us, while placing a plate of Rose's Newfoundland cabbage and pork chops on her lap, and showing me her half dimple. "You

136

have this Scottish look to you, like you just got off the boat and are still lost; it's very cute."

Something happens to you when you're sitting in the safest place in the world, and enjoying the sun, and eating food that you've known for years, and having people you love, and are soon to love, saying nice things about you. You almost get into a trance-like state, and that's exactly where I go. I feel as though I'm sleeping and awake at the same time. And it's fine. It feels good, everything is fine until I look over at Heather, and realize that she's taken off her jacket, and the t-shirt she's wearing has a peep hole in it that's right in the centre of her cleavage.

Heather is a beautiful girl, and truly, the first thing that you notice about her, are her eyes, her amazing blue eyes. But the second thing, or perhaps the third thing, after noticing her height, or maybe even her long, straight hair, is her breasts. She is the kind of a girl that my Scottish father would say, "is blessed. Very, very blessed."

Later, when she would tell the story, Heather would say I stared at her peep hole, for a full ten seconds; I disagree, and feel that it was no more than two or three. All I know is that I was enjoying staring at the glimpse of her full breasts, through that small peep hole, and somehow forgot that there was anyone else there. I just forgot that I was sitting on that porch, being the centre of attention, and being watched by three other people. And in those few seconds, the message from my brain, to the more sensitive and responsive area of my body, made a reaction in my shorts that did not go unnoticed.

"Malcolm, you're smiling in your shorts. Eat your dinner." Rose drops my plate of pork chops and cabbage unceremoniously into my lap, while shaking her head like the embarrassed surrogate mother that she is.

George can hardly get any words out as he's laughing so hard. "Is that a Scottish thing too, Mal?" He motions towards my now covered up erection when he asks.

My face burns beet red, almost glowing, and as I hurriedly eat my pork chops and fried cabbage with Newfoundland weeds, my new girlfriend puts her hand on my shoulder, and whispers mischievously, "We haven't found out if that's a Scottish or Canadian thing quite yet."

That night, when I'm in her apartment for the very first time, I get to know that the girl, who used to have green hair, still has two teddy bears on her bed and a poster of an old Punk rock band on her bedroom wall. She has no pictures of her family on her bedroom shelves and mantles; instead they are filled with candles and small glass figurines of mothers holding their children. She has a fluffy comforter with seven different pillows, and when you take off the blouse with the peep hole, she has the most perfect breasts that I've ever seen.

"Whisper Scottish in my ear," she teases me.

"I'm not sure I know how." I whisper back, in the familiar Kilmarnock Secondary School voice that comes so naturally to me.

"Well, that's a really good start," she half gasps as we lay on her bed, undressing each other.

"You're lovely. You really are," I whisper, looking at her almost totally naked body.

"Are you sure it's not what you were looking at earlier?" she asks, teasingly pushing her dangerous breasts together.

"No, it's all of you. It really is," I answer, and I mean it. Every word.

I do this thing sometimes, when I'm in a really good place. I ask myself if there is anywhere else in the world that I'd rather be than where I am right at that moment. And, as I kiss and caress the body of the beautiful girl, I know exactly what the answer is.

"You touch me like you mean it. I like that. It's like you're gentle and strong at the same time," she says.

We let the comfortable silence surround us, and I don't think about Terry and his maybes or his foreplay before the foreplay, or even Natasha and our failed relationship. I don't think about any of it. I just enjoy being with her, and for the first time in a long time, I know that I'm exactly where I'm supposed to be.

CHAPTER 18

In between working with my precious numbers, and Heather's job as Terry's marketing assistant, we phone each other's answering machines. We leave questions, filling in the gaps of our lives with the actual facts. Sometimes she sends an answer back, and sometimes, she evades it by sending me another question.

She tells me her middle name is Allison.

"Just like the song," I send my message back.

"What song?" she replies, mischievously underlining the difference in our ages.

I respond by tunelessly singing the Elvis Costello song, in my Scottish/Canadian accent, into her phone machine, wondering if I've ever sung for a girl before.

She leaves me a message that says, "I sometimes think we're sharing a head, or a mind. We seem to think the same things, at the same time. Are you psychic, Malcolm, or do you just know me this well already?"

We take turns, lying in my bed, looking out at the water, or in hers, staring at her little glass figurines. Sometimes, there's a faint dark flicker in her eyes, as though she's thinking about something else. It comes, and then leaves just as quickly, and she comes back to me, back to our shared laughter, our shared head.

I wait until we're in the darkness of her bedroom, surrounded by her little glass figurines, before I ask her why she looks so sad sometimes.

I can feel the warm air from the summer night coming through her window, hanging in the air between us, as she speaks. "My mother died when I was young. I was fifteen, almost sixteen. I think about her sometimes. I still feel a little lost sometimes. I just never had my mom when I needed her. That's it. That's all it is."

She tenses up beside me and I wait a moment before continuing. "I'm sorry, Heather. That must have been hard. It must have been really hard. Was it just you and your Dad. Are you still in touch with him? Are you close?"

In the dark, I can't see the flicker in her eyes, but I know it's there. I can sense it. I can feel it.

For the first time ever, she turns away from me, and there's no reply. When I tell her again that I'm sorry, there's still no answer. It's a long time before I hear her breathing change, and realize that she's fallen asleep.

You get to the point where summer feels like it's going to last forever, and other than the odd dark flicker, life is really good. Life feels right. Then, all of a sudden, everything can change. Everything ends. It has to. That's just the way things are. I know that something is wrong as soon as Weldon walks into my office, and I know it isn't work. I know it's personal.

Weldon Grimes is my office supervisor. He looks after our day to day business when I'm not there. He's a good man. He can rarely talk to me without telling a joke. It usually takes every bit of inner fortitude that I have for me to laugh at his jokes, but I do laugh. I do try. This time is different though. When he walks into my office, nervously rubbing his hands together, and fingering his wedding band, he isn't telling jokes. He's looking at me, concerned, and points to the phone, telling me to lift up the receiver, and take the call, before quietly closing the door behind him.

I think of my Dad right away. Then George, and Rose, or my mother, even, but it's not them. It isn't any of them. It's Hardly. I should never have doubted it. It was always going to be Hardly. Always.

"He's been shot, Son. Ireland. Feckin' Ireland. They sent him back to Ireland, again. It's his leg. He took a bullet in his leg. He's lost his leg, son. Are you hearing me, Malcolm? Are you receiving me?"

No matter how many times I tell him, my father still believes that you have to speak very loudly into the phone in order for your voice to be heard during long-distance telephone calls. In fact, throughout the years, perhaps because of Hardly, he's somehow acquired the voice of a military man, and speaks as though he's speaking into his radio.

"Yes, Dad, I can hear you fine. Take your time. Tell me what happened. Is he okay? Is Hardly okay?"

My Dad tells me about a routine patrol, and a couple of boys pointing their older brother's rifle out of a tenement window. Nobody knows what they were aiming for, and it could have been much worse. If it had been higher, if their aim had been more accurate, who knows where it might have hit him. The bullet struck him in the lower part of his right leg, shattering the bone. He's lost part of his leg. They had to take it off but he's going to be okay. That's all that we know. "He wanted you to know, Malcolm. He called me and wanted me to give you a ring."

Hardly, true to his word, tried to join the British Army the moment he turned 15. He was happy living with my Dad, but wanted to get as far away from Rab, his father, and Kilmarnock, as he could. So, he did. They resisted taking him at first, probably because of his small stature, but he was persistent, and finally, Hardly became a soldier. They sent him everywhere too, Germany, England, Ireland. Always, Ireland.

"I thought it was okay over there now, Dad. I thought there was a truce or something. He told me that. I'm sure Hardly told me that."

"It's better than it used to be, but it's not safe. It's not safe to be a soldier anywhere. This'll be the end of it, though. This has to be the feckin' end of it. He won't be on active duty anymore. He can come home. He'll be coming home." There's anger in his voice as he speaks. I can hear it. Maybe he's angry at the Army.

143

Or, maybe he's angry at the boys who shot Hardly. Or, maybe he's just angry at the decisions that Hardly and I have made. I can't tell. It's been too long, and there are too many miles between us.

"Malcolm, I should be signing off now, Son. I should be disconnecting. You can phone him, though. He's at the military hospital in Glasgow. He can take calls, you know. " His practical phone manners return, as he waits for me to speak.

"I will Dad. Tell him that I'm thinking about him. Tell him that I'll call him." I get the phone number from him, and try asking my Dad how he's doing, but it's too late. He's saying 'Cheerio', and hanging up the phone, while I'm still talking.

When I tell Heather about Hardly, I tell her all of it. I tell her about Rab, and how he hit Hardly with the iron, and the beatings, and my Dad taking Hardly in. I even tell her about getting pissed on at our tree. When I tell her the part about two boys shooting at him from a window, I can't talk anymore. I don't want to think of my friend out there on the street, dressed in his uniform, vulnerable.

"Are you going to go see him? Are you going to go to Scotland?" We're sitting on the edge of my bed, and the late September sunshine is streaking through the windows of my apartment.

"No, not right now. I'll try and go back once he's out of hospital. I spoke to one of his doctors. He's going to have lots of rehab, lots of work to do. They'll fit him with an artificial leg but he will walk. He will walk." I feel guilty as soon as I say it, and it seems as though she can sense it too.

"So, what are you going to do? Work? Should we just work all summer to forget about it?" She's not angry. She says it as though she really wants to hear the answer.

I look out my window, at the sun, wishing that summer was beginning, instead of ending and I know that I need to do something, anything to help me not think about my friend lying in a hospital bed. "Nope, let's get out of town. Can you get some time off from Terry? Let's get out of here and do something." It makes perfect sense. We both want to prolong the summer so, why not? Why not do what people do in every city of the world do when the sun begins to fade and the nights get shorter?

At first she just stares into my eyes, as though she's questioning my motivation, but after a moment there's no doubt. Her smile tells me that we're going. Her smile tells me that summer might last just a little bit longer.

Her idea is to camp in an old army tent, at a lake that she's heard of, that's two hundred miles away, in the interior of the province. She wants to sleep under the stars, cook over an open fire, and howl at the moon, while drinking a bottle of Indian whisky, that's been in her cupboard for years. I've never heard of Indian whisky, and even in my wildest days, can't remember ever howling at the moon.

I want to find a nice bed and breakfast, far away from the city, and gaze up at the stars from the comfort of a room that has a warm fireplace.

The compromise comes when I spot a 'For Sale' sign, on an old motorhome sitting by the side of the road. I phone her, and suggest that we can still go to her lake, and still cook outside, and yes, she can bring her bottle of Indian whisky. This way though, with the motorhome, we can be warm and dry, and it will give us some privacy from other campers.

And with the ease of an early relationship compromise, she answers, "Yes, I can't wait."

The motorhome is sound, and I fill four lined pages with notes from the operating instructions and tips that the previous owner has given me. It has a heavy feel to it on the road, and although it's smaller, compared to some of the others that pass us; it's still the largest vehicle that either of us has ever driven. I check the side mirrors, as I drive, then look over at her, and gaze just a moment too long at her bare legs.

"You're going to get us into an accident. Why don't you just pull over, gawk at my legs for a while? Then you can drive on safely." Her smile is playful, as she says it.

"You shouldn't have worn those shorts if you didn't want me to look at your legs." I smile back at her, trying very hard to keep my eyes on the road.

"I didn't say that I didn't want you to look at them. And if you want, I can take my shorts off." She means it. I can tell, as she bravely keeps her gaze on me.

"Keep them on. I'll concentrate on the road." I laugh, and it feels good, as I watch her, from the corner of my eye, mischievously pulling at her shorts.

The old motorhome bounces and coughs along the scenic roads, with the engine sounding like it wants to rest.

"It doesn't feel like it wants to go camping." She holds onto her seat as she says it, letting the sun beat down on her face.

"It's reliable. I had it checked out, old but reliable."

"I know you did. I trust it. I trust both of you."

We pass other campsites on the way to our campground, where other campers are also trying to pretend that it's still summer. We see boat launches and barbecue pits and signs telling us who the campsite hosts are. They all look like small miniature villages, with people pretending that this is their real home. I keep thinking that I'll see a fast food restaurant, situated right in the middle of one of them. As we drive on, I start to enjoy the feeling of being away from the city, and silently hope that our campsite will be more private, more remote.

As the afternoon sun fades to dusk, the other campgrounds we pass become fewer and fewer, until it seems that we're the only other people on the road, driving along in our clunky old motorhome. Just as we begin to think that perhaps our lake doesn't really exist, we see it. There's no sign, and although it has an official name, it's been called, 'the Lake at the End of the World' for as long as anyone can remember. It backs onto a mountain and is too cold to swim in for a long period of time, so families with children don't come here. When we pull up, we aren't surprised that there are only two other campers spaced out around the small beach.

"Let's park at the end, away from them."

"My thoughts exactly," I answer, steering towards the narrow road, and parking right on the gravelly beach, giving us a perfect view of the lake.

We sit for a moment, and look out the front windshield, enjoying the vibrant greenness of the lakes' colour, as the sun drops down behind the mountains.

The excitement of the trip, along with our Olympic flirting session since leaving the city, has tired us. Having memorized my notes the night before, it doesn't take long for me to set up the site, with the awning out and chairs underneath it, while Heather starts making a fire.

"We must be sharing the head today. We're working well together," I say, realizing that we automatically set about preparing the campsite, each doing different chores.

"Remind me again, what possessed me to let a man I hardly know take me out into the middle of nowhere? And for someone who does all his camping in hotels, you have a very sharp hatchet." She's chopping up some kindling, as she says it.

"You trust your instincts, and they told you that I was safe. It doesn't have to be complicated, does it?" I think of Natasha and how complicated our relationship seemed at times. Then I smile, and look over at Heather, standing so simply, and beautifully, wearing her shorts and tee-shirt, readying our campfire.

"I believe you, but I'll hold on to this tonight anyway, okay?" She's holding the hatchet across her chest, as though defending herself, smiling back at me.

The darkness falls quickly, and after a hurried dinner over the outside grill, we settle into a couple of chairs by the fire.

"Are there always this many stars out at night?" I look up, as I ask, amazed at all the different lights in the sky.

"Only if you look up, if not there aren't any. You gotta always look up."

The bottle of whisky appears, and Heather performs the ceremonial throwing away of the cork, explaining that it's traditional when you're camping, to drink the whole bottle. I smile back; knowing that even with our best efforts, there's no possibility that we'll empty the bottle.

She sets a candle on a rock, and we watch the glow from the light dance on the water's reflection. I take a blanket from the motorhome and lay it over her, and she smiles a thank you back at me.

"You looked cold."

"The whisky will warm me up," she coughs at the strength of her drink.

I cradle the glass in my hand, sipping the drink slowly. "I like you."

"I know you do," she says thoughtfully, "but you still haven't looked up yet. Look up and I'll tell you a story." There's too much darkness between us for me to be sure, but I'm fairly certain that the dark flicker, the hesitation, is back in her eyes.

I lay my head back in the chair and stare at the brilliance of the stars, waiting for her to speak.

"I have a daughter, a little girl." She pauses, "no, no, don't look at me. Keep looking up. This is the only way I can do this."

I want to look at her eyes. I want to see what her face is doing, but I don't move, in case she stops talking. The courage in her voice makes the words sound harsh and unfeeling, but I can tell that she's straining, straining to get them out.

"I wanted to tell you. I almost told you lots of times, but then something would happen; something would take it out of my mind for a little while. Then when you told me about your friend, when you told me about Hardly, I had to. I have to." She pauses between sentences as though she's weighing the impact of the words, listening to see what will happen once she says them. "It's like a door that I closed ten years ago, and haven't opened since. I think about her, but then I move onto something else, quickly, and then she's not in my mind, not in my thoughts. The nights were bad for a long, long time. I'd meet men and they'd amuse me. They'd save me from the alone nights, or I'd drink, like I am now," she half laughs, wearily.

"Where is she now, your little girl?"

She laughs again, but nervously this time. "Her name is Emily. That's what I was going to call her anyways, and I think she's in Ontario, back in my old hometown, but I don't know. I can't know that for sure."

The darkness and the silence envelope us. I feel as though I'm a long, long way away from my safe apartment that overlooks the water. It's almost like I've stopped breathing, as I sit there, waiting for more.

"Yes, I know. You deserve more of an explanation. What kind of mother leaves her daughter? It was complicated. I was eighteen. Michael was married, and older, much older."

I stare at the candle, watching it's reflection on the water.

"This man, Michael, does he have your baby?"

I glance over at her and her face is hard but her eyes are wet. She's staring ahead, not looking at me, trying to get through her story. "Yes, she probably doesn't even know that I exist. They kept me in a facility, told me they would look after me. I didn't know where I was exactly. They said that they would help me raise the baby. I believed them, him and that old nurse. The whole time I was isolated. It was some kind of mental health place. I never really saw anyone else while I was there. They kept me alone. I'd spend days and nights dreaming about my baby, and figuring out how our lives would all work. I knew by this point that Michael wouldn't leave his wife, but I still thought there would be a way to

151

keep everybody happy. Everybody was being so nice to me, anything I needed, anything, it was given to me."

"Then, she was born. She was so soft and warm. I remember holding her, I remember that. Then I just remember darkness and when I woke there was no baby, and I was in a different room, a different place, but with the same old nurse who had been looking after me."

She pours another glass of whisky and shakily holds it to her lips. She's angry now, and her face is smeared with tears.

"I don't know how long it was before I saw the light again. It was two weeks, maybe a month. I really don't know how long."

I stare at the water, the candle, anywhere, trying to let her tell her secret in the darkness between us. I wait for a while, before asking, "Why didn't you go back, find her, find Michael?"

"I was eighteen and scared shitless. They had taken me to some old musty hospital in Alberta. Alberta, I had never been a hundred miles away from home and now I was in Alberta. And this nurse terrified me, things became different, there were no smiles anymore. It just seemed easier, safer; to move on, try to forget."

"At the time, I did ask, I asked about Michael, where was he, where was my baby. Then the darkness would come again. When I awoke it was the same nurse, same room, but I felt different, lighter in my head, but still sad, really sad. I kept asking the questions, and each time the darkness would come, and each time I woke, the questions seemed to matter less and less, until finally I understood. I knew that if I stopped asking the questions she'd let me go. So, I stopped asking."

"She was drugging you." I look over at her face, wet with tears.

"Yes, I knew that at the time, but didn't know. It's hard to explain. The day they let me go, the old nurse followed me out, and told me that there had been another option. She told me her instructions had been to decide whether I walked out of there, or left on a slab. Those were her words; I still remember them. She told me that I was a good girl, and should get on with my life. She said that I should get on a bus to somewhere, anywhere, go find a new home, but to remember that she'd be watching me. On a slab, Malcolm. She said that I could have left there on a slab."

The fire is almost out. The few red embers are glowing in the dark, and the last of the candle has extinguished itself. I pull my chair until it's touching hers. I reach over and try to hold her. She feels cold underneath the blanket. My confident girl is shaking now, scared.

"I used to think I could see her, that insane old bitch, in crowds or when I was alone. Sometimes, I thought I sensed eyes. One day I'm sure I did. I was in a park; it was busy and I was running. I passed this old woman, who was sitting on a bench, and she smiled at me. Her eyes had that knowing look about them. It was her, older, but still her, and she nodded as though she was still telling me to keep my mouth shut."

"Your parents, your father is still alive, I thought?"

She pauses again, trying to compose herself, her voice changing again, becoming frightened again. "We weren't close. When my mother died he died too. He brought me up, and when I turned sixteen, he stopped caring what I did or didn't do. When I became pregnant I never told him. I just said I was leaving. He didn't care."

"Brothers, sisters, there was no one who would look for you?"

She seems frustrated now. "No, there's no one else. I just disappeared, Malcolm. I just came out here. I saw the ocean and knew that I couldn't get much farther away from them. I got a job, and then another one, and then started working for Terry. I just tried to disappear from all of them."

It makes sense. It all makes sense. There's always been something below the surface. There's always been a secret. "This man, Michael, who is he? Is he capable of hurting you, of hurting Emily?" I think of Hardly's father, Rab, and the bullies during my Kilmarnock school days.

She won't answer though. She just keeps staring straight ahead, barely acknowledging that I'm holding her. "No one knows. No one knows, only you. I wasn't going to tell you, but after what happened, after what you told me about your friend..."

By the time we make our way to the bed in the old motorhome it's pitch dark and the only sound is the whistling of the night air. She lets me hold her, and we lie there, fully clothed, feeling each other's warmth, until we fall asleep.

When the first lights of the morning squeeze through the blinds on the window, her breathing changes, and I know that she's awake. Her words come out firmly and without hesitation. "I keep dreaming about her, Malcolm. I see her face, her little baby face. I can't stop thinking about her face." She pauses and takes a deep breath before continuing. "Now that it's out, now that I've said it, I know what I have to do. I have to find her. I need to see her. I need to make sure that she's okay. I'm going back there."

CHAPTER 19

Things seem quieter, slower. It's as though the weight of the night before is holding me down, weighing me down. I tinker with the motorhome, checking fluid levels, inspecting the tires, and spend long minutes staring at it, trying to keep my mind busy. Heather soaks her feet in the cold water of the lake, staring out at its greenness.

We eat, almost in silence, respecting each other's thoughts. She touches my hand from time to time, and I try to smile, rubbing hers back, enjoying the comfort, the closeness.

I jump in the water, letting the coldness numb me, thinking about all the trips back to Scotland that I didn't take, and all the phone calls from Hardly when he would ask me when I was coming home. I swim out and back, and when I surface she's staring at me, waiting for me.

I pull myself up, and can feel the calmness coming from the still lake.

She's sitting on a rock by the edge of the water, leaning forward, looking as beautiful and helpless as I've ever seen anyone look.

I think about the movie of my life that plays in my head. I think about my Dad, and, I think about Hardly. I think about his phone calls, his letters. The same Hardly, the same Hardly that climbed the tree with me, the same Hardly that had to go home to Rab, his father, every night.

As I watch Heather, and think of the journey ahead of her, I decide.

It has nothing to do with the blueness of her eyes, or the way her face tries to look strong yet pleading, at the same time. In fact, it really doesn't even have anything to do with a little girl, who may or may not be called, Emily. It's about chapping on the door and staring into a man's face. It's about taking in a young boy when there's no one else to help him. It's about doing what my Dad would do.

"You're staring at me, Malcolm. Say something to me. Say anything." She's crying again.

"I don't want to get old and have a list of things I haven't done, Heather. I don't want to have regrets."

"I don't understand. What does that mean, Malcolm?" She's speaking quickly now, wiping at her eyes.

"I'm going to come with you. I'm going to come to Ontario with you. I'll help you."

She looks back at me, and shakes her head, telling me no, over and over again. It doesn't matter of course. It almost feels good to me. I don't feel like I'm the man who was pushed into the pool at his friend's party. Instead, I feel like the boy who punched Stuart Douglas in the face to help my friend, and I haven't felt like that boy in a very long time.

There's an old song where the singer sings about his girlfriend moving in with him, and that he had to buy her a washing machine. Well, I already have a washing machine, but after our night at the Lake at the End of the World, it makes sense to be closer. In the song it happens quickly, but with us, it took from the beginning of my summer, that was supposed to be about maybes, and sex, but wasn't, until early October.

The days after the trip we spend moving her belongings from her apartment to mine. She stops in front of my big windows, from time to time, looking out at the water, smiling. She's glad to be here. I can tell. We unpack only the bare necessities, knowing that we'll be leaving soon. We avoid talking about specific things, and in my mind I try to think of little beyond the obvious. I know that we're going to Ontario, to find a ten year old girl, who may or may not be called Emily. I know that I have to ask some questions though.

"You need to tell me about him, Heather; I need to know what I'm walking into."

"I know. I'll tell you what I remember." She sits on the edge of my bed, our bed, taking a break from arranging her figurines on top of a bookcase.

"He had this presence. It's hard to explain. He was a large man, but that wasn't it. He just had this way of being that made you want to listen to what he was going to say next. He'd talk about the power that he had in the town. He frightened me once. We pulled into a parking lot and he ran from the car to a group of men. There were lots of them, but when they turned and saw that it was him, they backed off. They let him through. He grabbed one of them, and pulled him to the ground. I looked away and couldn't see what happened, but I could hear the sounds of the man as he was beaten. When he came back to the car his hands were bleeding, but he was smiling, happy.

"The other men didn't step in?"

"That was the thing. They were afraid. There was always talk about him in town, talk that he was dirty, that he took the law into his own hands, but it's a small town. People talk about each other all the time."

"He? You mean, Michael? That's who you mean?"

She keeps looking at the walls, not facing me, avoiding my gaze. Her voice is almost automatic and it seems as though she's reading from a book, when she answers. "Yes, yes, of course, Michael. Michael."

It's not fear, or maybe it is. Maybe it's the uncertainty, the unknown, but I have to ask, have to see if there's another way. "I wonder if there's someone who specializes in this, a detective, an investigator. I wonder if there's somebody that could work with us, research it, find out more. There must be somebody that can help us to find Emily, find out where she is."

I know that she must have thought about it, considered it, and she doesn't hesitate in answering me. "I can't Malcolm. I just can't. I can't take the chance that he'll take her away, hide her away, if he knows that I'm looking for her. I have to do this myself. It's time. I left it too long as it is. She's ten, ten years old, and she's my girl Malcolm, she's my little girl."

I don't know children. I don't have brothers or sisters. I have an aunt, my father's sister, in Scotland, who has boys, cousins of mine. They're younger though, and I had left my Scottish school, by the time they attended it. I remember them as rambunctious, unruly, boys, who were always getting under my father's skin. My early girlfriend, who had wanted children seems like a long ago adventure, a youthful romance. When I think of her now, and my long ago reluctance to want a child, it seems like it was someone else living my life.

We sit in silence for a while, neither looking at each other, and I wonder what it must have been like for her to carry this for so long. I know what it's like to hate. I hated my mother for years. I hated that she left my father. She'd promised that she'd live in Scotland with him, promised us a normal life, and then just gave up. It wasn't until my parents were older, and years had passed, that I forgave her for denying me a normal childhood. I came to the realization, that although they were my parents, they were really just kids trying to raise kids, and grow up themselves at the same time. That's when I realized that with forgiveness comes freedom, and I somehow managed to let it go.

It was easy to get an invitation for Heather and I to have dinner at Terry and Jo's house. And Jo didn't sound surprised at all when I asked if we could do it quickly, even tonight possibly. We made a deal that she wouldn't tell too many embarrassing stories about me and that I'd pretend to like her cooking.

"You look different Malcolm, you're happier than the last time I saw you, maybe even settled. No hold on, not settled, you'll never look settled, just happy," Jo is enjoying herself, trying to make me squirm, as she sits by her husbands' side, across from Heather and I.

"It's the regular sex. It'll do that. I've been telling him that for years." Terry says it in his all-knowing, philosophical tone, forgetting that he's been preaching casual sex to me all these years, not regular.

"It must be the lasagne. It's very, very good Jo." I take Heather's hand as I answer them, and wait for them to smile knowingly, as we interact.

"You've got something on your mind Malcolm, I can tell. What is it your Dad says? What's the thing about the fart? Come on. I know you remember." He strains his face, trying to remember another of my Dad's colloquialisms.

"He says that I'm as subtle as a fart at a funeral, Terry." I can see my father's face saying it, dropping his Scottish charm right in front of us, then smiling, waiting for our reaction.

"That's it," Terry laughs, "that's it, and I know that something is up. You can't hide it from me. I've known you far too long Malcolm, and remember, I'm a salesman. I read people's faces for a living.

Heather returns his stare, and decides to lay our cards on the table. "I need to leave for a while. I need some time off, to go back east, family stuff, and Malcolm's going to come with me." She steps out of our shared head, and drops our intentions right in front of them.

They know that it's serious. They know by her tone, her look that it's about more than just visiting family back east. Terry puts down his knife and fork, clasps his hands in from of him, and is about to start his enquiries when Jo stops him. There must be something in our faces, or something in the way that I'm holding

Heather's hand. Jo knows, she just knows, and she does what only one person in the world can do. She takes control of her husband.

"Don't, Honey. Let it be." She says it firmly, kindly.

"I need to know. I'm concerned. Not nosy, just concerned."

And he is. I can tell from his face. He's looking at me, trying to smile, wanting answers, but I can't give them to him.

"I have a daughter, a little girl. I need to go find her, find out if she's okay." It's easier for her to say it this time. Her secret has been told once already.

We sit in silence for a moment, but Terry keeps looking at me, trying to read me. "How long will you be gone? Can you tell me that, or will you even be back? Is that too much to ask?" He isn't just asking about his marketing assistant. I know that, and it isn't just his natural inquisitiveness. He's concerned.

"Yes, of course we'll be back, and we'll call you once we're there. We'll know more once we get to Ontario. And, I'm sorry. I'm sorry to do this." She says the words with feeling, holding onto my hand, squeezing it. I don't know if she's sorry to be telling her employer that she needs time off, or sorry for taking away his friend.

"Malcolm, did you learn how to use that goddamned cell phone that I bought you?" He's frustrated. I can tell, but he's letting it go. He's letting it go.

"Yeah, Terry, and I'll call you." I answer my friend.

Sometimes, when you've known people long enough and they've been down the occasional dark road with you, they just

162

know when it's the right time to say nothing. And although it pains him to leave it alone, he does. And, with Jo's soothing hand on his, we finish our dinner without him asking another question about our trip.

His message on my answering machine wakes us early the next day. "Heather, Come back when you're ready. Your job will be here for you. And Malcolm, I expect a phone call when you get wherever the hell you're going and every day from that point on." Then there's the pause that married men often make when they're hearing their partner speak, "Oh, and Jo sends her love."

CHAPTER 20

The airline magazine on the plane shows a map of Ontario. Heather points to an area between two towns in the northern part of the province, Timmins and Sudbury, to show me our destination. I search the index of towns and cities looking for "Woodbine", but it isn't there. There's just a long curved line showing a road with nothing in between. Twelve thousand people living somewhere along a line, in a town that doesn't have its name on the airline magazine's map.

We stay overnight at a hotel just north of Toronto, intending to make the twelve hour trip in the rental car to Woodbine the next day. I've never travelled in Canada. My trips have always taken me overhead, bound for my other home in Scotland, so the weather catches me by surprise. Winter actually arrives during autumn in Ontario, so between our tiredness from the flight, and being unaccustomed to the cold, we can't wait to climb into bed and feel warm. I hold Heather in my arms as we listen to the fan from the hotel room heater blowing warm air into the room.

"Unless things have changed, there should still only be one elementary school. Emily will be in fourth grade. We can start there. We can go the school, once we arrive there." She makes it sound like a question, sounding like she wants some reassurance.

"What about Michael? What about just going to his house and confronting him? Or at least taking a look and see if we can see Emily? Wouldn't that work better?" I picture a confrontation with Michael and then the police being involved if need be, and then the happy ending, Emily being re-united with Heather. I don't feel concerned or intimidated by the man at all. It doesn't have to be complicated. We're the ones that are doing the right thing.

She's shaking her head while I'm talking and tensing up in my arms. "Not yet, Malcolm, not yet. You don't know this man. This is his town. Please let me try this my way. Let's just see where she is, how she is, please, Malcolm."

I pull her tighter towards me and it's hard not to agree with her. She's probably right. If we can scope out the town anonymously for a couple of days and check up on Emily without causing any commotion then that's probably our best option. "This is a really small town." I think about the absence of the name on the map. "We need to be careful. Somebody might recognize you, Heather. If we're doing this your way, then we want to be invisible for as long as we can. I think that's important." I'm making it up as I go along, not really knowing what we're going to do next.

"It's winter here already, and I'm going to be wrapped up in enough scarves and hats that I'll look just like the locals. Nobody will know who I am. Nobody will recognize me." I don't ask any more. But I know, now. I know that she has a plan.

When she emerges from the bathroom, the next day, she's a brunette. Her long hair is gone, and it curls around the edge of her face, hiding the shape of it. She's wearing no makeup, and her colour is a pale white. I have to lift her hair to see her half dimple. It isn't a disguise, but it has the look of someone who can blend into a crowd. She isn't the girl with the green, or even red, hair anymore, and I suspect she doesn't look like the scared eighteen-year old who left town ten years earlier. She doesn't look like anyone, and I suppose that's exactly how she wants to look.

It's dark when we drive in, but the streetlights give me my first view of the secluded little town. It's old in an almost charming, but not quite yet rundown, kind of way. I survey the main street, and it seems to me that it's the kind of town that will always look old. It's too far away from major cities to warrant things like a mall or a large retail outlet. Instead, there's an old hardware store, a pub, a bank, a couple of coffee shops and restaurants, and a community centre. We spot a motel as we drive in, right on the highway, at the edge of town, and decide that we'll stay there. We're tired and Heather is anxious to get out of the dark cold night, and check into our room, but I want to see what the town looks like. I want to see the place where she grew up. So, we drive up and down the streets, trying to get a feel for the place.

She's sitting low in the passenger seat, her head turning as we drive, remembering her hometown. "Holy shit, it hasn't changed. That's new, or maybe it isn't." She points to various buildings, trying to remember.

We pass a library, and then I pull over in front of the high school, surprised at the sign in front of it. "It's your name, 'Postman Secondary School'. Why is your last name on there?"

She slumps even further down in the seat. "My great, great something or other. My family's name's all over here. We even have a street named after us. Can you keep driving please?"

She's looking away from me as I pull back onto the road, and drive towards the motel. I hear every sound as the wheels crunch along the icy road. There is no warmth here, just coldness, everywhere.

I can smell the liquor, and hear the television program coming from the doors behind the front desk. The manager is a thin, sallow faced man. His grey hair is matted, greasy, untidy. He ambles out slowly, almost staggering, pushing his long unruly hair away from his face. He seems disturbed that I'm taking him from his television program, and I can smell the alcohol on his breath, even before he speaks. He only brightens up when I tell him that we'll be staying for a few days, perhaps even a week.

"Malcolm Wilson, do I detect a little bit of an accent, Mr Malcolm? Is that a Scotland accent that I hear?" He takes my credit card and processes it through his old fashioned machine, while speaking with his own French-Canadian accent. "I'm Claude, nice to meet you, Mr Malcolm."

"Well, I was from Scotland once, now I'm not so sure where I'm from, Claude." I laugh, tired of telling my half-Scottish, half-Canadian story once or twice too often, and try to keep my distance from his breath.

"A true Scotsman is always from Scotland." When he answers, he sounds almost belligerent, putting my credit card back on the counter, and staring through his glassy, drunk eyes.

All of a sudden, I don't like him. I don't like this man who wants to tell me what it means to be from Scotland. It's been a long drive to a town that I know little about, and I'm tired. I drop my Canadian half for a bit, and give him my best Kilmarnock

Secondary School glare along with my genuine Scots accent. "I grew up there. I know exactly what it means to be from Scotland, Claude."

He seems to catch a breath of sobriety as he answers me, in a steadier voice. "Well it's good that you're proud of that." Solemnly, he puts the room key on the counter, and makes his way back to his television program in the other room.

Walking to the door, I realize how weary I am, and wonder why I'm trying to intimidate a man who's going to have access to my room for the next few days while Heather and I spend our time being amateur stalkers. I wonder if I should have tried to check in with an alias and paid cash. It's too late now so I do my best to make my peace with him. "Listen, Claude, I'm sorry. I'm just tired. I didn't mean to snap at you. Have you been here long, in Woodbine, I mean?"

"It's fine. I can see that you're tired, Mr Malcolm." His own demeanour changes back to almost friendly, but he still edges himself towards the sound of his television. "The girlfriend and me, have been here for a few years now. Came out here to hide from my crazy ex, and decided to stay. It's a nice little town, quiet, miles from everywhere. You and your wife, you have business here?" He motions towards the car where Heather is still sitting, slouched down in the passenger seat.

"Not really, just kind of taking a time out."

"Well, maybe we'll see you in the morning." He looks at me as though he's heard my lie many times before.

Nodding, I venture back out into the cold night, not sure if I've just made a friend or an enemy, but glad that he's a man hiding from something. I've had clients over the years that are hiding. Some from an ex like Claude, some from more serious circumstances, and they all have one thing in common. They tend to live quietly and not cause any commotion. I hope that's the case with Claude. I hope there won't be any more questions.

I grab the luggage and hold the room door open, letting Heather hurriedly walk inside, her scarf covering her face, with her hat pulled down low. She looks like any other traveller trying to get out of the cold night.

The room is larger and cleaner than I expected. It looks like a thousand other motel rooms in a thousand different cities. There's a small desk at the edge of the room, a bed, and a table mounted to the wall, with a portable coffee maker on it. The water is running in the toilet, but with a jiggle of the handle, I make it stop. I pull the sheets back to make the bed look more inviting, as Heather turns up the furnace thermostat.

"You don't know a Frenchmen called Claude, do you? I'm not sure if he lived here when you were here or not. He's a drinker too, by the smell of it." I don't expect her to know him, but I want to make sure that Claude didn't recognize her as she went from the car to the room.

She replies almost immediately, setting her suitcase down, and unpacking. "Nope, I'm pretty sure that I don't, Malcolm. Why, did he say something to you? You gotta remember, I was eighteen when I left. It's been ten years. He could have moved here since then you know."

"No, honey. He didn't say anything. I just wanted to make sure that it wasn't somebody that you knew."

We stand and look at the room with its musty smell, and bright floral curtains on the front window. It'll be our home base for whatever period of time it takes to find Emily.

"It's bigger than the motorhome." I try to make it seem more appealing than it really is.

She laughs and pulls the scarf from her face. "I love our motorhome. I miss it."

The next morning, I wake up staring up at the shiny sparkles embedded in the ceiling of the motel room, remembering a motel room from a long time ago, that I shared with my mother.

Leaving Heather asleep in the room with the sparkles, I drive into town and find a coffee shop. I pick up a couple of breakfast sandwiches, a tea for Heather and a coffee for myself. There are a couple of workmen picking up their own breakfasts, but nobody seems to notice me; nobody seems to care. Things do seem to have a different pace from the city though. Nobody is in a hurry. Nobody seems too anxious about anything. It seems like just an ordinary little town.

Heather is awake and dressed, and ready to go, so we quickly eat in our room, then leave to go to the elementary school, before it's even seven thirty. As we drive, I watch her and almost want to smile. If she wasn't slunked down in the seat, semi disguised with

170

her woollen hat on, it would almost have feel like just another adventure. But this is different than finding the lake at the end of the world. This is about finding a little girl.

Her idea is for us to park on the street, by the rows of houses, across from the school, and watch for a girl who might resemble her. She tells me that she'll know her; she's sure that she'll know her own child. It isn't a great plan, but it's what she wants. When I suggested driving past Michael's house she shut me down again, telling me that she doesn't want to see him yet. For now, she just wants to see Emily.

It's October, and although it's cold for us, we hope that the local kids won't be in their winter outfits yet, and we'll be able to see their faces. We have two old childhood pictures of Heather, on the dash of the car. They're the only pictures she has, and I've tried to burn their image into my head. In both of the pictures, she's alone, sitting on someone's living room couch somewhere, with a tentative look on her face. It's odd to see such a serious expression on a little girl's face, so different from the smiling girl that I first met. She thinks she must have been eight or nine when the pictures were taken, just a little younger than Emily would be now. So, if Emily looks like her mother, like Heather, then we'll have an idea of what she looks like. I touch the old photographs with my fingers, hoping that the same face will come walking down the street.

"I have something for you." She hands me a small plastic ball from the pocket of her jacket.

171

I hold the ball in my hand. "I'm sorry, what is this for?

"We might not be able to tell if it's her from the car. This way you can go and kick the ball around the park, or play with it somehow. You can get a better look that way. I brought it with me." As she says it, I can almost see the reality of the statement hitting her. I can see her becoming deflated, as she realizes that it really doesn't make any sense for me to be playing, alone in a park, with a little ball. I try not to smile as she forces it into my hand. "I don't know, Malcolm. I just thought it might help."

As we lay in the room, the night before, we talked about sitting outside an elementary school in a rental car, watching young children when you're thousands of miles from home. We decided if a concerned neighbour, or a teacher, or even a policeman, knocked on our window with questions, we'd tell them we'd stopped for a few minutes to reminisce about Heather's old school. We were on our way to points north, taking a trip down memory lane. It sounded plausible to me, but to be actually in the school yard, where the children are, and with a small ball, this added a whole new dimension to it.

I hold the ball in my hand, thinking about how difficult this is going to be, not wanting to see her disappointed.

"Hey, they're starting to come. Look up the road." I see a few children, some walking together, a couple by themselves, farther down the street coming towards us, and we're right. These are hearty, small-town kids and the cold weather isn't bothering them at all. They're wearing jackets, and some of them have

172

woollen hats on, but none of them seem to be wearing scarves, or anything that might cover their faces. They all walk, none of them are driven. Some are even coming out of the houses that we're parked alongside. She was right. This is a small town, with small town sensibilities. Children find their own way to school in Woodbine.

She peers intently, crouching uncomfortably, even farther down in the vehicle, her eyes just barely above the dashboard. I look at the old photographs of her, and wait as dozens of little legs sluggishly make their way towards the school. They come at us from both ends of the road, almost simultaneously. There are little boys, and bigger boys, walking together, and then little girls, in twos or threes, never alone. We're parked across from a park that joins the schoolyard. It takes a great deal of concentration to look in one direction, and then back in the other, all the while trying not to look suspicious.

The children walk along the road or on the sidewalks, not even glancing our way. Some of them cut across the park, making it impossible to see their faces. At first there's only a few, but then they come in bunches. They're talking in loud, excited voices, some pushing at others, doing anything I suppose, to not think about spending the next few hours in a classroom. I spend my time straining my eyes, trying to compare their faces with the photos, while looking up and down the road just in case another vehicle comes along, or a parent wanders by wondering what we're doing there.

"This is difficult. I can't see the ones in the park." There's frustration in her voice.

"Look, those are all girls, see what they do. They all walk along the side, off the road. The boys don't care. They're in the road, showing off for the girls. Shit, we try to impress you guys even at that age." It's interesting to me to see the patterns, to see how the young children show off for each other.

The girls stick to the sidewalk, or if they're really daring, they walk on the outside curb. But the boys bounce between sidewalk and road, not caring about the odd car that comes along. We search their little faces, trying to find some kind of a resemblance, something that will make us look twice. I want them to turn their heads, to give me more than just a glance. I want them to give me something that looks familiar.

Heather holds her own photograph in her hand. "This is too hard. I'll know her. I know I will. I just can't see them all, not from here."

She says it again, that a mother knows her child. She's convinced that she'll recognize Emily. I let my silence tell her that I agree, but secretly I think that we might need to find another way. And then, just as fast as it started, it ends, and they're all in their classrooms, away from us. It seems like it has only been minutes from the time they came walking down the road to the time they're all behind the school doors. There had been perhaps a hundred children, all different sizes, but most of them could have passed for a ten year old, and we saw the faces of maybe thirty. At least half

174

had crossed through the park. We need a way to be in that park, and we both know it.

"I guess I could be in the park at lunch time." I reluctantly hold the little ball, tight in my hand.

"It's the only way. I'd do it, but I might be recognized. I can't be, not yet." She touches my face as she says it.

"There might be another way. What would her last name be?"

"Postman, I mean, no, no. It would be Michaels' surname, Adrian, maybe. I don't know for sure. I don't even know her first name. Why, what does it matter?" She's exasperated now. "It's not as if we can call the school, and ask for her. She's ten years old. That just doesn't happen, Malcolm."

I silently start the engine and pull the car out onto the quiet road, heading back to the motel, trying to think of an excuse to be in a schoolyard during lunchtime. "I have an idea. Are there maps in the glove compartment?"

A couple of roadmaps fall out, as she opens the compartment. "I'm going to sit on that bench over there, and read these maps at lunch time. I'll be just an ordinary traveller, trying to find my way."

She pulls herself up, leans over, and kisses my cheek. Her lips are cold, even in the warmth of the car, but it feels good to have the closeness after staring out of the car window at little faces for so long. "That's it. Now you're thinking like a detective. Thank you." She goes back to her down low position, pointing me forward. "No don't turn. Keep driving. I'll show you something."

She quietly gives me 'lefts' and 'rights', guiding me along streets lined with old houses, until she whispers for me to pull over.

"It's the one with the porch, the big green porch," She's still whispering, pointing towards the house that she grew up in.

"I didn't want to ask. I wasn't sure if you'd want to see your Dad or the house." I stare at it, trying to imagine a little girl there. "It's nice. It looks like it would be a nice place to grow up."

She lets out a small almost anguished sound and keeps whispering. "It was Malcolm, but only for a little while. Then it was bad, really, really bad. Can we drive on please?"

There are times that you ask questions and times that you don't. So, I don't ask. I think of a girl, fifteen, almost sixteen, losing her mother, and living with a father who doesn't care. I steer the car down the street, past the house, and notice a large black sport utility vehicle, parked in the driveway. Its windows are tinted, and it's decked out for winter. I look over to see if I can see the expression on her face, but she's turned away, and her door is locked. At some point between leaving the school and driving to her old house, she locked her door.

CHAPTER 21

I hold open the door and wait as Heather hurries from the car to the room, with her hat pulled down low, over her face. The tension of the morning seems to leave us for a moment as I watch her pull off her jacket, toss her hat on the floor, and step forward, staring hard into my eyes, and pushing her body into mine.

"Are you sure? Now, is now the best time for this?" I ask as I slip my hands under her sweater, and cup them around her breasts.

"I want you, Malcolm. I want you to fuck me." She drags the words out, long and emphatically, sounding like someone that I don't know, kissing me hard, and biting into my lower lip.

I push her onto the bed, pulling off my jacket and sweater. I have an overwhelming urge to feel my skin on hers. She writhes up the bed towards the headboard, staring at me with a devilish look in her eyes, almost daring me to come and get her. I pull her shoes off roughly and, leaning forward, rest my body on hers, as she seems to almost struggle underneath me. She kisses me hard, over and over again. She holds my head, pulling it towards her, almost begging me to be harder with her, rougher with her. I reach down and loosen her jeans, slipping them down her legs, and slide my hand gently between them. I try to whisper in her ear, whisper Scottish in her ear, the way she likes, but she pushes my head away from her face.

"No, no, not this time, Malcolm. Fuck me like you mean it. Please, just fuck me." She spits the words out, firmly pushing her body up into mine.

I stand up and pull off the rest of my clothes, as she removes hers. I kneel over her, watching her eyes, not recognizing the hard look of desire that she's giving me. As I place my mouth on her breasts, she pulls my head hard, down on top of them, again begging me to be rougher with her. I quietly oblige, squeezing and touching, and tasting, and then, when I can't stand it any longer, I raise her legs, and place myself between them. She grabs my hand and places it on top of her wrists, over her head, forcing me to hold her down even more firmly. I hold my body there for a moment, waiting, staring at her, not recognizing her. It's only a moment before she pushes herself up into me again, her body asking for more.

I keep kissing her roughly, watching her eyes, as they dare me to drive myself deeper into her. Her lower body keeps pushing back, almost wildly, into me, as though she's trying to buck me off. I push back, staring at the wild look in her eyes, overpowering her strength with mine. She groans and writhes, biting into my shoulder, as though she's silently trying not to scream. I look away. There's an old battered headboard on the bed, and diamonds on the ceiling above us, diamonds that are just sparkles in the paint. I close my eyes, still pushing myself into her, wondering what's really happening. When I open them, there's a small, noise from her, and there's sweat on her face mixed with tears.

I pull myself off, as she starts to sob. "What are we doing? What was that? I thought you wanted me to. I'm sorry." I blurt out excuses and questions, as she covers her face with her hands.

"It's okay. You were okay. It's me. It's just me." She says it with resignation, with finality.

I reach out to touch her, but she's up quickly, and as she turns, I can see a hardness in her face that I've never noticed before.

We get back to the school just before lunch time, and watch the quiet school grounds and the adjoining park, knowing that it will soon be bustling with children. I grab the maps and kiss her gently, before getting out of the car. She slides into the driver's seat, and rolls the window down to talk to me. "I haven't thanked you for helping me, Malcolm." She pauses as though she doesn't know what to say next. "We're in this together now. It isn't my secret anymore. It's ours, both of ours."

She's looking into my eyes but she can't see me. She's somewhere else for a moment then smiling, she comes back. "I do love you, you know. I honestly do."

The usual feeling isn't in her words but I take them, accept them. "I know you do. It's going to be fine. It's going to be okay." Just like my Dad told me when he taught me how to punch bags of leaves in our front yard so many years ago. Everything is going to be okay.

She hands me the small ball and smiles as I stuff it into my jacket pocket, making my way to the park bench. As I wander over to the park, I think of all the variables involved with finding someone when you don't even know for sure what their name is. Does she actually attend this school? Does she still live in this town? And, will we even recognize her if she passes? I think of how we could have done more research, found more information. There are so many things that have to fall into place for us to find Emily, or whatever her name might be now.

I take up my place on the bench and spread one of the maps out beside me, all the while watching the large doors at the side of the school where the children entered in the morning. I can see the back end of the rental car where I parked, but I can't quite see Heather in the driver's seat. She'll be hunched down again, trying to stay out of sight.

The doors open, and a cascade of children come tumbling out, some running, others walking. They hold lunch kits and bags of various sizes and colours, and just as we predicted, most of them come walking towards the park. From my vantage point, I see them this time. It's much easier than sitting in the car. I think of the images from the old photographs that I left in the car, then look at the faces coming towards me, trying to see a face that might look familiar. Some of them stop and sit on other benches or wander around with half eaten sandwiches in their hands. Others stay in the schoolyard, hurriedly eating, probably trying to get the maximum amount of playtime in before school resumes. When they reach me, most pass right by as though I'm not there. Some of the cheekier ones make a face or whisper to their friends and laugh. It doesn't matter. I'm close now, close enough to see them.

I have no time for the boys, but I search the faces of all the little girls, looking for a half dimple or a cheeky smile, or something, anything that will make me think that it's Heather's Emily. I hold my jacket tight against me, shielding myself from the cold, enjoying watching their smiling faces, even smiling back at some of them. There doesn't seem to be as many as there were in the morning, so I assume that some are inside, eating or staying warm. The heartier ones run amongst the trees, playing on the schoolyard swings, shouting at each other, trying to be noticed, trying to do something that makes their long schooldays a little easier to bear.

There are two groups of little girls sitting on benches that face each other at the edge of the school yard, where it joins the park. I can see their fair hair, and hear their high pitched laughter, but I can't see their faces. It's hard to tell exactly what size a ten-year-old should be, especially when it's a long time since you were ten. These little girls look ten to me. They look like ten-year-old girls.

I leave my map on the bench and walk closer, trying to get a better look at the little girls. I can't see the car at all now, but I know that Heather will be watching me or watching the other children in the park. I focus my eyes, trying to see them as they giggle at each other, jumping excitedly while eating their lunches. As I get closer, I see them more clearly. There are two on one bench, and three on another. One girl is talking over the others, always interrupting. I hope that she isn't Emily. I'm a few feet from their benches, and can see one little girl, sitting at the end, listening, and I wonder if that might be her. I stop every few feet, focusing on the little girls, trying to see something, anything. As I try to remember the face in the old photograph, I hear footsteps coming up fast behind me. Suddenly, there's a strong hand coming down on my shoulder and I hear a man's voice.

I freeze in position, and watch as the little girls look at me, then turn back to their lunches, giggling. "Is there something we can do to help you sir?" He asks it in a condescending way, as though he isn't really interested in the answer.

When I turn, I see two of them, the man who stopped me, and a woman coming behind him. They've been walking fast to reach me, but don't seem out of breath. The man stands with his arms by his side, hands raised out, clenched into fists, as though he's ready to attack me if my answer isn't to his liking. "I'm sorry. I'm lost. I was looking for some directions. I have a map. I'm not a local here. I'm just passing through."

I stumble with my answers, and as I motion towards where I'd been sitting, I notice that the map is gone and that there's only an empty bench. I look around for the rental car, and the man seems to think that I'm looking for an opening, trying to make a run for it.

"The police are on their way, Buddy. Just relax. You can tell them your story when they get here." He pats the kids on their heads as they pass him on their way from the schoolyard to the park. Some look up and wonder what's happening while others just laugh and run by, continuing their games, ignoring us. Although the man looks to be about my age, he stares at me as though he's older, like a parent, scolding a child.

"The police? What are you talking about? Listen, I don't know what you think is happening here, and I'm sorry if I've caused you some confusion, but I really am just lost. I thought somebody could give me directions." I look at him, hoping for some understanding, knowing that I haven't done anything wrong.

The woman is standing beside him now, closer, waiting for his lead. The two of them seem fearless, protecting the children in their schoolyard. I look from her face to his, trying to appeal to them. "What did you think I was doing?" I say it as though I'm offended by their vague implications.

"Well, I get a call that there's a man lurking around the park, watching kids, staring at them, trying to smile at them." He answers me as though he's talking to one of the children. "I don't know what to make of that. So, I sit by my window, watching you. Then, when I see you sneaking up on those young girls, I think, well, I'll just come over and investigate for myself, see what kind of a man tries to talk to kids while he's got a bottle of something or other stuck in his jacket pocket in the middle of the day." He motions towards the bulge in my pocket, still never taking his eyes from me.

I laugh and without thinking, pull the small ball from my jacket. "It's a ball, just a little ball. That's all." It isn't until I say it that I realize the stupidity of my remark, and see the police cruiser pulling up beside us.

"Oh, that's much better. That makes much more sense," The woman speaks now, sarcastically, then walks over to the policeman as he gets out of his car.

I stand silently, not wanting to look away from the man, while the woman speaks to the policeman. Finally, after listening to her and nodding in a tired way, he motions for me to walk towards him. The man shadows me, watching my every step. "Do you have some identification on you sir?" The officer speaks with an official tone.

I pull out my wallet and hand it to him, thinking that it's better not to speak.

"Our school monitors here, tell me that you were asking elementary school kids for directions. Is that correct Mr Malcolm Wilson? Is that what you were doing?" He pronounces every syllable in my name, as he reads it from my driver's licence.

"Yes, I'm lost. I said that. I did have a map, but it must have blown away. I just wanted some help. I'm sorry if I caused any confusion." I try to appear exasperated, as though I'm being inconvenienced, but he can see that I'm worried, all of them can.

"You're on foot, Mr Wilson." I can't tell if he's asking me, or telling me, as he keeps holding onto my licence, staring at it.

I look up and down the empty road, seeing no sign of the rental car, or Heather, and feeling very alone. I nod quietly back to the three of them, as they stand watching me, acknowledging that yes, I am on foot.

The burly officer stares at me for a moment, trying to measure the situation. Then, he holds the back door of his car open and says something that I've only ever heard on television, "Get in. Let's take a ride."

I reluctantly climb into the back seat and let him close the door behind me. He shakes his head in silent dismay and nods his thanks to the man and woman. They just stand there and watch us as he gets into the front seat to take me to the police station.

CHAPTER 22

I feel nauseous as I sit in the small interview room. I'm frustrated and tired but I know that I've done nothing. It's a small town and I'm sure they aren't used to strange men walking around school grounds, but I know that I haven't broken any laws. I had a small ball in my pocket, that's not against the law anywhere. I tried to speak to some of the little girls. That's not against the law either.

185

They're being careful. They're just being careful and I haven't done anything wrong.

After taking my belongings and identification to have it checked out the officer comes back only once. I suppose to make sure that I'm still there. The station, from what I see when I'm led in through the back door, is small, but seems to have all the modern equipment that any other big city office might have.

I try to remember the name of Terry's lawyer, just in case they find some way to lay a charge against me. I met him at one of Terry's summer parties, the same summer parties that now seem so far away. I wonder if it's appropriate to ask to call him now, or wait until they decide whether or not to charge me. I think of calling Terry, telling him everything, or George, telling him to get on a plane and get out here. Get out here and help me straighten everything out. I wonder about Heather, where she is, why she didn't stay. I know that she must have had a reason. Something must have happened to make her leave me there. I don't know much about the police and I don't know anything about small-town police but instinctively I think that my best plan is to not talk, and to give them as little information as possible. I'm just about to stand up, when the door opens, and the first officer comes in with an older man, who looks official, senior.

"Malcolm, you don't mind if I call you Malcolm do you? I'm Staff Sergeant Macklin. I'll get right to the point. What are you doing here? What are you doing in Woodbine? And, more importantly, what were you doing in the schoolyard?" He wastes no time, leaning forward on the desk that separates us, asking his questions in a friendly, almost familiar, tone.

I'd made a deal with myself as I sat waiting for the officer to come back. I decided that I'd keep Heather's secret, our secret, for as long as I could. I decided that I wouldn't say her name, or Emily's, but if I heard the sound of a cell door closing behind me, I'd tell them everything. If that did happen, I thought the worst case scenario would be that they might be understanding, and perhaps even help us find the little girl, or at least tell us if she still lived there.

"I'm travelling, just passing through. I told the officer this already. I'm staying at the motel out by the highway. It's the Blue something." I speak in my genuinely frustrated and tired voice.

"The Bluebird, yes, you're registered there, Malcolm. Go on," Macklin says it in a quiet way, as though he's a great detective solving an important crime.

"I took a walk, tried to find my bearings, and got lost. I was going to ask someone for directions, anyone. I wasn't thinking about the fact that I was in a schoolyard. I was just lost. That's all." I'd had hours, sitting in the interview room, trying to think of what I was going to say, and it sounded plausible in my head when I thought it out. It sounded like it made sense, right up until I said it.

The first officer stays quiet, seeming to measure my reactions, while Macklin keeps asking his questions. "The ball Malcolm, why were you carrying the little ball? Were you going to play with the children?"

He asks his question in a way that makes me want to leap out of my chair, and grab him and push him against the wall. The quiet insinuations from the other officer, the way the man and woman in the park looked at me, patronized me, and now Macklin's blatant attempt to bait me into admitting to something that isn't true. I hold the arms of the chair very tightly, and watch as the two of them confidently sit there, judging me.

"I found it. It was lying in the park. I picked it up, and then forgot about it. I didn't even realize it was in my pocket." I lie, all the while staring at Macklin's face, daring him to doubt me. It's as though my anger is propelling me forward. "Now gentlemen, I've been very patient with you. I realize that you have a job to do, but by now you must have checked me out, and found that I've never been in any kind of trouble. So, I would ask that if you don't have any more questions, I'd like to go home."

They don't budge. It probably only takes seconds, but feels much longer, and I can feel a small drop of sweat, dripping slowly, from my forehead. They just keep looking at me, and then Macklin smiles. "This is a small town, Malcolm, and as you saw from our concerned monitors earlier, we look out for each other here. So, I suggest that you do go home, all the way back home to Vancouver. And, if I see you near that school again, I will charge you. And, I can guarantee you that charge will not be one that a good businessman like yourself will want following you around. Is that clear, Malcolm?"

The first officer stands up and opens the door, and as I nod, I hold my anger back and walk towards them. When I make my way to walk to the left, back the way we had come in, to the back door of the police station, Macklin speaks again. "Out the front door please, Malcolm, out to the entrance on the main street. You have nothing to hide, do you?"

I turn and walk past the closed office doors, as a couple of other officers, who're sitting at their desks, look up at me, probably trying to memorize my face. I hold my head high, staring straight ahead, and make my way out to the lobby. The officer at the front pushes my wallet towards me on the counter. As I turn and walk to the front door, I notice the officers' pictures, all lined up on the wall with their names on small placques below them. I don't let them see my reaction when I quickly glance at the picture that's at the top, above the rest of them. The resemblance to Heather is uncanny. I let the heavy door close behind me and I wait until I'm outside, before fully realizing that the plaque below the picture, with the distinguished looking senior officer looking sternly into the camera says, 'Inspector John Postman, Commanding Officer.'

My usually perfect navigation system is off from being too tired, too hungry, and I take two wrong turns before I realize that I'm walking in the wrong direction. Eventually, I find my way back to the main street of the town, to where we'd driven the night before. I have to get to Heather, find out what happened, but my hunger gets the better of me, so when I pass a small corner store, I stop and pick up an apple and a sandwich.

I walk fast, back down the road towards the highway, and our motel, trying to stay warm in the cold night air, trying not to think about where I spent the past few hours. As I get closer to the motel, I picture the rental car, sitting in front of our door. I visualize it, hoping that it's there. I'm close enough to see that the lights in our room are off, and that there is no car, before I realize that Heather has the key to our room.

Claude is sitting on an old chair in the office, sipping on a drink, when I come in. His thick, grey hair is again ruffled and unruly, and the smell of alcohol and tobacco fills the whole room. "You're a popular man today, Mr Malcolm. Had two different cops here looking for you."

"It's been a long, long day. I'm sorry, but I don't seem to have my key. Can you let me in my room please, Claude?" I ask him, plead with him. I just need somewhere that I can go and think.

He slowly takes another sip of his drink, and pauses, as though wondering what he's going to say next. "I need to tell you that the last thing the old lady and me need is somebody staying here who's going to cause us trouble. We're respected here, upstanding citizens."

He pronounces the words as though it's funny to him that he's respected anywhere. I'm too tired and frustrated to follow where he's going. I stand in the doorway, glancing over to our door, wondering where Heather is. "What did the cops want, Claude?"

He looks at me as though I've asked him something that's really funny. "That's what I'm trying to explain to you, Mr. Malcolm. I know cops. I've always known cops, and I don't want to know them anymore."

He pauses, looking at me directly for the first time, and then sighs. "I don't tell cops nothing that they don't need to know. I don't know what they wanted with you, but whatever it is they're not getting it from me."

I start to thank him, and then see the calculating look in his eye. I let him have his moment and wait for him to try and close the deal. "All of a sudden you've become a high risk occupant, Mr. Malcolm. I believe that this particular situation entails what is commonly referred to as a small surcharge." He says it smugly, confidently.

I pull some bills from my wallet, and quietly hand them to him. "Can you open my door now please, Claude?"

"It's open. I didn't lock it after the last cop left, the one that was on his own. He wanted to look around in there." He quickly pockets my money as he says it.

For a split second, I think of punching Claude, in his drunk, conniving, head, and taking back my money. I think about aiming for the wall behind his head and driving my fist through him. I know that my anger isn't really with him though. He's just an old time hustler, trying to take advantage of a situation. And, it's a long way to the next town, and the next motel, especially with no car. So, I turn and walk away, leaving him with his little victory.

The room looks just as we left it that morning, with both our suitcases lined up beside each other. I look in the bathroom, the drawers, the cupboards, trying to find a note or some trace of Heather, trying to see if she's been back. If the cops did look through our things, then they put everything back the way it was before. They were very careful, very tidy. It looks as though nothing has been disturbed. I walk back into the parking lot, thinking I'll see something, some sign of her. There are no other cars, no other people. The highway is quiet with just the occasional vehicle speeding by. The office light is off now and all I can see is the glow of a lamp, coming from the back of the house, where Claude is probably holding my money in one hand, and his drink in the other, laughing alongside his girlfriend.

I pick up the phone that's on the table beside the bed. It rings several times before he picks it up. "Mr. Malcolm, did you think that surcharge included room service?" He cackles so loudly at his own joke that I have to hold the phone away from my ear.

"Claude, the woman that was with me, when was she here today? Did she come back? Did you see her leave?"

There's a long pause. He must be taking a pull from his drink, or thinking of a way to extort a further surcharge from me. "There was no woman. There was you, and then two cops earlier, then one by himself, later. That's all I saw."

"The woman that checked in with me; we talked about her; you asked me about her, remember? Did she come back to the room? She would have been driving our rental car, Claude. You would have seen her."

He answers right away. "I told you already, Malcolm. I didn't see a woman."

I give up. I hang up the phone, realizing that he probably didn't see Heather at all. I was so careful hiding her and helping her come into the room undetected. I walk around the room once more, lifting up her suitcase, checking everywhere, looking again for a note, or some trace of her. I check the garbage can in the bathroom. I lift up the television set. I open and close the drawers again but there's nothing. Nothing.

I open my suitcase and search around for a minute before I finally find the cellular phone that Terry gave me. I try turning the power on. I push every button on the front, waiting for the little light to activate. I push the volume control on the sides, trying to power the little phone to life. Finally, I pull off the back and see that the battery is missing. I try to remember if I put the battery in the phone before leaving Vancouver. I can't remember. I throw the phone back into the suitcase and collapse on the bed.

I've been asleep for some time when, suddenly, I'm awake, wide awake. There's a small gap between the curtains on the front window. The light from the street is streaming through it and shines on enough of her face for me to know that it's her. She's sitting on the chair, facing the bed, quiet, as though she's been sitting there for a while watching me. I don't panic. I sit up and try to wipe the sleep from my eyes, try to focus.

"You grind your teeth when you sleep. Did you know that?"

I remain silent, watching her.

"You grind your teeth, and sometimes make a little sound. Then, you make another sound that sounds like you're making an apology for the first sound. I could have heard that sleep on a tape recorder, and known that it was you." She laughs softly, in a nice way. It's the same warm laugh that I loved when she first mistook me for a banker, back at the party.

I wait, still. There's no point in asking the questions. She knows what they are already. I just pause, knowing that she's come back, so there has to be answers.

She laughs again, nervously this time. "I feel like we're back at the lake, when I first told you about Emily. There are no stars this time though that I can make you look up at. No stars."

I get out of bed and stand up and stretch. I pass her on my way to the bathroom and I'm not sure if I want to hold her, or hold onto her until she tells me everything that she knows. She tenses up as I make my way past.

The water from the bathroom sink is cold in my hands and feels good as I splash it onto my face and drink it. She hasn't moved when I sit back down on the other side of the bed. The clock radio on the side table says one thirty a.m. "Where have you been, Heather?"

"I'm sorry you had to go through that at the police station, Malcolm. It wasn't fair. When I saw those people coming towards you, I knew that I couldn't stay. I'm sorry. I just left. I had to."

I watch her, believe her. She slouches over. I still can't see all of her face in the half darkness, but I keep listening.

"I went to the library. I didn't want to come back here alone. I took a chance that I wouldn't be noticed, and it worked. It was good. I saw something there. I remembered something." She sits up straight now, looking right at me and that's when I notice it. There's a mark on the side of her face. I see it in the light as she meets my eyes, looks at me.

I lean forward, trying to touch her face, trying to touch the mark. "What is that? What happened to you?"

She touches it quickly, and pulls away, as though just remembering it. "It's nothing. I saw someone I thought I knew, and left the library quickly, and walked into a door. It was stupid, no big deal." She turns her head to hide it, dismissing it, wanting to continue her story. "Listen to me, Malcolm. I know how to get closer to her. The schools have a library day, every Thursday and Friday. That's tomorrow. Tomorrow is Thursday. I saw the sign on the wall when I was there. I remember now. I went there as a kid too, every week, one day a week was library day."

I keep looking at her, trying to see the lump on the side of her face, trying to understand.

"She'll be there. I know she will. They take the smaller kids the first day, then the older kids on Friday, that's two days from now. We could see Emily, on Friday, in two days."

Her eyes are glassy with tiredness, but there's a little bit of optimism in her smile. I barely dodged the bars of the jailhouse, and she somehow walked into a door, but all of a sudden we have a way to move forward. We have more of a plan. I keep sitting on the bed, trying to inspect her face, almost cruelly waiting for the tears to come. She keeps sitting upright in the chair, watching me, silently pleading for my forgiveness. Then, the tears do start coming down her face onto her cheeks.

I get up and walk to the other side of the bed, pulling the covers back. She quietly starts to sob, as I stroke the side of her face, gently touching her. I take her top off, and slip her into the bed, covering her over, before climbing in myself. I raise my arm and let her pull her body beside me, joining, as though we're one, just the way we do back home, back in Vancouver, with our view of the water. A part of me still wants to know more, but the other part of me feels the pain from her. My heart is melting, and I'm not sure if it's from sharing our common head and feeling her sorrow, or if this is what it feels like when you love someone. I squeeze her tight to stop her from shaking, shivering, and let my eyes close, fairly confident that she'll still be beside me when I wake.

CHAPTER 23

I dream of chasing and of being chased. Mostly in the dreams I'm alone, but sometimes, I can just barely see Heather, standing on the edge, trying to reach me. I always stop at some point, and everything else stops too. There's no one behind me, no hand on my shoulder, and no one in front of me either. I wake up gasping for air from my imaginary run and hear the shower running in the bathroom.

She stands in the doorway of the bathroom, naked, drying her hair with a towel, "That must have been a hell of a door you hit." The lump is becoming a bruise, and it's puffy, on the right side of her face.

"It hurt. It was stupid, but I thought I saw this kid that I went to school with at the library. I turned quicker than I should have and got out of there. Nobody noticed me though, I'm sure of that."

"Honey, where did you go when you left the library? I was worried about you."

"I just drove and drove and drove. I drove out to the cemetery. I drove out to the mill, past town. I drove out to the hills. I parked on different streets, thinking about growing up here, about what it felt like. I sat and thought about Emily. I know that she's still here, that she still lives here. I just know it. And then, I thought about you, and dragging you into all this. I just needed to stop and try to breathe. I wasn't thinking." She sighs, as though remembering the night before, "I'm sorry that you were worried, Malcolm."

I hesitate and then ask, "Did you park outside Michaels' house?"

She doesn't want to answer my question. I can tell by the way she pulls her clothes on quickly with her back to me. She takes a while before answering. "No. He lives out by the hills. I parked at the bottom, on the road. I didn't want to go up. I parked outside my old house, where I showed you yesterday. I was on some kind of black nostalgic trip. Everywhere I went I kept feeling worse and worse, remembering all the shitty things that happened to me here."

There's a tone of finality in her voice as she finishes dressing. It feels as though I've asked enough questions for one day.

"You're going back to the school, aren't you?" I sit up, still watching her.

"No, I have a better plan than that." She sounds almost smug now. "It's Thursday today, so it'll be the smallest kids visiting the library. I don't think that she'll be there, but you never know, so I'm going to go anyways. I can at least see how they handle the kids, see how supervised they are."

"Heather, I'm not so sure I should go with you. This cop, this sergeant, he warned me to stay away from the kids. I think maybe I should wait for you here."

She sits on the edge of the bed, ready to leave now. "It's fine. I can do this Malcolm. I feel like we're getting closer to her, much closer."

She reaches over to kiss me, and I hold on for a long time before letting her go. I watch her walk out, and close the door behind her. The car is gone by the time I've pulled the curtain away and looked out the window. So, I just sit on the bed, shaking my head, not quite believing that I've forgotten to ask about her father, the policeman, or whether she's seen the battery for my cellular phone.

The inside of the room starts driving me crazy as soon as I'm up and dressed, so I decide to walk. I cross over the highway and take off in the opposite direction, away from the town. I don't take a direct route as I amble aimlessly up and down the streets. I walk past old houses, and small businesses until I reach an industrial area that has the sounds of tools banging and men working. My breath snaps the cold air in front of me as I walk faster, trying to stay warm. After a while, the shops become streets again, and I see more blocks of old buildings. Then, just as the streets seem to stop, there's an oversized house with a sign on the outside, 'The Woodbine Hotel, since 1902'.

Needing some refuge from the cold, I push open the large doors at the front and walk in, adjusting my eyes to the darkness and artificial lighting of the bar. I make my way through a series of small outer rooms, and can see men sitting at tables, hunched over their beers. Some look up, and the ones that probably aren't supposed to be here, either look away or keep staring at their pint glasses. I walk into the larger room and see a long bar with bar stools, a pool table, and more tables, almost all of them empty. The bartender sees me come in, and nods, motioning towards the empty tables, letting me take my pick. I sit against the wall, watching the slow movement of the other men as they carefully lift their glasses to their mouths.

"Are you eating or just drinking, because the girl did make some stew this morning and there's some left, if you want to eat." He's standing by my table, motioning towards the bar.

After walking around the streets for miles, I'm hungry, glad to sit down. "Whatever you have will be fine. Stew sounds good and a pint of whatever's on tap, thank you."

He's probably in his fifties, maybe even older, but still is a big man with an intimidating presence. As he lumbers back to the bar, he sways from side to side as though his legs and hips don't support all of his weight. I imagine he's had to remove his share of unruly customers over the years. When he comes back, he places his big hands on the table, leaving a bowl of stew and a pint of beer. I reach for my wallet to pay him.

"Leave it. Pay me when you're ready. We're not going nowhere." He keeps standing at my table as he says it. "You're new here. I haven't seen you."

"Passing through, just here for a few days." I decide to keep it simple, instead of trying an elaborate lie.

He nods and looks at me for a split moment too long, as though he doesn't quite believe me, but doesn't really care what my business is.

I empty the bowl and drink the beer as though I haven't eaten or drank in days, and I notice the bartender's burly frame standing over me again. "You're a thirsty traveller. I'll tell Beth you like her stew?" He asks the question, smiling, waiting for my answer.

"It was very good. You know; I think I'll have another beer too."

Maybe it's sitting in the warm bar and feeling so anonymous, or maybe it's just stupidity, but as he walks back to my table with another beer, the words came out of my mouth as though someone else is saying them. "I think I have an acquaintance that might live around here, maybe you know him, Michael Adrian. Is that a name you recognize?"

His expression doesn't change. He places the beer in front of me and pulls a chair out, turning, so that he's facing me, and lowers his big, bulky, frame into it. Then, he stares for a moment before answering. "Well, you're not a cop, and you don't look like trouble, so why would you be looking for Mike, I wonder."

I want to reach for the beer and casually sip it, but I'm afraid that my hands might shake, so I keep them on the table before answering him. "No, I certainly don't want trouble. I went to school with a man by that name, and heard that he lived here. It was just a question."

He seems to keep weighing me up, as though he isn't sure what to do with me. "Yeah, Mike's a friend of mine. He lives here. And who should I say was asking about him?"

I decide to play the stupid card and offer my hand to him. "I'm Malcolm. He probably won't remember me, but if he's the same Michael, who went to school in Vancouver, tell him I said hello."

I've had enough clients lie to me over the years that I know how to recognize the sound of a lie, and when I say it, I know that it sounds untrue. He puts his big hand in mine and shakes it, and without taking his eyes off me, smiles. "I will Malcolm. I will."

I half expect him to pick up a phone when he gets back to his place at the bar, and whisper some muffled instructions into it. In the movie of my life that plays in my head, I see a group of menacing looking characters being summoned to my table, and interrogating me while the rest of the solitary drinkers stare into their glasses. But he doesn't. Nothing happens. He polishes some glasses, wipes the table in front of him, and fishes through some paperwork below the counter.

202

I quickly drink my beer and get up to pay him. "That was good, hit the spot thanks. Will this cover it?" I hand him a couple of bills.

"Perfect, thanks," he answers.

As I turn away, he calls after me. "Wait, here, take this. I found it back there. It's Mike's card, in case you want to look him up."

He hands me a business card, 'Adrian Landscapers, Michael Adrian, President.'

I look into his face trying to see some kind of an expression, but he just nods and turns back to his work.

The cold air hits me as soon as I start walking again. I think of Heather and wonder what's happening at the library. There's no way for her to reach me, no way for her to tell me whether she needs my help. I'm lost in my thoughts, making my way back through the streets towards the motel, and barely hear the pickup truck pulling up beside me, with the window rolled down. "Get in. I'll give you a ride. It's too cold to walk."

It's one of the men who had been sitting drinking at one of the corner tables in the bar. I hardly noticed him, and didn't think he seen me at all. He's alone in the vehicle, and has a bottle of beer open in the cup holder. I hesitate, still thinking about my conversation with the barman.

"Don't worry Buddy, you're not my type. Get in if you like. I'm headed into town if that's where you're going." He smiles, showing the gap between his front teeth, and I climb in, deciding that it's small town hospitality, nothing more.

"Actually I'm at the motel out by the highway. The blue something,"

"I know it. I'll get you there." He turns the heat up in the truck, seeing me shiver from the cold, as he takes a swig from the bottle of beer.

He drives through the industrial area where I walked earlier; looking at the different shops as though he's giving me a tour. "Any kind of fabrication you need, we can do right here now, you know. We used to have to go clear into Timmins, but now we do it right here in town."

I smile and nod, smelling the stale beer in the truck, and seeing the empty bottles in the back seat. "That's handy, much better to keep it local."

"I heard you asking about Mike. If you're looking for work, you're better off checking out the shops back there. I mean Mike might talk to you, but this is his slow time of year, and he's got those sons of his to keep busy too, remember." He slurs some of his words, and focuses on the road while talking to me.

I sense an opportunity and decide to take it. "Sons are good. I always wanted a son. He doesn't have any daughters does he? I'm sure they'd be much more trouble."

His response comes right away. "Nah, just the two boys, both the spitting image of their Dad. This is you, your motel."

He pulls into the empty motel parking lot as I look around for the rental car. "Thanks for the ride and the advice."

"Anytime, you take care," he answers and drives off just as quickly as he appeared.

I sit by the window, with the curtains open watching the darkness fall, and think about my intoxicated, truck driver friend. I wonder if he might be mistaken. He might not know that there's a little girl too. A man like that wouldn't take notice of a daughter. He'd know about sons, sons that are the spitting image of their father. Or maybe he does know, maybe he knows why we're here too, looking for her. Maybe he knows that I spent the day before being questioned by the police. My mind starts to race ahead. I think of a little girl hidden away. It can't be though, she has to be here. It feels like she's here. I have to deal with facts and concentrate on what I know. I touch the letters on Michael's business card, and then tuck it back into my pocket.

I can tell by the expression on Heather's face that it's been an unsuccessful day. It's early evening when she pulls into the parking lot, and quickly comes into the room. She sees the concern on my face. "It's okay. I'm okay. She wasn't there today. It was smaller kids, younger than her, just as I thought. There were only a few of them with one teacher. She'll be there tomorrow. The older kids are there then. I'm sure she will be, too."

"I think I'll come with you. I can't sit by this window all day. I'll just sit in the corner of the library somewhere, and read a book. I need to be closer to you, to make sure that you're okay." She looks at me and smiles, as she settles into a chair. "That way you won't bump into any more doors."

"You can come. Just don't talk to any more kids. I'll do that," she says, half-smiling.

"Have you thought about what you're going to say to her, what you're going to do?" I ask.

"I'll know when I see her. I'm sure I will. I just need to see her. I need to look at her eyes, and see if she's happy, Malcolm." She has an intent look on her face, as though nothing will stop her.

"We might see your daughter tomorrow, Heather. It's amazing isn't it?" I answer, as the very real possibility suddenly dawns on me.

She nods, smiling, then almost breaks into laughter. "I smell liquor. Is it beer? Have you been drinking? Your eyes look glazed over, and your hairs all mussed up."

All of a sudden, I realize that I probably don't look myself. "I went to a local tavern, 'The Woodbine Hotel.' I mixed with the locals for a while. It's quite a town you've got here." I purposely slur my words, as I answer her.

"The Woody Hotel, you're so funny. We never went anywhere near there. It's too rough. Are you sure nobody hurt my big city accountant?" She mocks me when she asks, showing off her half dimple.

"They loved me. I even got a ride home from one of the regulars there. And their stew was delicious."

"Oh, that reminds me," she says pulling a sandwich from each pocket, "Here, have some supper. I picked these up after I left the library."

I like it. I like the way it feels between us in our room, the room where we share our secret. I know there are things that I don't know yet, questions that are still unanswered, but I'm not in a police station tonight. I'm with Heather, with my Heather, and tonight I'll be lying with her, cuddled beside me. So I leave them. I leave all of my questions for another day and just enjoy the way she's smiling at me, as I take the plastic off of my dinner and eat yet another sandwich.

CHAPTER 24

The library is larger than I imagined. There are a series of small reading rooms that have no doors, each dedicated to a different category of books and one main, larger area. When we walk in, we see a main desk with two librarians, both preoccupied stamping and sorting books. I walk closest to the librarians, smiling, while Heather walks on the other side of me, looking in the other direction, hiding her face. There are two women sitting in the periodical section, reading magazines and a man in one of the far rooms, searching amongst the titles. No one seems to look up as we make our way in opposite directions from each other.

I sit in one of the corner rooms and grab a title from the shelf closest to me as Heather takes her place in the main part of the library with her back to the wall, quickly hiding her head in a large reference book. I open my book to a random page, and read a passage that seems to jump out, 'God grant me the serenity to accept the things I cannot change, the courage to change the things I can, and the wisdom to know the difference.'

I close the book to look at the title and realize I'm holding the handbook of 'Alcoholics Anonymous'. I stifle a laugh, thinking of my excursion the previous day to the local bar, sitting amongst the afternoon drinkers. I wonder if the barman had a copy of this book under his counter along with Michael's business card.

One of the librarians shuffles by a couple of times, smiling and nodding, as though she wants to be asked a question. I keep my face in the book, reading about alcoholics, and don't look up, trying to look as though I'm intent on my reading. The other occupants come and go, until there's only Heather and myself, and one other woman. Heather doesn't move. She just keeps looking at her book, turning pages sometimes, and occasionally glancing at the clock that hangs on the wall. It's one o'clock before the door opens, and we hear the sound of excited chattering children, and a voice behind them saying "Shh."

They come in groups as though they've been divided up according to their ages, or perhaps their classes. They're partnered together, holding hands, smiling, laughing, trying to be quiet. Heather is right; these are older children. The first ones that come in seem to be the oldest ones. They're like younger versions of young women and men. The girls have the beginnings of makeup on their faces, and the boys have the beginnings of teenage acne. The next group is younger. This is the group that Emily should be in. They're smaller and don't have the sullen look that's already developing in some of the older kids. They hold each other's hands tightly as though they'll be lost if they separated.

I settle in my chair, moving a stack of books, trying to see their faces as they spread in different directions. There are two young female teachers, and thankfully no familiar school monitors who might recognize me from my schoolyard mishap. The teachers seem to be spread too thin, trying to look after too many children.

They follow after them, showing them where to find their books, all the while trying to make sure they respect the quietness of the library. I watch Heather. She puts her book down, and looks at their faces too, studying them, trying to find a resemblance. All of a sudden her eyes grow wide and she looks over at me as we make the same discovery simultaneously. The children are wearing nametags.

There are different coloured tags and in large black letters their first names are spelled out. The writing seems to be child's writing, and the colours must group them together, presumably by age or classroom. I can see Heather as she props her book up against a stack of others as though she's reading. I can see her head move as the children walk by, carrying books, looking amongst the shelves. She's reading their tags.

I do the same and place my alcoholics book open, facing me, and look in the opposite direction, trying to read their names. I see 'Justins' and 'Jacquies' and 'Williams' and 'Lynns'. I move in my chair as they walk within reading distance of me, and keep looking at the tags on their chests. I sit up suddenly as I see an 'E' on a young girl's nametag. She has a book in front of her, holding it as though it's a treasure, hiding the rest of the tag. She smiles shyly at another girl, who sits at a table across from me. They exchange glances for a moment, as though they're sharing a secret. I keep my eyes on the 'E', trying to get a better look. I look at the face of the girl, hoping to see something that will help me to recognize her. Her hair is dark and curly, cut short. Her skin is rich and dark too. I wonder if Michael is of Mediterranean descent. I can't see a resemblance to Heather. The little girl keeps holding the book over the rest of the tag. I look back at the other girl. She's a 'Hannah'. She looks at the first girl with the same cheeky but shy expression as though she's waiting for her to say something.

As the girl with the 'E' passes me by, I whisper to her, trying not to attract any attention, "What are you reading? Is that a good book?"

I just need her to lower the book, let it drop so that I can see the rest of her tag, but instead she holds it firmly against her body, even tighter, and whispers back. "I can't talk to you. I don't know you."

I quickly look around at the teachers, who both have their backs to me, helping other children. There are kids everywhere now, and I've lost sight of Heather. I want the little girl to drop the book so that I can see her tag, but she won't. I try smiling. I try to do the same cheeky smile that she exchanged with her friend. I forget for a moment my visit to the police station, my time in the school grounds. I sit back in my chair, giving her space and try a harmless question. "What's the name of the book? That's all I want to know."

She steps away from me, and lets out a small shriek, still holding the book close to her, "I told you. I'm not allowed to talk to people that I don't know."

To my surprise, the shouting actually starts away from me, at the front desk, and it all happens very quickly. The librarian is standing now, on tiptoes, looking around the library and yelling at the teachers. "We have a problem here. Miss Thompson, quickly, we have a problem."

The teachers are scanning the children, looking around, mentally doing a head count. The librarian keeps talking, quickly, as though she can't believe what has happened. "We have a problem. She's gone. The girl-she's gone. They just walked out. I didn't notice. It looked so natural. They're gone." She's pointing outside now, panicking, but is still rooted to her position behind the desk, waiting for the teachers to take control.

My girl with the 'E' retreats to her friends table, still clutching the book over her tag, watching me carefully. The other children seem to automatically find each other, while the teachers' panicked voices tell them to 'partner up, stay with your partners and don't move.' I try to find Heather, but there's too much movement, too much confusion. The other librarian is talking into the phone now, asking someone to come quickly, and saying what I don't want to hear, "A little girl, she's been taken."

One of the teachers runs out the front door, as the other one walks from table to table, looking at faces and nametags, trying to see who's missing. I still don't understand. I still don't know what happened. I sit for a moment before realizing that the phone call was probably to the police, and that this is the last place that I probably should be. I get up and take a last glance at the little girl in the table behind me, as she clings to her friend, still hiding her tag. I walk past the tables filled with children, trying to look normal, trying not to look suspicious, as they sit firmly holding the hands of their partners.

Heather's table is empty except for a stack of books where she's been sitting. I quickly walk from small room to small room, then back to the main area, before I realize that she isn't here. I have to get out of the library. I pass the teacher who's still inside, as she frantically holds a little boy who's crying and I say to her, "I'll go look. I'll help you."

The teacher nods, thanking me for my help. I'm almost at the main door when the first little girl comes running forward. "He tried to touch me. He tried to talk to me."

She has left the book on the table, and her name tag is in plain view. 'Ella' stands behind her teacher, pointing accusingly at me.

I make my way past the main desk to the door, as the librarian puts her arm on mine, trying to restrain me. "The police are coming. You should wait here. They'll have questions for you."

I can see the teacher's lips moving, but I can't hear her words. I panic now too. The children are talking, some of them are crying, some shouting. It all sounds like one big noise. I shake loose from the librarian's grip and get to the door. I swing it open and make my way through. As the door closes behind me, there is a little voice from one of the children saying, "Where's Emily? Is it Emily who's gone?"

The cold, blustery air hits me hard and I remember that my jacket is hanging on the back of the chair, inside the library. I quickly look up and down the street, but the rental car is gone. The other teacher is coming towards me, her arms open, desperation in her eyes. "I can't see anybody. There's nobody here. Who would do this?"

I start to tell her that I'll look farther down the street just as the first teacher comes running out. "Don't let him leave. He touched Ella. Try to stop him."

I turn away from them, and start running, before realizing that I'm running in the direction of the sound of sirens. Quickly, I cross the street and run the other way, without looking back. My breathing is short and panicked as I try to think and run at the same time. I need to get somewhere that I can regroup, to try and figure out what just happened. I run to the end of a street and duck down an alley, all the while thinking that Heather will be just around the corner. I know that there's an explanation. There has to be. I want to see her sitting there, waiting. There has to be something that will make sense of it all.

I'm in a parking lot and keep running. I run until the sounds of the sirens get fainter, and the buildings become fewer. I run until the shops and offices of the town became houses, and I run until the houses became fields and farms. I hear dogs barking, but don't look to see if they're close. I just run until I can't hear the sirens anymore.

There's a broken-down section of a fence, and I try to jump over it but my tired legs trip and I fall. I can't move any farther. I see an old barn and make my way over to it. The fields around me are empty. I collapse behind the barn and try to breathe. My shirt is covered in sweat. I wipe my face with the back of my hand, and realize how wet it is. I shiver as the cold air hit my warm skin. I try to stand up and realize that I've ripped my pants on the fence and cut my leg. I reach down to touch it, wiping at the blood on my knee with the back of my hand. I put my weight on my leg, thankful that I'm not limping and look around, trying to get my bearings.

All I can see are fields past the barn, and a farmhouse, off in the distance. Some of the fields have dilapidated old fences around them and look like they're in need of repair. My wet shirt clings to me, and the cold wind makes my whole body shiver. I hold my sides to stop the shivering, as I make my way to the front of the barn, and squeeze through an old door that's jammed halfway open. Inside there are several empty sacks from the feed and bales of hay. I pick one up and then, finding a nail sticking out of the wall I rip a slit in it. Removing my wet shirt, I put the sack over my head, holding the dry material against my cold skin. I marvel at how ingenious I'm being, standing there, in the freezing cold.

There's a ladder leading to a loft upstairs in the barn. I climb up, testing my footing on the old planks of the loft, making sure I don't fall. My breathing is starting to return to normal. It's as though some kind of survival mode kicked in and all I knew to do was run. I throw my wet shirt over a rafter on the roof, and settle in a corner of the loft, wrapping the remaining material from the sack around me, trying to warm up.

I reach in my pocket and pull out Michael's business card. I think of the library, all the faces of all the little girls. Emily was there. She was in the library, and now she's gone, and so is Heather. I think of possibilities, some far-fetched and some almost plausible. Nothing makes sense anymore. Heather must have seen Emily, must have spoken to her, and somehow she left with her. I try to think of anything that she might have said that would tell me why or where she would have taken her, and why she would have left without me.

The wind hits the old boards of the barn, and makes them rattle, and with every sound, I shiver more. I rub my legs, trying to keep them warm, trying not to cramp up in the cold loft. I hug the material against me, holding it, trying to will it to warm me up. I think I hear sirens in the distance, but then realize that it's just the rattling of the barn. I hear a dog, barking, coming closer, but as I strain to hear I realize the sounds of my own heavy breathing and the howling wind outside is playing tricks on me.

I stand up and gingerly put weight on my leg again, testing the resolve of the loft with every step I take. I try to think about what's happened. I need to get to Heather, and more importantly, I need to get myself some help. If I can get to a phone, I'll call Terry. I'll ask him to contact his lawyer. I'll tell him everything. A missing child is big news, and if they haven't found Emily and

Heather yet, and cleared up whatever misunderstanding has happened, there will be people searching everywhere. I wonder what they think my part in all of it is. What do they think I was doing, talking to a different little girl? Do they think I was a diversion?

I think of warm nights in my bed, back in Vancouver with Heather. I think of our view of the water from my bedroom, the safeness, the comfort. I can't stop shivering. I lie back down in the corner of the loft, holding myself again, trying to warm up.

When you stop making sense, and start to go into a state of shock, a strange sensation comes over you. You absolutely know that your thoughts aren't making sense, but you also know that there's nothing that you can do to stop them. If you try to stop your mind from going sideways, it actually starts to go there faster. So, you give up, and just carry on with the ride. I keep holding myself in the corner, trying to imagine that I'm lying in bed with my Heather again, and not in the cold loft of a barn. I listen to the almost rhythmic slamming of the boards of the old barn as the wind hits them. I listen to the way the wind whistles through the half-open door. I can hear them in the distance, coming, getting closer. I touch my knee, and feel how the blood has dried over already. The wind keeps slapping the sides of the barn, and the partial light that shines through the slats in the wood gets fainter and fainter, and in the distance, I hear them coming. I hear them getting closer.

I close my eyes tighter and can actually feel Heather's body, sidling up to mine, joining it as though we're one, the way we like to do. I can feel her settling into me, pushing the covers under her chin, and then pulling her chin back down to cling to me even tighter, and I still hear them getting closer. I'm shivering, but Heather is pulling her arms around me now, trying to warm me up. I try to stop my teeth from chattering; try to sigh, the way she likes me sighing when we're locked in our bedtime embrace. I open my eyes and close them again, and I can see her in our bedroom. I'm lying back, watching her as she places all her little glass figurines of mothers holding their children, all around the room. The noises are closer now, they're almost here. I try to get my mind to stop, to get it to listen to the other noises. I strain and strain, and still they're getting louder, closer.

I hear dogs now as though they're right outside the barn. I push myself up and kick the ladder down from the loft, then crouch back down in my corner. I hear vehicles, but no sirens, just dogs, lots of dogs barking. It's some time before I hear the voices along with the barking. I huddle in my corner, back in survival mode. I try not to breathe, as I listen to the muffled sounds of men talking, giving orders, asking for advice. I hear a word here and there, but the wind carries most of them away, until I hear the door being pushed open, and the dogs sniffing in the barn.

There are heavy footsteps, and men giving encouraging words to the dogs. The dogs bark and keep sniffing, not giving up. One of the men tries to get the dogs to leave, but they won't. They keep sniffing and yelping and barking. Finally, one of the men speaks, "He's here. They smell something."

The man and I probably look up at the roof of the barn at the same time, and see my wet shirt hanging in the rafters. "Get a light in here. Now. If he's not here, he's been here. Get a light, and make sure your weapons are drawn, gentlemen. We don't know what we're dealing with, remember."

I draw my breath in, realizing that I've been found. I wait. It seems like an age, until the strong light shines on the back walls of the loft, and the man's voice reaches me. "Show yourself very slowly, Mr Wilson."

I raise my hand, and hear a loud, simultaneous, clicking noise. "Hands down, asshole. Get on the floor, and crawl towards the edge of the loft. And if you raise your hand again, I'll blow your fucking head off." His voice is confident, commanding.

I crawl in inches, slowly and carefully towards the edge of the loft. I keep my hands on my head, and my face down. I can't see them. All I can see is the battered floor of the old loft, but I can feel the anticipation of the men down below. I can hear their breathing, and it feels as if everything is happening in slow motion. Nothing matters other than getting to the edge of the loft, without making any sudden moves that might cause one of them to shoot me.

Suddenly, I don't feel anything below my hands, as I reach the edge of the loft. I stop, waiting for their instructions. "I should just let you keep crawling, you prick."

219

I lie there on the cold floor of the loft, shaking, shivering, waiting, for the man's instructions when I hear the ladder being placed against the side, and the sound of a dog trying to get up the ladder. "Hold onto that ladder and come down backwards." His commands are more measured now that he can see me, see my fear.

I slowly make my way down the ladder, and as I reach closer to the bottom, several sets of strong hands, pull me to the ground roughly. They keep me on my stomach, emptying my pockets, searching me, patting me everywhere. Then, they turn me to face them. I open my eyes, and see a crowd of police officers, two of them holding dogs on leashes. The dogs are yelping, trying to get at me. My face is covered in sweat again, and the drops are falling into my eyes. I blink the sweat away, not wanting to move my hands.

They pick me up and tighten the handcuffs roughly around my wrists. One of the dogs is allowed to jump up on me, growl at me. I pull away in panic, as the officer gives the dog some leash, and lets it intimidate me. Another man pushes me from behind to the door of the barn, and back outside.

I'm shoved towards a police car, but before the door is opened, one of them turns me around. I don't recognize any of them from my trip to the police station the other day. They all look the same. They all look like angry, young policemen. The officer who told me what to do, takes off his hat, and slowly, looks at me. He clenches his fists as though he's about to strike. His eyes are menacing and he leans into me, "I've only got one question for you. Just one, where is she? Where's the girl, asshole?"

My back is against the car, and I start to slide down. I buckle from the exhaustion, the cold, the unanswered questions. It's worse than I thought. They still haven't found Emily. They don't know where she is. I'm picked up from either side by an officer, just before I hit the ground. "I don't know. I really don't know." It's all I can say. It's all that I know.

He stares at me for a moment, then looking at the other officers, motions for them to put me into the back seat of the car. I slide in and feel the warmth and temporary relief from whatever harm is about to come my way.

CHAPTER 25

The police station is buzzing with activity, and the room they put me in this time is different. It says 'Interview Room' on it, and as I'm pushed through the door, one of the officers slides the sign to read 'Occupied'. My handcuffs are taken off, and I'm handed a clean, grey t-shirt to put on in place of the old sack. There's constant activity in the room as I'm pushed into a chair, and handcuffed once more. The officer who spoke to me at the barn, sets up a tape recorder on the small table between us while the others watch, placing chairs, or standing, around the room.

He seems ready to proceed when we hear the noises. Loud banging noises come from the outer offices, along with yelling. I can't make out the words, but I can hear the anger. Somebody is very angry. The noises get louder as the commotion gets closer to us. The officer with the tape recorder bristles and hesitates as though he doesn't want to turn it on yet. I can hear somebody saying, "Get out of his way," just as the door is thrown open.

He stands in front of me and looks me over for only a moment. His mouth is frothing with anger, and his teeth are clenched. His breathing is heavy, and he's exhaling, powerfully. He unbuckles his belt and quickly slides it from his pants, wrapping it around his right fist. His eyes are glazed over, but I know the eyes. I've seen them before. They're Heather's eyes. His nametag reads, 'John Postman, Commanding Officer'. "Hold him down. Hold him the fuck down." His voice is breaking, and as he says it, his eyes dart around crazily.

The two officers on either side of me flinch, until he repeats his order, and they each grab my shoulders from the top, and push down heavily. I squirm in my seat and try to use my legs to push up, but it's no use. These are big strong men holding me down. I manage to turn my head and his first punch grazes me, but as I try to right myself in my seat, his second one comes faster than I anticipate, and hits me square in the face. I feel the pain in my mouth, and blood trickling down my chin.

He adjusts the belt around his hand, as I try to stand, but the officers are steadfast and keep pushing down on my shoulders. I look up and can see the disbelief on their faces, as though they can't believe what they're witnessing. I try to speak before the next round of punches comes towards me. "You don't understand. It's Heather. The little girl, Emily, she's with Heather. She's with your daughter." John Postman has to be Heather's father. The resemblance is uncanny.

He cocks his fist back and hits me again and again. I feel the blows against my eyes, my mouth, my cheeks, and when my head droops, he punches me on top of it. He's grunting between punches. "I know who she's with. I know she's with that little bitch. Where are they going? Where are they going?" He keeps asking the same question, and hitting, again and again.

The question rings in my ears, as he stands, ready to strike again. Nothing makes sense. Every bit of me wants to find a way to explain things to the man, but I can't even explain it all to myself. I feel as though I can't stay conscious any longer just as the door opens.

"John, for Christ sakes, John, think. Think." Macklin, the sergeant from the previous day, is standing at the open door, behind Postman, looking at me, then, looking at his commanding officer. I hold my head up, trying to show him what's happening.

Macklin cautiously lays his hand on Postman as though he's afraid to touch him.

Postman, stops and looks at Macklin, then at the other officers, before speaking, looking like he's been awakened from a daze. "I want to know, Sergeant. I want to know where she is, and I want to know within the next five minutes, or I'll see this son of a bitch leave here on a slab." His hands fall to his sides. He's almost vibrating from pounding me. His gaze never leaves my face, and he looks at me with disgust as he talks to Macklin. He just keeps staring. I want to spit my blood in his face, push away the other officers, and hit him as hard as I can, but every time I try to stand, the officers push me back down. I have no energy left.

I take a long look at him through my sore eyes, as he leaves the interview room. He's probably in his mid fifties, and isn't a big man, but from the way he carries himself, and the power of his punches, I know that he's solid, strong. It seems to take every bit of determination that he has, to pull himself away from the room, saying to Macklin, "Five minutes, sergeant, and them I'm coming back in for him."

It feels like no one in the room breathed while he was here. The only thing I heard was *his* breathing, and the slap of the belt, and his fist against my face. I try to catch my breath and start choking as the two officers release their grip on me. I can see blood, soaked on my t-shirt.

Macklin takes a deep breath before he starts to speak. "This is going to be really easy, Malcolm. Every time you open your mouth I want to hear the truth coming out of it. I want you to answer my questions honestly, and if you do that, then maybe we can get a doctor in here to work on that face of yours." As he speaks, he stares at me, and his face has the same trademark expressionless cop look to it that it had during our previous interview, but there's a difference now. There's something in his eyes, something that isn't quite right. His face doesn't soften, but I can tell. I can tell that this isn't something he's used to. I don't know the relationship between him and Postman, other than the fact that Postman is his superior, but I have a feeling that this isn't behaviour that he's seen before.

"We have a child missing, as you know. We know who she's with, and we know that this woman was with you." He pauses briefly, before continuing. "I need to know where they're going."

They know about Heather already. I can't comprehend. It just doesn't make sense. We were so careful hiding her, hiding her from everyone, but somehow they know that Heather is with me. My voice doesn't sound like it's mine when I speak. The words are numb sounding. It feels as though my mouth is frozen and I can't make the words sound the way that they're supposed to. I'm done. I'll tell them anything they want to know. Heather has left me, perhaps even used me. I don't understand it. I just know that I need to save my own ass. "They have my car. It's a rental. The paperwork on it is back at the motel."

He cuts me off before I finish. His impatience shows as he keeps staring at me, his lip quivering again. "We know that. We know they have your car. I need to know where they're headed. Where are they, Malcolm? Where is she taking the little girl?" His voice is raised now, almost shouting.

I don't want to say it. I don't want to say the words because I know what the consequences will be, but I have no choice. I don't know. I don't know where she's going, or what her intentions are. I know that in the days leading up to our trip out here, and then when we got here, she changed. It felt as though sometimes I would talk to her, and she couldn't hear me properly. It was like she was so focused on finding Emily that it blocked everything else out. Macklin's face falls. He knows what I'm going to say before I say it. "I don't know. If I knew, I'd tell you. I didn't know she'd take the kid. She just wanted to see that she was okay." My voice is different, and the words still don't sound right. My mouth is numb, sore from the punches.

Macklin looks confused and disappointed at the same time, and his response is immediate. "You don't seem to understand, Malcolm. That man, that officer in the other room. He's going to come in here in a minute, and if I don't have an idea from you, an answer...Well, I can't be responsible for his actions." He says it almost as though he fears the consequences as much as I do.

It's hard to talk. My words are desperate as they come out of my mouth, mixed with the blood and tears that are running down my face. "She could be going anywhere. She could be going back to Vancouver. I don't know. She just wanted to see if she was happy, to see if the little girl was okay." I want to say that Emily is hers, her little girl, but I don't. I try to lift myself up in the chair with my elbows pushing on the armrests, to emphasize what I'm saying, but there's no strength left. There's no need for the officers to get up and hold me down this time. I have no strength. My body is defeated, and I fall back down into the chair.

He keeps looking at me, as though he either doesn't care what I'm saying or doesn't believe me. He starts speaking again when the door is suddenly thrown open, and his superior is once again standing there. "Get out here now. We've found her. We got the little bitch." Postman's eyes are gleaming now as though he's entered into some kind of madness. His gaze shifts from Macklin to me and then back again, his face lit up, gleefully.

Macklin motions for one of the young officers to stay as he and the others leave the room, and I take comfort in the sound of the door closing behind them.

I have no concept of time as we sit in the interview room. I hear the noises of radios crackling and words being spoken, but I can't decipher what is being said. There's excitement, then orders barked, and then silence, presumably as they wait for a response. Postman's voice is louder and stronger than the others, but his words are fuzzy. I wonder if he's damaged my hearing as he punched my head. The remaining officer shifts in his seat for a while, then, as I try to wipe the blood away with my hands, he hands me a handkerchief. It's heavily soiled with blood when my still handcuffed hands, shakily place it on the table in front of me.

I stare at the unused tape recorder sitting on the table. I wanted to ask for a lawyer when the first officer was setting it up. I've never been in any kind of trouble with the police before, and I know that I must have some rights, even when it involves a missing child. I had been ready to ask, ready to demand, that I be able to contact a lawyer before Postman barged through the door. By then it was too late. He was madness itself, and my only option had been to not talk. But now it sounds as though they've found them. It sounds like they have found Emily and Heather, and I know that the first thing I have to do, for all our sakes, is to find out my own status.

I turn my head and try to look up at the young officer. His nametag reads, 'Ellison'. He can't be much more than twenty-three or twenty-four. His eyes are trained on the door as though he doesn't want to look at me. "I want to talk to a lawyer." I mumble it, my mouth still not working properly. "I want to make a phone call and call a lawyer." I keep staring at his nametag.

His expression doesn't change. He keeps looking at the door as though he hasn't heard me. I try more forcefully this time. The words come out mixed with spit as I hope for his pity. "I am entitled. I want to speak to a lawyer."

He hisses back at me, immediately this time, in a low voice. "You're entitled? You don't get it, do you. You have no idea what you two have done here. You don't know who that little girl is, do you?"

"I do know. We do know." My voice sounds pathetic, as I start to ask again, pleading with him to help me. "I want to call..."

"Don't ask me. Don't do it." His head is steady and hard as he angrily answers, still not daring to look at me.

"I just want to..." I try again, not looking in his eyes, still staring at his nametag, thinking that I have nothing to lose, just as the door opens once more.

Macklin comes in again with another officer, and thankfully, Postman is nowhere to be seen. His face is more relaxed now as though a great weight has been taken from him. "We're going to put you in a holding cell until we can determine your part in this, Malcolm. At this point the senior officer has not determined whether or not you will be charged. We've called for a doctor to come from the hospital, and he will attend to you as soon as he gets here." He's all business now, more relaxed, official, and says it in a steady tone, as he motions for Ellison, and the other officer to take me away.

I try again, this time turning my head to Macklin, as they grab me under my arms. "I want to call a lawyer."

Macklin's expression doesn't shift as he looks down at the blood on the table, and moves some papers around. He lets the two officers pull me away, and doesn't look up as he speaks. "So noted Malcolm, so noted."

The clanging of the cell door behind me is a relief after the ordeal that I survived back in the interview room. I sit on the small narrow bed of the cell and listen to the buzzing of the faint fluorescent lights that hang from the low ceiling. I touch the lumps on my face, trying to determine what damage has been done. Nothing makes sense. Heather hasn't been with me the whole time we've been in Woodbine, but when she was, I hid her. At the schoolyard and at the motel, we kept her concealed, under hats and scarves. Her name isn't on the rental agreement for the car or at the motel, but somehow, her father knows that she's in town, and it was her who took Emily.

I think of the library, of looking over at Heather, as she hid behind the stack of books. Did she know that she was going to take Emily with her? Had she tried to take me with them? The street had seemed so empty when I ran away from the two teachers. The car was gone. I'd been left. Heather had taken Emily and left me. My head pounds. I touch my temples and feel the pain pulsating beneath my fingertips. I need to think clearly. I need to talk to someone.

I close my eyes to try and stop the pain, and fall into a sleep. I'm awakened by the noise of footsteps coming towards my cell and the door being opened.

Ellison, the officer from the interview room, lets a man with a large black satchel into the cell. "It's mostly his head, doctor, but take a look at the knee too." He points towards me as he says it.

He stands relaxed, holding the door of the cell, watching as the doctor holds my head between his gloved hands, focusing on my eyes. The doctor takes some gauze and liquid from his bag and treats the cuts on my head, then touches the lumps on my face as I wince in pain.

"Stitches? Hospital?" Ellison asks him in a matter of fact way.

The doctor looks at my face, then my knees as though he's trying to determine. "You know, I think we'll be okay. He'll bleed a bit, but if you keep cleaning it up, I think it'll heal itself."

He holds some bandages up as though asking for permission to put them on. When Ellison nods his approval, he wraps one around my head and the other around my knee. There's no compassion from the man it's all business, but I have to try. I have to ask. I lean forward although I know that Ellison can still hear me. "I need to make a phone call. They haven't let me call anyone. I need to call a lawyer. I need some help." I'm almost pleading, hoping.

There's no movement, no reaction. The doctor just continues to work on me. He takes my pulse again, then shines a small light into my eyes. He checks the bandages. It's as though I haven't spoken at all. I watch Ellison as he waits for him to finish, then they look at me with glassy stares, ignoring my request. I realize

231

that there must have been many, many men held in these cells that have made the same statement, asked the same question, probably to the same doctor.

He finishes his work and stands back, looking at me as though he's been working on the engine of a car. He looks back at the officer and nods, lifting his satchel, then follows him back to the hallway as the solid door of the cell closes on me once more.

I sleep on and off. Sometimes it seems like minutes, but probably it's hours. At one point, I wake, and there is a bottle of water, lying on the floor in front of me with a towel. The small hard pillow below my head is soaked from my sweat. I wet the towel and wipe the cool water on my forehead. They must be watching me, checking on me. I try to stay awake, but the tiredness keeps coming over me. I try to fight it, but my body just lies back and falls on the bed. I see food too, on a tray that has been slid through the opening in the cell door. I want to be awake when they deliver the water or pick up the food, but my tired body won't allow it.

The cycle is repeated, over and over, until finally I wake and have enough strength to keep my body erect. I drink the remainder of the water and put my hands to my head. The pounding is less now but still there. It feels like a night and a day since I've been here, but I still don't know. I prop my body against the back wall of the cell, and sit upright on the bed, determined that I'll be awake when they next come with food or water. I work my jaw back and forth. I feel my face, feel my bruises. I bend my leg, checking for movement, making sure that I can still use it with the bandage tied tightly around it.

I close my eyes and count, then open them again, and count again, monotonously waiting. It seems like hours, but finally I hear footsteps coming towards me, and to my surprise, Sergeant Macklin stands outside my cell door. He stares at me for a long time before speaking. "We're letting you go. We're not going to charge you, Malcolm."

He speaks in a soft measured voice as though he's doing me a favour. "We're comfortable in the knowledge that you didn't know what Heather was going to do." He pauses again, watching me.

"Where is she? What's happened? Where's Heather?" I have so many questions as I look back at the man.

He just keeps staring in his non-committal way. "I can't comment on anything else concerning this," he stops again, choosing his wording carefully, "incident, other than to tell you that we have no further interest in you, Malcolm."

He slowly starts to walk away. "The doctor will take a look at you again before you're released. Then you should go home, Malcolm. Go home to Vancouver."

I shout, scream. I try to make my words as forceful as my still swollen mouth will allow. "Fuck, Macklin, tell me. Where is she? What's happened?"

He turns back, and for a moment it looks like he might answer, but he just shakes his head and turns away, telling me to go home, once more.

The doctor is quick and businesslike, just like the first time he examined me. He changes my bandages, and tells me to check in with a doctor in a day or two, and if I feel dizzy I should probably have an x-ray taken. I coldly thank him for his help, and as he leaves, another officer motions for me to follow him. I'm led back upstairs, to another room in the police station, and then to a counter where a plastic bag containing my personal belongings is given back to me. I take my wallet and put it in my pocket, along with the key to the motel room and Michael's business card.

I mentally try to remember what else was in my possession, when Ellison appears, and hands me a set of keys. "These are yours too. The car is rented in your name. You can have it back. It's outside." He points towards the door down a hallway, motioning for me to leave.

It seems too simple. How do you lock someone up, beat them up, and then just let them go? I pause, not quite able to take in everything that's happening.

They must have found Heather and Emily with the car. Why would they not need it? They must need it as part of their case against her. Nothing makes sense. It feels like something else is going to happen. It's just too easy. "I don't understand." I look at Ellison, waiting for him to explain.

"You should go. You're free to go now." He points towards the door, imploring me to leave.

I leave. I walk away, right outside to the parking lot. My eyes squint as they adjust to the glare. It's a bright, cold day and there's a light dusting of snow on the ground. The rental car is parked right in front of me, at the edge of the lot. I walk around it, inspecting it, trying to get it to tell me what has happened. It's dirty and unlocked. I open all the doors, looking for something that will tell me, give me a clue. The seats are empty. The glove compartment is empty. It's just an ordinary car that needs to be washed.

I slide behind the wheel, being careful of my bandaged leg, and turn the key. I slowly ease the car out of the lot, carefully looking at the building that I've just come from. As I look back, I see someone at a window, standing there, staring at me. Postman perhaps, but I can't be sure. I drive onto the main road and point the car in the direction of the motel.

CHAPTER 26

"You've been evicted, Mr Malcolm. You're no longer welcome here." Claude sees me coming towards the office. He's standing at the door waiting, not letting me in. "I told you. I don't like cops. You're trouble, lots of trouble, and we don't need that here."

He looks tired, like he's been up all night. His hair is rumpled and his red eyes have bags under them. I think of him and his girlfriend, who I still haven't seen, being questioned by the police. I wonder if Claude has seen Heather; if that's how they know she's here. As I get closer to him, his eyes widen when he sees my bandaged head, and sighing, he reluctantly steps aside, letting me walk into the office.

My body collapses into one of the old chairs in front of his counter. There's an old Coca Cola sign on the wall that's showing 10:05 AM. I glance at it while he closes the door and takes one last look outside, as though he's looking to see if anyone is watching us. "Claude, what day is it? How long was I in there?"

"It's Sunday, and you look like shit." He pauses, wiping the sides of his mouth with the back of his hand. I've been in the police station for almost three days. I must have been passed out for longer than I thought. I put my head down in my hands, and try to figure out how I lost the last three days of my life.

Somewhere between hearing Macklin say I was free to go, and driving to the motel, I started making a plan. The only thought in my mind the whole time I was locked up was Heather, wondering where she was. Now that I'm out, I know that the police aren't going to give me any information, so I have to do it on my own. I know where I have to go next. I don't know what I'm going to do there, but I know where to go. I just need a little more help from Claude first. I need a little bit of breathing room. I pull out my wallet, and take out a credit card. "I need my room, Claude. I need it for one, maybe two more nights."

He interrupts me before I finish. "No, no, I can't do it. You have to go. Even the cops said that. You have to go." His pleas sound real, as his French-Canadian accent becomes stronger, but he keeps staring at the credit card.

"Claude, this is what I want you to do. I want you to go to your machine behind the counter, and punch in a cash advance. I want you to take out one thousand dollars. Then, you need to give me five hundred of that money, and you keep the rest. Will your machine let you do that, Claude?"

He keeps shaking his head, speaking in French now, and saying, "No", over and over. I'm a risk. His forehead is sweaty, and he's nervous, shifting from one foot to the other, but, he keeps staring at the credit card.

I hand it towards him, willing him to take it.

"Two days, that's it. Tuesday morning, you're out of here, no longer, and if the cops come back again, then all bets are off, and I'll have *them* kick you out." He grabs the card from my hand, and takes it over to the counter.

I listen as he punches the numbers into his machine then opens the safe and counts out the bills. He gives me back my card, with my share of the cash, all the while trying not to look at me. I push down on the sides of the chair, and stand up, feeling the soreness all over my body. As I turn to leave him, I have to ask, have to know. "Tell me, did you tell them about Heather? Did you recognize her? They must have asked you, Claude."

He answers immediately. "I'll tell you what I told them. I saw a woman in the distance, that first night in the car. After that I didn't see her no more. I can't give a fucking description, because I don't know what she looks like. And no matter how many times that crazy son of a bitch cop asks me, I still don't know who she is, or what she looks like 'cos I didn't fucking see her."

He's yelling now. There's desperation and frustration in his voice. He sounds like a man telling the truth. I turn away from him and hobble towards the door. As I make my way through, I suddenly have a thought and stop the door just before it closes on me. "What cop, which one was it?"

"The boss, the chief, the one with the crazy eyes, the one that looks like he's always ready to kill you." He pulls the door from me and closes it, leaving me out in the cold.

The room is messier this time. Clothes are strewn about, suitcases turned upside down, and papers are lying on the floor in disarray. I take a long look around, wondering if our belongings gave the police any clue to where Heather had taken Emily when a thought strikes me. Her stuff is here, all of it. Her suitcase, her toiletries, her reading books, it's all here. If Heather had intended to snatch Emily from the library, if it were premeditated, she would have taken something with her. It would have been easy for her to sneak some clothes or belongings into the trunk of the car while I was sleeping or in the bathroom, but she didn't. I smile as I look through her things, confident that nothing is missing. Whatever happened at the library, she didn't plan it. It just happened.

When I was in the cell, I thought about trying to get back to Vancouver, back to the safety of my numbers, to pretend that none of this happened. There are desperate thoughts that go through your head when you're locked up and have no answers. I only have to look at Heather's things, to look at her suitcase, her clothes, to know that I have to stay. I have to find out what's really happening, and to do that I have to find her.

I quickly shower and change, and make my way back out into the cold. The snow has fallen again, and there's a build-up of it covering the ground. I can hear Claude, scraping the sidewalk around the side of the building, out of sight from my room. There's a small laundry room with a storage area beside it that's part of the motel, directly across from me. I can hear the washers running from behind the door that's slightly ajar. I quickly cross the parking lot and take a look inside. There are three well-used washers with dryers beside them and a small table, presumably for folding clothes on. At the back of the laundry area, there's a door. I push it open and see that it leads to a small utility area. There are blocks of fuse panels and breakers, making a slight buzzing noise. On the back of the door there is a key. I quickly put it in my pocket and make my way back to the front door.

I can still hear Claude scraping the snow from the other side of the building. I try the key in the lock of the laundry room door. It easily turns it. I have options now, and I put the key into my pocket, looking around, making sure I haven't been spotted.

I jump back into the rental car, and as I leave the parking lot, I see a woman sitting in the office, furiously sucking on a cigarette. It must be Claude's girlfriend. I wonder how much money he told her he's taken from me this time. I drive away quickly before she can turn around. I assume there will be some alcohol consumed tonight, thanks to my generous donation.

I lay the business card on the console between the seats. The address below the business name says that it's a mile and a half off the main highway on the north end of town. It's Sunday, so he may not be there, but I want to see the place, see where he works. I want to see the man who is responsible.

It's easy to find. There are signs immediately as I leave the main road. They keep changing. They read, 'Adrian Landscapers, proud sponsor of minor league baseball'. Or, they say, 'Adrian

Landscapers, proud sponsor of minor league hockey'. There is even one that says, 'Adrian Landscapers, yearly benefactor of the Adrian Scholarship for Scholastic Achievement'.

It's a large fenced yard, and the main gate is half open. There are piles of lumber, and sacks of soil, and what looks like grain or feed, stacked neatly around the perimeter. There's a young man on a forklift, moving pallets slowly from one area to another. I park outside the fence and walk in, rubbing my hands to keep them warm against the cold.

"I'm sorry, we're closed. Unless it's salt you need." Another young man is behind the highest pile of sacks of salt I've ever seen. He's sweating from whatever work he's been doing, and smiles a kind, confident smile at me. "First snowfall of the year, we can help you out with salt, if you're worried about the snow."

Our Vancouver winters rarely require large amounts of salt to melt the snow and ice, but as I look at the huge pile of sacks in front of me, I realize what he's talking about. "Actually I'm looking for Michael, if he's around." I smile back. "And I'll bet he's your dad, isn't he?"

He keeps smiling, but stares at the marks on my face, as though he wants to ask what happened, but is afraid to. "Yep, Dad's here, up in the office as usual." He points towards the main building, and a set of outside steps. "I'll take you up if you like."

I can see the other boy now, on the forklift, and realize that my truck driver friend, from what seemed like a hundred days ago, was right. They do look like each other. They're young, eager-

241

looking boys. "You know what? You keep going with your work. I'm sure I can find my own way." He nods and walks back around his piles of salt sacks, leaving me to make my way to the stairs.

The building is old, and I try to imagine Heather coming here, meeting Michael. I think of the story she told me, the story of him beating up a man, while the other men watched, afraid. I knock on the door as solidly as I can, thinking about how far we've come from that night at the lake at the end of the world.

The man quickly opens the door and seems a little taken aback at my appearance. It doesn't last though, and he quickly recovers giving me the same kind, confident smile his son gave me in the yard. To my surprise, he's a slight man, and I tower over him. "Hello, come in. I saw you talking to Tom down below. Is there something I can help you with? I'm Michael Adrian."

I shake his hand firmly, letting him lead me into his office. "I wanted a quick word, but I'm not sure I have the right man. Is there only one Michael Adrian?" I ask stupidly.

He laughs back at me. "No, I imagine there's a bunch of us, but I'm the only one around here. Been here all my life, almost sixty years now." His grey hair is combed back and he's wearing jeans and a plaid shirt, and when I look down he has house slippers on his feet. "You'll have to excuse that." He sees me eyeing his slippers. "I take some liberties when I work here on Sundays. It makes me feel like I'm at home."

It doesn't add up. It can't be the same man. I stand in the doorway of his office, trying not to show the shock on my face.

242

The man just doesn't strike me as the bad, criminal type that Heather has described.

He takes a moment, surmising me, deciding on whether or not to let me in, his businessman's smile never leaving his face. "Listen, why don't you sit down? It's cold out there. I'll pour you a coffee if you like. I need a break anyway from this paperwork." He motions towards a seat for me, and makes his way to a coffee machine that's sitting on a counter covered in books and papers.

My face is still covered in bandages. I changed them at the motel room and tried to clean up, but the sight has to be making him wary of me. Maybe he thinks I'm a hobo looking to warm up for a few minutes on a cold day. I glance around the office, looking at piles of books, the computer that he must have been working on, and the family pictures on the desk behind him. There are pictures of him with the two boys, at different stages of their lives. There are family shots of Michael and a woman, obviously his wife. And there are pictures of the four of them together, holding each other close, and smiling the types of happy smiles that come easy to people who love each other.

"I'm Malcolm, Malcolm Wilson. I wanted to talk to you about someone. You used to know her a long time ago. She grew up in this town." I wondered whether he might know my name. The police must have been in touch with him about his daughter. I'm unsure of everything now though. I watch for his reaction as he hands me the cup of coffee.

"Well Malcolm, if she worked here, I'm not sure if I would remember her. They all work here you know, all the kids. It's like a rite of passage in this town. They all seem to work at the yard at some point. It's just too hard to remember all of their names, but I'll try." He smiles, as though he's humouring me.

I wait for him to sit, then stare at his face, watching for any type of reaction. "Heather, Heather Postman, do you remember her at all?"

The smile remains. There's just a slight hesitation in his eyes, as he puts down his cup of coffee, and gives me his full attention. "Heather, yes, I remember Heather, of course." He pauses then adds, almost as an afterthought, "Her family were originals in Woodbine, been here for years, and her father, he's the police chief, has been for a long, long time."

I pick up the coffee cup, never letting my eyes leave him, waiting to see if he's going to speak again. My hand doesn't shake. It's solid as I keep my eyes on him. I can hear one of the boys outside calling to the other in a good-natured way. I can hear the sound of a clock ticking on the wall, and smell the strong coffee. The office doesn't feel warm and inviting anymore, but I feel comfortable with this man. I feel like I'm my dad, standing at Rab's door, all those years ago. I feel like, if I need to, I could pick Michael up and throw him down his stairs.

He starts to reach into his desk, and I can feel my eyes growing large at the prospect of facing a gun for the second time in the past few days, but all he comes out with is a pack of cigarettes

244

and a lighter. "My one bad habit; the boys think I've quit." He stops smiling now, and his hands shake a little as he lights his cigarette.

He puffs for a moment and stares out the window at the purple sky that's clouding over, promising more snow. "Who are you, Malcolm? What is it that you want with me?" He asks it firmly but still politely.

In the days after Heather told me about Emily, and told me about her relationship with Michael, I thought about this moment. I thought about confronting him, trying to physically overpower him, and taking out some kind of revenge, for what he'd done to her, what he'd done to both of them. The anger had consumed me at times although I was careful not to show it. I thought of pounding my fists into him, just the way my dad taught me years ago. It seems different now though. He doesn't look like the monster I envisioned. He looks like a family man, a man whose sons smile when they talk about him, a man of the community.

"I'm a friend of Heather's. We came into town together a few days ago. She told me about you. I wanted to meet you." I tell him the truth, or at least the part of the truth that I'm going to let him in on for now.

He seems to lighten up. His hands stop shaking and he looks at me in a reassured way. "Heather's in town? Where's she been? I always wondered what happened to her. She had a hell of a rough ride after her mother died." He seems to contemplate that for a moment before continuing. "You tell her I said hello. She was a good little worker."

I keep pushing. I need to get a real reaction from him. I need to know where Emily is and why she isn't in the family pictures. "It's Emily actually that I want to know about, how Emily is doing. That's why we're here, back in town I mean."

His response is immediate. "I don't think I know Emily. Did she work here too? The boys might remember her."

He doesn't know. He's telling the truth. If he is lying, then he's a master deceiver. I keep staring at him, and he looks back as though he wants me to explain who Emily is.

"You really don't know, Michael? Isn't Emily your daughter?" I'm out of options. I don't know what else to say.

Again, he answers right away. "I don't have a daughter. I have two sons. You met Tom, outside, remember." He looks at me as though he thinks the coffee is clouding my mind.

"You had a daughter though, Michael. You had a daughter ten years ago. Emily, I'm talking about Emily. She went missing a couple of days ago. I know all about her, Michael." Still, I push, wanting to hear an explanation from him.

The man shows no signs of panic or fear. He's sitting, facing me. He faces a man bandaged, and cut, and bruised. I know I look desperate, because I feel desperate, but he still shows no signs that he recognizes Emily's name. "You're mistaken. I told you I don't have any daughters, just sons. Now what exactly is your relationship to Heather, and what is it that you want from me?" He has his businessman voice on now, and I can tell that he's tired of our conversation.

I lower my head into my hands, forgetting about the bruises, and wince in pain when I touch it. It doesn't add up. It didn't add up from the moment I walked into the yard, and saw his sons working. It hasn't added up from the time that the drunk gave me a ride home. This man doesn't have a daughter. I look up and decide to try a different tact. "Heather had a daughter. She had a daughter ten years ago. Her name is Emily. She lives in town here." I let the words hang in the air, watching him.

He takes the words in thoughtfully, watching me, and then turns to glance out the window at his sons, working. "Ten years ago, ten years ago, she would have been here." He stands up suddenly, spilling his coffee on the desk. "I don't know how. I don't know how that could have happened."

He's mumbling now, and keeps talking to himself, as though he's trying to remember something. His face turns an ashen colour, and he paces back and forth in front of the desk. He keeps repeating that it was 'ten years ago'. He touches his lips the same way I do when my numbers temporarily don't add up. He looks like a man who can't quite make sense of the situation. I try again, still trying to believe that I'm talking to the father of Heather's child. I sit up straight in my chair, and look at him accusingly. "She had your child, didn't she, Michael? You and Heather were together?"

247

Before I can finish, he's answering me, not shouting but talking firmly, positively, adamantly leaning towards me, trying to make sure I don't miss a word. "No, no, no. Of course not, she was a child, a little girl. I wouldn't touch her. They all come here and work for me. Heather had some problems." He pauses, looking at me, his eyes softening for a moment, as though he can tell me what the problems were without using words.

"If I'd known...If I'd known that it was that serious. I didn't know she was with child, that she was pregnant. How could I know? She left. She just left." He's almost in tears now. His face is still colourless and his skin is sweating. His eyes are wet as he looks at me pleadingly.

It still doesn't make any sense. I still don't know what happened. He's in front of me now, wringing his hands together, nervously. He looks like a man with regrets. I need to know what those regrets are. "What do you mean, Michael? What problems? What do you mean, if you'd known?"

He sits back down on his seat on the other side of the desk and tries to regain his composure. He wipes his eyes with the back of his hands, and leans forward on the desk, before speaking again. "That father of hers, the cop. She told me. She came right in here and told me, not in so many words but...if I'd known how serious it was. If I'd known what was really happening in that house..."

All of a sudden, I know. Maybe I knew for a while and hid from it, I can't say for sure, but now I know. Now, I know. My stomach has a lump in it, and I feel sick. The anger takes a moment to come, but I know it will. It'll come. I stare at him as he put his hands on the desk, looking at them. He just keeps looking at his hands, shaking his head. I want to hit him. I want to hit him the way my dad taught me to hit the boys at school. I want to hit him even though it's not him that I'm angry at. I reach across the table, and almost do it, but I can't. I know that he might have been able to stop all of the pain that Heather suffered, and all of the pain that she's suffering now, but although I want to take my anger out on someone, my fight isn't with him.

Minutes seem to pass, as the gravity of it all slowly hits us. When Michael finally looks up, his eyes are red and his face is wet. He wipes himself with his sleeve, and when he speaks his words are clear. It's as though he's making a confession, which I suppose in a way he is. "I knew who she was of course. We all did, John Postman's daughter. And I knew what happened. Her mother died. Her mother never seemed like a happy woman, and she was always sick. It's a small town. You know these things, especially when it's the police chief's wife. Tom and Mark were a few years younger than Heather, so I'd see her parents, see them at the school or in town."

He keeps going. It's almost as though he's afraid to stop now, and wants to get it all out. "Well, Heather turns out to be a great kid, a good worker, quiet and withdrawn, but a good hard worker. Her dad would pick her up, waiting in his cruiser right over there, never wanting to come into the yard. He'd nod at me, if

I saw him." He shakes his head as though he doesn't want to remember the memory.

"She's here for six, maybe eight months, works through the summer, and then some weekends. She'd sit and eat her lunch right out on those steps that you came up, sometimes all by herself. She was getting more and more withdrawn the longer she was here, wasn't talking to the other kids. My boys were real young then, eight, ten years old themselves." He pauses, thinking, I suppose, of his own children.

"Anyways, I ask her one day; ask her if she's okay. I take her up here into the office, let her eat her lunch sitting at one of the desks while I work." He stares out the window again. I can tell that he doesn't want to look at me. I can see the pain in his face as he contorts his mouth, trying to say the words. "She tells me that things aren't good at home. She says that she and her dad, they don't get along. She says, he sometimes, I think she said, took liberties with her. I tried not to understand what she meant. I tried to explain it to myself, tell myself that it was a teenager not getting along with her father."

The snow is starting to fall outside, just as the sky has been promising all day. I can see Tom, in the yard, looking up at his dad, holding his hands out at his sides, indicating that the weather is changing. Michael forces a smile back and raises his hand in a wave. He turns and looks, continuing his recollection. "It's sometimes easy to look the other way. Her Dad was respected here, still is. I looked the other way. And then one day, she's gone.

I heard that she moved away, moved out west, and I never thought about her again." He stops suddenly, trying to make himself believe. "I wish I could say that I didn't know what she meant. I wish I could tell you that, but I'm not sure. I just don't know for sure."

He's a beaten man. His confession to me hasn't made his face look any less heavy than it was when he began. He'll have to carry the knowledge around with him for the rest of his life that he might have been able to do something, he might have been able to help. I suppose that there are some amends that never really can be made. I think about getting up and leaving him right where he sits, and going home, but now that I know, know for sure; in many ways my journey is just beginning. I still don't know where Heather is, but the reason that we first came to Woodbine, all of a sudden, is more important than ever. I have to find Emily.

I look over at him as he sinks into his chair. "There's something that you can do for me, Michael, something that might help you feel better."

CHAPTER 27

The anger doesn't go away. It doesn't subside. It simmers. It finds a place deep inside, and stays there, waiting. I've been lied to the whole time I've been in Woodbine, longer even. I've been lied to ever since the camping trip at the lake. And now, the man that I've come to confront, to hunt almost, has turned out to be just a decent man who has pictures of his family on his desk. He made a mistake. He turned a blind eye when he should have done something, but it isn't up to me to be his judge.

He reverts back to being the businessman that he was when I first came in his office. He knows police officers. Most of them worked for him when they were kids. And when I tell him the story of my police station beating and jailing, he says that he knows Ellison, the young officer who was with me. He trusts him, and thinks that he can get some information from him. The phone call starts out as an almost jovial chat, but soon reverts into a low voiced conversation. I can tell that he's pressing the man on the other end of the line, almost begging him for information.

He listens intently for a moment, his eyes darting back and forth. I can tell that his mind is racing. Then, he speaks firmly to Ellison again, telling him that he just needs a little information, a little help.

He hangs up and looks at me as though he's proud of himself. "She's not at the police station. They were en route there, but then got ordered to take her to Thornside. She's still there, but under guard."

He answers my perplexed look before I can even get the question out. "It's a hospital, a facility for the mentally challenged. Oh, and there's more, he says it's very interesting, but there haven't been any charges laid, none at all. It's all being handled by a senior officer, her father, presumably, and nobody seems to be saying what's happening. In fact nobody seems to know what's happening."

My mind races; if she's in hospital then she's probably okay. She has to be. And, no charges, that doesn't add up, but then again maybe it does. Maybe her father thinks that this will all just go away again. "Where's Thornside? Is it local?" I look at the snow coming down, outside the window.

"No, it's about an hour from here. You're not going to get there tonight. They're real good at clearing the roads, but I'll bet that it'll be tomorrow morning before you can travel on them. There's the main highway, and then the one that takes you to the hospital. They'll be treacherous in this snow."

My mind is working again. I can still feel the anger. I can still feel the betrayal, and want answers to my questions, but I know that I have to take one step at a time. "Let's call the hospital. Let's call Thornside, and see if we can check on her status." I have an ally now. I'm not sure how much help he's going to give me, but I'm going to take advantage of it while I can.

He looks up the phone number and quickly calls them. The conversation is businesslike again. I think of the mental image I had of this man. I'd considered him a monster.

He hangs up the phone. The discussion was short. "They confirmed that she's there. She was admitted three days ago. She's medicated and resting. That's all I could get out of them. But it sounds like she's okay."

"You did good, Michael. You did really good." He has done well. He's gotten me more information than I'd been able to get, stuck in a jail cell, yelling my questions at Macklin.

I stand up to leave not knowing whether or not I should shake his hand. He speaks first. "I wonder if you'd do me a favour. I wonder if you'd meet my boys, meet them properly."

For some reason it's important to him. It's as though he needs to show me, show me that he really is a decent man. I nod as we make our way out into the snowy afternoon.

When we reach the yard, we see that the boys have been clearing the snow. Tom has a shovel, and the other boy has a small plough attached to the front of the forklift, and is methodically clearing the yard. They have playful grins on their faces, as though they know that it's falling faster than they can clear it. Their father waves them over towards us, as we stand in the shelter of the building. "Guys, this is Malcolm. He's a friend of Heather Postman's. You probably remember Heather from when she worked here."

The young men each hold their hands out for me to shake, both confidently looking into my eyes. The forklift driver speaks first. "It's good to meet you. I remember Heather. She'd climb all the way to the top of the feed sacks, and sit up there eating lunch all by herself sometimes." He smiles at the memory. His face changes as he seems to remember more. "She dyed her hair once. I remember that. Her dad didn't like that. He didn't like that at all." He looks at us as though we should know what he means.

"I don't remember that. Didn't she always have the same hair colour?" Michael asks.

"Nope, she dyed it. Her dad hated it. It wasn't a good scene. We didn't see her for a few days. Then when she came back, her hair was back to normal." He looks from his father and then back to me, as though he's trying to get us to read between the lines.

We let the silence surround us as the snow softly falls on the ground.

I still don't really have a plan. I have an idea. I ask Michael for help one more time. "Michael, can I ask a favour? Do you have a vehicle I can borrow, something that might drive a little better in this weather than my car?" I point towards my rental car, sitting on the street.

He doesn't hesitate. I suppose some of it is his conscience, but I have the impression that he's the kind of a man who'd help a stranger out in almost any situation. He quickly organizes the boys to bring an old pickup truck around to the front, and it's decided that we'll drive in a convoy, back to the motel, me in the rental, Michael in the truck, and the boys in the family sedan.

When we arrive, the parking lot is empty, and Claude is nowhere in sight. I leave the rental car parked in front of the motel room, then jump in with Michael, as he backtracks, and we park the pickup right along the side of the main highway.

We jump out of the old truck, and he gives me the keys, not asking why I'm leaving it at the edge of the road. The boys sit in the family car, parked behind us, waiting. "It burns a little oil, but it runs great. And there's some weight in the back of it, from the wood piled there, so you should have good traction, but wait till tomorrow, or you just won't get through." He's talking about the truck, but keeps looking at me, making no attempt to go join his sons. "We'll give you a ride to your motel. It's probably a mile's walk to get back there."

I shake my head. I want to see exactly how long it'll take me to trudge through the snow, with my bandaged leg. Somewhere, my plan is becoming clearer. I shake his hand, but he still doesn't turn to leave. He has a questioning look on his face. "She told you it was me. She told you I was the father. I wonder why. I wonder why, me?"

I want to give him an answer. I want to somehow make him feel better, but I have the same questions myself, so all I can do is guess. "I suppose that there was a time when she trusted you, liked you." It still doesn't add up for either of us, and he keeps staring at me. "I don't know. Maybe she knew this would happen. She must

256

have known that I'd come to you, come to see you. Maybe she wanted to give you another chance. Maybe she knew that you'd help me."

He looks down at the ground, as the snow keeps falling around us, and when he looks up he seems to be himself again. He passes me a small piece of paper, with numbers scribbled on it. "It's my number, my cell phone number. Use it if you have to." I take the number from him and watch as he turns and walks away, before jumping into his vehicle and driving off with his sons.

It takes ten minutes, walking quickly in the cold, to reach the motel. I open the door of the parked rental car, and slam it a couple of times, until I see Claude at the window of the office, peering out at me. I half-heartedly wave at him, trying to appear distracted, hoping that he didn't see me walking down the highway. I walk deliberately to my room. I want him to know that I'm here.

Heather packed a small carry-on bag for the plane trip. I empty it out and pack some bare necessities in it, my identification, some clothing, toiletries, only the things that won't weigh me down. Then, I zip it closed. I want it to look like I'm coming back to the room. I pile the bedding to one side of the bed, and push a couple of pillows under the sheets. It almost looks like someone is sleeping in there, and in the dark, it might gain me a minute or two. Somewhere in my mind, my plan continues to take shape.

I stand at the bottom of the bed, enjoying the heat and letting the sweat from my walk run down my face. I think of the lake at the end of the world. I think of a scared girl, carefully placing all of her little figurines on the shelves around my bed. I think of the way she looked at me when she did it, the way she looked at me for my approval. I don't think of the lies, or the betrayal. I think of a girl with a half dimple, sitting at the lake at the end of the world, afraid to tell me who the father of her child really is. I open up the small bag once again, and go around the room, picking up some of her things, and adding them to mine.

Thornside, is listed in the telephone directory that's in the drawer of the small bedside table. The listing shows an address and some basic directions. Michael was right; I'll have to change from the main highway to another one, and then to a road whose name I don't recognize, but I'm fairly sure that I can find it. I dry the sweat off my face and find some leftover fruit and granola bars amongst our things. I eat silently, sitting by the window, waiting for the darkness to come.

The snow subsides for a moment, then starts again, falling even harder, and faster than it was before. I look across the parking lot, at the closed door of the laundry room, feeling the key, still in my pocket. I wait until I see the lights from the motel office go off. I picture Claude, retiring to the back, a glass of whisky in his hand. I wait, watching for any movement, but there is none. The main highway is quiet with just the odd car every few minutes, struggling along slowly, through the snowy night. I listen, hoping to hear the rumble of a snowplough, but it's quiet, almost serene.

I close the curtains, and unscrew the bulbs from the overhead light and the bedside lamps. Quietly, I open the front door, still looking, listening, for any activity. I lock the door behind me, watching the dark office, and the laundry room door. As fast as I can, I make my way across the snowy parking lot, carrying the small, bag that's packed with our things. The laundry room door lock turns just as easily and silently as it did earlier, and I enter the dark room.

There are no rumblings of washing machines this time. Fortunately though, it's still warm inside, and I can hear the faint humming noise from the electrical panels in the back utility room. I feel my way around in the dark, getting my bearings. I look in the back room, to see that it's just as I left it, earlier in the day. I suspect that the key I took was a spare, and that Claude, or his lady friend, automatically locks the laundry room door at a designated time each day with their own set of keys. There is a small window at the front. I tilt the venetian blinds on it and can look directly across the parking lot at my idle rental car, parked in front of my room, right where it should be.

My breathing returns to normal. I hadn't noticed how tense I'd been as I stole my way across the parking lot, watching for any sign of movement from the road or the office. I can see the snow, falling lazily now, not with the force it had earlier, filling the footprints that I left. There is no noise. The highway remains eerily

259

quiet, and the weather drops a muffled blanket over any outside sound. There is a room with a light coming from it at the far side of the motel; another overnight traveller I suppose. After a while, it goes out and the darkness quickly settles over everything. I've rarely seen Canadian snow during my mild Vancouver winters, but I have seen Scottish snow. I've experienced that.

I went back to Scotland for a month after I graduated from college and travelled around the country. I took my dad, and my girlfriend of the day to all of the places that we never visited growing up. My dad gave us a running commentary on the battle of Culloden when we reached Inverness. He told us about William Wallace when we visited a monument in Stirling. We reached the gateway to the highlands; I drove us through the snow, even farther. I took us as far north as we could, all the way to John O' Groats. I was born farther south, in Kilmarnock, but this still felt like my country, all of it.

My mother met my father when she took a trip to Scotland as a young twenty-something year old girl. My father charmed her as the Scottish gentleman that he is, and she charmed him into thinking that she could be a good faithful partner. When she tired of what she called his 'dour Scottish moods and the gloomy climate', she took me back to the motels of Vancouver. My father never did recover from her leaving, but he was always glad to have me back in Scotland.

He talked to me during that trip, talked to me as an adult. We drove through the early winter snow in the north of the country, over roads that tourists never make it to, and he talked to me about the past. I drove carefully along the twisting highland curves, as my girlfriend slept in the back seat, with my dad beside me, reminiscing. He told me how I had kept his life complete, even though he didn't know anything about raising a child. He told me how I'd intimidated him with my knowledge and the ease with which it took me to acquire it. I looked straight ahead at the road as he talked, not wanting interrupt the emotions that were finally coming from him. He tried to turn me into him for a while, he said, a brawling, football playing, man's man, but it didn't work. I became me. He said that he loved me and smiled, saying that he liked what I'd become.

The snow continues to fall outside the laundry room, as the night gets later and later. I'm tired and let out a yawn. I wonder if I should try to sleep. I wonder if I'll hear his vehicle outside if I just lay my head down on the floor, and sleep for a few moments. I think for a moment that I might be wrong. He might not come. He might be at the hospital. He might not be thinking about me, worrying that I might know what he's done, and what happened in his home ten years earlier. I might be wrong.

I barely hear the vehicle, as it creeps into the parking lot. At first, I think it might not be him. It's not a police car, but then I recognize it. I remember the big sports utility vehicle, sitting in his driveway. The snow is still soft, and there's little noise, as it slowly makes its way towards my room. He sits there for a minute; then two minutes; then five. I strain my eyes and can see Heather's father, sitting inside the car. I can make out his head, the greyness of his hair. He turns around and looks at the office, then over to where I'm crouched by the window. He pauses, looking in my direction for a moment too long, but then he returns his attention to my room. I exhale, realizing I've been holding my breath in again, just like back at the barn.

He slowly makes his way out of his vehicle, and reaching down below his seat, pulls out a small bat or baton. Quietly, almost gently, he pushes the car door closed behind him. He looks over his shoulder to the office and the parking lot one more time as he walks to my room door, and tries opening the handle. He stands for a moment, and I ready myself. I grab the bag, and put my hand on the inside of the laundry room door. I hold onto the door handle tightly, and wait as he returns to his vehicle, and once again opens the car door. His head ducks down into the back seat, and he comes out with a tool. His back is to me. I bend open one of the bottom slats in the blind just in time to see him walking back to my door. I have a clear picture of him now. I almost feel as though I'm standing right behind him. He's working the tool on the door, quietly, efficiently, trying to pry it open at the lock. His body doesn't bend the way a weaker man's would. He stands erect, using the strength in his arms to force it open.

He jumps slightly as it pops open, but he still doesn't move, waiting. I can see him so well now that I feel like I can hear him breathing. The motel room door opens in his hands, yet still he doesn't move. He waits. His back to me. I can see him watching,

262

waiting for some movement from inside the room. Slowly, gradually, he moves into the room, and I reach for the laundry room door and open it.

I move with a speed I didn't realize I had and bolt from the laundry room, out into the parking lot. I only cover a few steps when I have a change of heart, and go back towards his vehicle. He didn't take the keys. They're still hanging from the ignition. I imagine him in my room, trying the light switch that won't work as I quietly open his door, then reach over and grab the keys that he left there. I quickly pull them and close the car door behind me, as quietly as I can. I look once to the room and the door that he closed behind him.

I run. I run with a panicked, frantic pace. My legs slide and I right them, trying to move forward. I run in the snow, along the side of the highway. I focus on the road in front of me and nothing else, as I try to make my way back to the parked truck. I hold the small bag in one hand, and his car keys in the other, forcing my legs to move quickly through the snow. I listen as I run, trying to hear any noises, over the sounds of my heavy breathing. I hear what sounds like a car, slowly, methodically, coming down the highway behind me, pursuing me. I feel his keys in my hand. He might have spare keys for his vehicle, but it isn't likely that he has them with him. It can't be him, not so quickly. But still the sound gets closer. I can't look back. I continue moving towards where I parked the truck. I keep moving forward. I can feel the weight of the snow, as my feet keep moving with all the speed that I can muster, but still I hear the vehicle. The sound gets closer. I feel like he's watching me, but still, it stays back. I run frantically now, along the side of the snowy highway.

As the lights from the vehicles headlights shine on my back, and light up the ground in front of me, I desperately jump to the side of the highway. I stay clear of the ditch, still trying to move forward, still not wanting to look back and see him. I stumble, but catch myself before I fall. I stop, clutching the small bag in one hand, holding it, ready to swing it like a weapon, as I turn my head back towards the vehicle.

There's a large, dark, van with a young bearded man, rolling down his window, laughing at me. "Out jogging?" He turns to the driver, another young man, involving him in the joke.

I stop, looking behind them, down the road, searching for another vehicle. I'm out of breath, sweating. "No, I'm sorry. I thought you were someone else." I wonder if they see the relief that I'm feeling. They let their vehicle idle on the deserted road, looking at me incredulously. "My truck, it's just down the highway. I'm just getting back to it." I can see the truck now, just off in the distance, where I left it.

"We'd drive you, but you look like you're gonna make it okay." The passenger smiles at me, and I can hear the driver telling him to roll up the window. "You are going to be okay aren't you?" I can't tell if he means it, or if it's the beginning of another sarcastic remark.

I nod, and before I can answer him, the van drives away, and I continue quickly towards the truck.

Even as I sit in the pickup truck, I feel as though I'm still running through the snow. I turn on the engine, and just as Michael promised, it quickly turns over and fires. The sweat from my run rolls down my forehead, and stings my eyes. I let the defrost fans unthaw the windshield, keeping a watch on the road, checking to see if there's anyone following me. I pull the old truck out onto the snow-covered highway, barely giving it enough time to warm up. I gently touch the brakes and the back wheels slide immediately. I right the vehicle by turning the steering wheel in the same direction. I follow the tracks in the road, from the van with the young men, and continue along their path, trying to find some traction in the flattened snow.

The highway has two lanes, but with the fallen snow it looks like one extra wide track. They drove right down the centre, far from the shoulders. I hold the steering wheel tightly, gingerly trying to accelerate more, then, fall back to a slow steady speed, as I try to stay straight on the slippery ground below me. I look in the rear view mirror, searching for other cars, looking for him. I wait until I'm some miles up the road, then I roll down the window, and throw Chief Inspector Postman's car keys as far as I can out into the snowy night.

I memorized the directions from the phone book that was in the room. After what seems like hours, I finally see the entrance for the next highway. The van that was in front of me stayed on. It didn't take the exit. So, I need to break new ground on my own now. The entrance sits on an incline, and then slopes back down again once it reaches the other highway. I need to maintain some speed in order to take the curve, to make the entrance. I let the truck hit the tilt of the road as fast as I can safely push it, and then allow it to slide down the other side. Again, I swing the wheels the same way to correct myself. The snow has stopped falling and it feels like there's no one else alive, as the old truck silently, solidly, hugs the highway and straightens out. I can feel the cold from outside coming in the truck. I turn the heat up, glad of the noise of the fan.

The minutes pass by and turn to hours, and as the monotony of the slick, snow covered road passes me by, I think of Vancouver and home and how it's never going to be the same again. I think of Heather, stuck in a hospital. And, I think of Emily, a little girl that I don't know. What happened to make Heather come for her now? How had she managed to get her to go with her back in the library? And, I have the same question as Michael, why me? Why did Heather bring me along? Why did she let me come? And, why had she not trusted me with the truth, with her truths?

I hear a noise ahead of me. I turn the fan down to listen, and as I drive forward I see it coming towards me, on the other side of the highway. I let out a laugh, and hold tightly to the wheel, as I see the snowplough, working its way down the other side of the freeway, clearing a lane for any drivers that might be going in the other direction.

The sky is lighter now. Daybreak is coming. It'll be morning when I reach the hospital. Still, there are no cars behind me. It's a surreal experience, being the only vehicle, driving slowly on the snow-covered highway. I think of Heather's father, creeping around my room, trying the light switches that won't work, poking at the pillows with his baton. Then, realizing that I'm not there, getting to his car to find no keys. I wondered if he'll waken Claude, and enlist his help in finding me, finding his keys. I wonder what Postman had intended to do to me. What would he have done in order to make sure that I don't reveal his secret? I can't go back to the motel now. There's no amount of money that Claude will take as a bribe. I laugh at the image of him, out there in the parking lot, with the furious, crazy cop, telling him that he doesn't know where I am.

I'm tired, but have to go on. I open the window a crack, and let the cold air blow on my face. The snow is crustier now, giving me better traction. I drive on, faster, as the old truck holds solidly onto the road. There's a bank of signs ahead, just as the sun appears and starts shining. The light from it seems to illuminate the

267

road sign, allowing me to read it. I'm almost there. The sign reads that I'm five miles from Thornside Hospital.

I pull onto the exit and take the road for the hospital. The snow is easier to handle now, as though it was cleared, and then fell again. I push the truck forward, increasing my speed, still trying to keep it straight on the road. I take a look in the rear view mirror again, and still can't see another vehicle. The panic from earlier is gone now. Maybe it's from being too tired, or maybe I've just stopped caring whether he catches up to me or not. I'm there now, closer, almost to Heather.

Within minutes, I see the big grey building up ahead. I pull the truck into the hospital parking lot, confident that it won't be recognized by Heather's father, even if he has found a way to follow me. I back into a parking spot and look around, still seeing no one.

Sitting there, I try to remind myself that I'm not under arrest. I'm not under suspicion, in fact I haven't even been charged. And, more importantly, I haven't done anything wrong. I've stolen some car keys, and thrown them away on a highway, and if they can prove that, then I'll gladly accept their punishment. I stiffly pull myself from the truck, and close the door behind me. My muscles ache from the hours spent driving along the treacherous road, and my leg is still sore and bandaged from the fall that I took back at the barn. I take a handful of snow, and use it to wash the sweat and tiredness from my face, then walk towards the large entranceway to the hospital.

CHAPTER 28

I decide on the truth. I've always tried to live that way, and more importantly, I have nothing to hide. So, I tell the man at the information counter the truth. I'm there to visit a patient who was admitted a few days ago. I'm sorry for the early hour, but if it isn't too inconvenient I'd like to see her. The young man sleepily gives me the room number, and directs me to the third floor, suggesting I take the elevator. Much to my relief, he doesn't ask who I am or what my business is. He just gives me directions. It's easy, much easier than I imagined.

I take the stairs, remembering that Ellison told Michael on the phone, that she was under guard, and not wanting to announce my arrival with the noise of the elevator. I carefully open the door to the third floor, and see the police officer, sleeping in the patient's lounge. His breathing is heavy and he's sleeping soundly. There's a nurse, with her back to me, sitting in an open office behind a counter, a few feet away from the lounge. I stand there looking at the policeman for a moment. He looks like he might be one of the officers from the station, but I can't be sure. I slowly make my way past the lounge, and then quietly past the nurse, who still doesn't turn around. I look at the room numbers. I can smell the same, industrial type smell that all hospitals have. I can feel the emptiness of the early morning. There's no one there, no one at all. I find the room and gently turn the door handle.

There's a bed in the centre of the room, but she isn't in it. There's a girl crouched in a corner, holding herself, a blanket draped over her shoulders. She's shivering and her face is covered in bruises, and soaked with wetness. It's not her. It can't be her. I involuntarily let out a small sound. It might be from the anger of seeing her like this, or from seeing the look of fear in her eyes, as she looks at me. But it is her. It really is Heather. I stare, trying to match up the picture of the girl that I've come to know with the girl who's crouched in the corner.

I'm not sure if she knows it's me. She looks in my direction, shivering, showing no signs of recognition or familiarity. I walk towards her. She pushes herself back harder against the wall, making a hushed, yelping sound as she cowers away from me. I kneel down, feeling defeated, still staring at her. She keeps looking at me, her eyes large and hesitant.

We sit for a few moments before she speaks. Her sentences are in fragments at first, incomplete. "He touched... He always touched me." Her voice is small, and doesn't sound like the confident girl that I know. She speaks slowly and carefully, watching me, sometimes looking at the door as though she thinks we'll be interrupted any minute.

"I know. I know that now. You could have told me. You should have told me." As I speak, she shakes her head, saying, "No, no," over and over again, so furiously I'm afraid she'll hurt herself.

"I was ashamed, ashamed. Don't you see? Don't you understand? I was so ashamed." She says the word as though it is dirty, as though it hurts for it to come from her mouth.

I look away, waiting, not knowing how to react, how to comfort her. I try opening my mouth, but nothing comes out. I don't know what to say.

"You can't talk." She whispers it in an almost hoarse voice. "You have to let me talk, Malcolm." It almost sounds as though she's angry with me.

As she says my name I feel a sense of relief that she might be okay. I don't know how much of Heather is still there, but she said my name, and that's a good thing. I sit on the floor, leaning against the bed, waiting for her to speak again.

"It started when I was small. He'd touch me, always at night. I hated the nights. I used to pray for morning to come. Mornings were good. Mornings were the sunshine coming in my windows, and no touching. They were the time when I'd try to block out what he did to me the night before. He never came to me in the mornings." It takes all of her strength to get the words out. She looks down at her hands as she speaks; sometimes clenching them together so tightly that it seems to cause her pain.

"It got worse when Mom died. It happened more and more. It was just the two of us in that house." She stops, and then looks up suddenly, wiping the tears from her eyes. "It wasn't Michael, it never was, you know. It was never him." She says it urgently, forcefully. "He was just, I don't know. I just had to tell you that it was someone, anyone."

I whisper back to her. "I know Heather. I know that. I went to see him. I spoke to Michael." I inch my way forward, trying to hold her, trying to take away some of the pain, but she just shakes her head again, and pushes herself back hard, against the wall.

She wipes her tears, and pulls the blanket tight around herself again, looking up at me almost shyly. "When I knew that I was pregnant, I tried to hide it, tried to keep it from him but he knew. He always knew." Her eyes are cold again.

There's anger in her now as she speaks. "He sent me to that hospital, the one I told you about in Alberta, with the crazy old nurse. And he was nice to me there. He stayed with me, saying that it would all work out, but of course it didn't."

"I should have come back. I should have found a way, but I was just so glad that I didn't have him..." The fear is still in her eyes, and she keeps squeezing her hands together, wincing at the pain.

"When I met you, and we spent that time at the lake, I felt like I could do anything. I had always thought about Emily, about coming to get her, but the fear always stopped me. I always blocked it out, pretended that, maybe it never happened. And then, with you, with us, I thought I could do anything."

She raises her eyes and looks at me, answering the question that's hanging in the air between us. "I knew you'd come with me.

I told myself you decided on your own, but that night, when I told you, I knew you'd come."

I move closer again, and this time she doesn't move away. I reach out to touch her hands. She lets me touch them, and I gently separate them, stopping her from hurting herself. I rub the tops of her hands, warming them up, trying to stop her from shaking.

"I lied to you, the lies about Michael, about having a relationship with him. I lied to you over and over, but I didn't mean for all this to happen. I just needed to see her. I needed to see if he was...I needed to make sure she was safe. I just needed to see her."

I rub her arms, her shoulders, over the blanket, and watch her frightened eyes as they talk to me.

"That night, the day you went to the police station, I did go to the library, but then I went to his house, to my old house. I waited until I saw him leave, and then I went in. Emily was there, and she let me in. She's beautiful Malcolm, so beautiful." The tears in her eyes glisten as she pushes her head forward, emphasizing the words.

"We spoke, and she knew about me, knew that I'd left. He's told her I left both of them. I asked her about her mother, and she says that her mother died. That's all she knows, but she kept staring at me, noticing the resemblance. I know she doesn't know who I am to her, who I really am." She pauses again. "I touched her face, and she touched mine and smiled, giggled. I tried to ask her, ask her what it was like at home, but she just looked down and

273

said it was fine. I had no way to know, no way to know if things are okay. We sat there talking for a long time and then, it happened."

She touches the bruise on her face, and I start to feel the anger simmering in me again, as I realize how she got her bruise. There had been no door that she walked into at the library.

"I didn't hear him coming in. He was behind me, and all of a sudden I saw Emily's eyes get very wide. He picked me up, and turned me around, yelling at Emily to go to her room, telling her to get away. He's just the same, the same as before, except this time I wasn't so afraid."

"I tried to talk to him, tell him that I wanted to spend some time with Emily, get to know her, but he wouldn't listen. As I picked up my things to go, I threatened him, told him I'd tell, tell what he'd done to me. And, that's when he slapped me."

She stops, catching her breath, remembering. "Emily saved me. I could hear her crying upstairs, whimpering, and he could hear her too. He looked up at the stairs and I left. I walked away, ran, I suppose, frightened once again, but I knew this time I would do something about it." She stops, and looks at me. "I knew I had to do something about it."

I try to hold her, try to pull her close. Finally, she buries her head in my chest, and lets me put my arms all the way around her. I feel like that day at the lake again, the day I hadn't decided whether I'd go with her or not. This time I feel like I know the truth, all of it. I think there are times in life when you're given decisions to make, and there are times when the decision is so clear that you just have to follow it. I don't feel like I'm making a decision as I hold onto her, on the hospital floor, I'm just following it.

"We have to get you out of here. We need to figure out how to get to Emily." The words come from my mouth instinctively, as though it's the most natural thing in the world to say. She whimpers in my embrace, and holds on to me tightly for the first time in days.

She speaks again, between her sobs. "At the library, I knew when I looked at her and she looked at me, I just knew. I didn't even have to ask her to come with me. She just did. I looked at her as she walked in, and as I got up, she just took my hand and followed me. It was so easy."

She pulls away from me, still trying to explain. "I thought of you once we were outside. I realized that I'd left you, but by then it was too late. We were in the car and driving. I didn't know where to go, or what I was going to do. I just knew that I had to get her away from him. I thought about you, but then I would look at Emily, into her eyes, and the only thing that mattered was making her safe. I'm so sorry I left you, Malcolm. I'm so sorry."

"It's okay. It's all going to be okay." I gently pull her hair back, and kiss her forehead, burying my nose into her skin, enjoying the feel of her. I hold her tightly, feeling as though I can protect her from anything now.

"I don't want you to think I forgot about you. I don't want you to think that I didn't care what happened. I just saw my little girl, and all of a sudden, nothing else mattered."

I hold her tightly, trying to squeeze and comfort the fear away.

The anger is back now. It fills my head, makes my whole body tense up. In my mind, I see him as he punched me with his belt, wrapped around his fist. I see him as he slapped Heather, and I see his maniacal expression, when he came into the office, and said that he'd found her. My heart pounds, as I try to focus, try to think of what our next move is, but all I can see, all I can think of is Postman. And, the only thing that I know for sure is that I have to see him again.

I help her put on her clothes. Her body is weak and limp from whatever she's been put through the last few days. She doesn't ask questions. She just leans over and lets me help her. I sit her on the bed, and then carefully open up the room door, to look outside. There are large overhead 'exit' signs at both ends of the hallway, and they all point towards the same area that I came in from. We have to pass the lounge with the policeman again, but it doesn't matter. She's leaving with me, and no one is going to stop us.

I shepherd her under my arms, trying to take as much of her weight as I can, leading her down the hallway. The nurse's area is empty now. I hear some low noises, coming from the back offices behind the counter, but there's no one in sight. I think of excuses, reasons, stories. I think of what I'll say if we're stopped. We quickly, steadily, make our way to the stairway, trying to pass the lounge unnoticed.

There's no one there. The officer that was there earlier is gone, and the lounge is empty. All I hear is the normal working noises of the hospital, from down hallways and behind closed doors. There is a patient speaking loudly somewhere and a nurse answering. I keep moving her along. She's light now, like a child.

She doesn't have the strength for the stairs, so I her into the elevator, and it quickly moves us down to the main floor. The creaking door slides open to the lobby, and we can see that there are people there now. There's a patient, in a white gown, sitting in a chair by the wall. There's movement, with other patients and nurses, slowly moving around, going about their work. The same young man is standing at the front desk, but an older woman is beside him now. And another police officer is sitting in a chair by the door, reading the newspaper, with his back to us.

It's a different man now, a different officer. I keep shuffling Heather along, trying not to look at him. She keeps her head down, oblivious to everything, other than the motion of me leading her forward. I avoid looking at the officer's face. He doesn't budge as we come into the lobby. All I see are his arms, holding the newspaper, head tilted down reading. Suddenly, I have a sense of panic that it might be him. It might be Postman, sitting there waiting for us. But, still I don't look. I just keep holding onto Heather, our backs to the officer, concentrating on leading her towards the front door.

I know that the older woman will speak. Her eyes trail as soon as we walk from the elevator, into the lounge. We're almost past her desk, when she taps on it to get our attention. "Excuse me? Can I help you with something? Where is it that you think you are going?" There's a sense of indignation in her voice as her eyes widen and she looks at us.

"We're checking out. I mean she's checking out. She hasn't been charged with anything, and I'm her next of kin, so I'm taking her home now. We're going home." I keep staring at the woman, not wanting to see the face of the officer sitting just a few feet behind us, hoping that neither of them can hear the desperation in my voice. My ears are primed as I listen for any sound from him. I'm ready to turn around and face him if I hear the newspaper start to rustle. There's nothing though, just the sounds of the fluorescent lights buzzing away in the lobby, and the occasional voice of a patient or nurse, somewhere down the hallways.

I stand my ground, and the woman and I continue to stare at each other for a moment. She seems to be searching for a reason to keep us there. The young man from earlier, stands beside her, with

278

his hands on his hips, waiting for her direction. Finally, she breaks the stalemate and looks behind us. I know that she's looking over at the officer. Her eyes widen, and her mouth opens in mock surprise as she seems to be asking him a question without speaking. She wants him to make the decision. She wants his approval.

I recognize his voice from my days at the police station immediately. "It's fine. He's right. There are no charges. They can go."

I look over just once, as I hurriedly pull Heather towards the main door. Ellison still hasn't looked up. He just keeps looking down, reading the paper, acting as though he hasn't seen us at all. I push open the big, heavy door, not wanting to look back, just in case it didn't happen at all.

As we hit the bright, cold, lights of the morning, I realize that we've had someone looking after us while we sat in the room, talking. Ellison must have relieved the other guard at some point, or maybe there had been two of them all the time. Either way, the young officer who wouldn't let me call a lawyer, has let us leave the hospital.

CHAPTER 29

It feels so good to have her with me, to not be alone. She sits curled up, looking exhausted, and holds onto the passenger door while I drive. She stays awake but doesn't speak. There are other cars now, and as I drive around the roads from the hospital, the snow seems to take a break. Some of the roads have been cleared, but some are still slick with the remnants of the previous night's storm. I drive until I can see buildings, shops and restaurants. The hospital is in its own small town, but it's very different from Woodbine. Although the hospital is an old building, the rest of the town is newer, fresher. There are fast food restaurants, and the same type of chain stores you see wherever you go.

I keep my hands tight on the wheel. My eyes constantly check my mirrors, watching for any car that might be following us. I keep looking over at her, not quite believing I have her beside me, not quite believing that we were able to leave the hospital so easily. I fight the urge to reach over and touch her. I think about pulling over just to hold her, to feel her close, to feel like I'm not alone, but I just keep on driving.

There's a large hotel, situated in the centre of a busy block, and I immediately recognize its familiar, large emblem, high on the sign out front. I circle the block three times, then pull over and park at the side of a road, waiting, watching. There's only the normal flow of other vehicles. I see men and women in their business suits, and workers in coveralls and work shirts, all going about their business, oblivious to us. There are no police cars, no vehicles driving slow to look at us, no one watching. So, I pull into the hotel parking lot, and after leaving Heather in the car for a few minutes, check us into a room.

I register in my own name, and they don't ask if I have anyone with me. It's a different town and Postman is back in Woodbine. I keep telling myself that we have nothing to hide. Heather hasn't been charged, and legally, nobody should be looking for either of us.

The room is on the first floor and this time I'm too tired to hide her. We walk in just as anyone else would, without looking over our shoulders at all.

The room is large and warm and clean. I barely have enough strength to remove my jacket and pants, and shirt. I pull back the duvet, and we climb under the covers. I've been awake for more hours than I care to remember. I look at the clock, and it's just before ten in the morning. Heather falls asleep immediately. I have no way of knowing if she slept at all while she was at the hospital. I stare at her poor, sore face, wondering what she must have been put through over the past few days. Quietly, I pick up the phone that's at the side of the bed, and make the call that I promised I'd make before leaving Vancouver. It's seven a.m. on the west coast, but he'll be up, looking at his computer, getting ready for his day.

"Terry Allister, good morning." It's one of the most comforting sounds I've ever heard in my life. I should have made the call days before, but I didn't know what I was going to say to him. I almost tear up, listening to his impatient tone, as he speaks again. "Good morning, this is Terry. Who's there please?"

"Terry, it's me." I say the words slowly, and then pause, knowing that I won't get a word in anyways, as I wait for his questions.

"Malcolm, where the hell have you been? You stupid Scottish shit, Jo's worried sick about you. What's going on, and what happened to my phone calls?" He sounds irritated, but he's almost laughing too, unaware of what we've been through.

I have to cut him off, and I almost wish Jo was there too, to help settle him down, as I start to talk to him. I look over at Heather, but she's fast asleep, and no amount of excitable Terry will wake her up now. "Buddy, you need to listen to me. Grab a pen. You need to write this down." He starts to speak again and once more I cut him off. "No Terry, just listen for now. I really will explain everything later."

He grunts a yes to me, and I give him the name, and phone number of the hotel, with our room number. It's probably a world record for Terry, as he manages to do what I ask of him for at least thirty seconds, before he starts asking questions again.

"Malcolm, your voice, it doesn't sound right. It doesn't sound like you. You gonna tell me now?"

He isn't laughing, and sounds worried, but more than anything else, he doesn't have control, and Terry always needs to be in control. That's probably the secret of his success, and those of us who love him, or even like him, tolerate it because after a while, we learn that he really is a good, caring man. "Terry, please listen to me. We've gotten into a bit of a problem here, nothing that can't be sorted out, but I do need your help."

When I ask him for his help, I can almost see him on the other end of the phone, his body hunching forward at his desk, all alert and ready to do whatever it took to help me. "I'll let you know everything that's happened, but I can't right now, that'll have to come later. For now, I need you to do a couple of things for me. Call me back in four hours, and if Heather or myself don't answer, call the front desk and have them call the police. Don't give up trying to get in touch with us until you hear my voice."

There's a slight silence before I hear him again. "Fuck, Malcolm, what's going on there?"

"Terry, just call me back, call me back in four hours. I'll fill you in then, I promise." I lay the receiver back down on the phone, and barely have enough energy left to roll my head over onto the soft, white pillow. I know Terry. I know he'll call back.

I still have only the beginnings of a plan forming, but it's hard, hard to focus. I keep thinking about Postman, about what he's done. The anger isn't going away. I think about Ellison. Why did he just let us leave? Was he told to, or did he decide on his own? Or worse yet, was he somewhere out there, still watching us? I think about Emily. I hear the faint sounds of the street noises, outside the window. I hear Heather's heavy breathing, as she sleeps beside me. I realize I'm clenching the pillow, holding onto

283

it. I release my grip, and try to concentrate on my breathing, try to focus. It's not Heather or Emily or even John Postman that I see as I try to fall asleep. It's my friend, Hardly, and I remember. I remember that he too is in a hospital somewhere, with a hole in his leg.

Taking the piece of paper from my wallet, I punch the long distance code into the hotel phone and amazingly I'm connected almost immediately. I almost ask for Hardly but then, I remember, it's Gerald. He used to be Gerald.

"Hullo, who's calling please."

His strong Scots accent comforts me, and I lay my head back on the pillow enjoying the familiar sound. It's been years since I've seen him and almost as long since we've spoke on the phone, but it's still him. He's still the same. I can tell. "It's me, Hardly. It's Malcolm, how are you feeling? How are you doing?"

There's no pause, no hesitation as my childhood friend answers immediately, the gratitude evident in his voice. "Malcolm, Malcolm, where are you? It's good to hear from you. I'm fine, mate. I'm fine, just a couple of bullets. I might even walk again. Not as bad as getting pissed on from a tree, Malcolm. Not even close." He's laughing now between words and I feel guilty about the struggles that he's gone through and fact that I haven't been there, haven't been there at all.

"I'm okay, Hardly. I'm okay. I'm in Ontario, still in Canada, helping a friend. I just wanted to hear how you were doing. I wish I could have gotten there to see you. I really do." My words sound empty and he certainly has the right to question my friendship, my loyalty, but this is Hardly. That isn't what he does.

"It's okay, Malcolm. You have your life over there in Canada. I know that. It's the way things played out. It's not your fault. You did what you had to do to survive, and I did what I had to do. Different roads, mate, different roads, that's all. One day we'll meet up. I know we will. I've told your dad that. One day we'll all meet up again."

I have to suck my breath in hard to stop the emotions from coming out. I pause before continuing and he asks me to excuse his slurping as he sips some water.

"I have to ask you something, Hardly. I always wanted to know, do you think I did enough? Do you think I did enough to help you, to help us, when we were back there in school?"

This time there is a pause and I think of a mixed up version of a young Hardly and an older military man. Hardly perhaps touching his face or scratching his head before answering me.

"Malcolm, those were hard times. We were wee waynes, children. We got through it together. We got through it alive, didn't we? I mean here we are, you in Canada, across the ocean, and me here in Scotland and we're talking. I'm talking to Malcolm. We're right, Malcolm. We're right as we could be."

It's not enough though. As my tiredness starts to get the better of me I feel as though I'm awake and dreaming at the same time, talking to Hardly and dreaming about him too.

"I always felt like I left you and then when I didn't come back. I felt like I'd left you and my dad. I just, I didn't know. I didn't know where home was or what it was. I just stayed. I stayed away, away from it all." My head is on the pillow now and my eyes are barely open, but I can see him. I can see him as he sits in his hospital bed with tears in his hard little eyes while he talks to me.

"Malcolm, don't worry. You know where your home is. You know inside. You do know that, don't you Malcolm. That doesn't go away. You always know that."

I'm nodding to him and falling asleep at the same time. I think I answered, yes, before clumsily putting the phone back on the receiver. I hope I did. I hope he heard me saying, yes.

The ringing sounds like it's supposed to be there. It feels like it's part of my sleep, part of my dreams. I jump as I realize that the phone on the bedside table is ringing. It feels as though I just laid my head down. I look over at Heather, still sleeping soundly beside me, as I pick up the receiver and say hello to Terry.

He doesn't say hello back. He's all business now. "Malcolm, I've got Brennan's number here too. He's my lawyer, you'll remember him. He came to my party a couple of years ago. I want you to call and talk to him. Oh, and Jo's here too, right beside me."

286

I rub the sleep from my eyes, trying to catch up to all the information that he's giving me. I should have realized that when I said 'police' to Terry earlier, that it would have scared him, and of course he has Jo beside him now. He needs her level-headed good sense. We both need it.

I tell them almost everything. He has one of his gadgets attached to the phone, so that Jo can hear me, and I can hear her. At times, he exclaims, or asks me what the hell I was thinking, but Jo just keeps steady, sound. I can almost hear her breathing. I feel like I can see her, nodding in the background, telling Terry to be patient, to wait, while they listen to me speak. I leave out the part about the lies Heather told me. That isn't important anymore. That's our business.

"You need to get your ass back here right now, Malcolm, both of you. We'll sort this out from here. You need a lawyer, a prosecutor." He's angry, but he's worried too. I can hear it in his voice.

I let him talk for a moment. He keeps going, making plans in his head as he speaks, telling me what the best course of action is, the best way to 'make the bastard pay'. He talks about 'legalities' and 'prosecutions' and 'consequences', but never once does he mention Emily. And, never once, does he talk about the type of retribution I've been dreaming about. He doesn't realize this isn't a business deal, and it has nothing to do with legalities anymore. It's personal.

Something happens when you reach a certain level of anger. It consumes you. My fear left me, somewhere along the highway, between Woodbine and the hospital, and now the feeling that's in the pit of my stomach is anger, rage. I don't think about the police, or being locked up, or even charged. I think about Postman and Emily and Hardly, always Hardly.

"Give me Brennan's phone number, Terry. That's a good idea. I think I do remember him, too." Heather is awake now and looking at me sleepily, as I write it down.

He gives me the numbers, trying to interject with advice, with cautions, until finally he offers his own services. "Malcolm, I've decided. I'm coming out there. If you're not going to come home, I'll come to you. This doesn't sound like you, this just isn't you. I'll fly out. I'm coming out, today."

Jo still hasn't spoken. I don't know what she's thinking. I can't tell what her reaction is. "Terry, I need you there. I need you on that side, helping me. And, I need you to not worry. You have to trust me." I speak to him firmly; probably more forcefully than I ever have before.

He doesn't listen. His interruptions and objections keep coming. He doesn't have control, and I know it's killing him. He sounds like he thinks he really can fix it all, if he just comes to Woodbine. I don't let him finish this time. I raise my voice. Heather sits up, listening. "Terry, you don't understand, nothing's really changed since we got here. It's still about a little girl, except now it's even more important. We have to go. We have to get

Emily." I know I have no choice. There's no decision to be made. I'm just running, running on instinct.

Heather keeps staring at me, watching me. I hold the phone, and listen to the silence on the other end, imagining Terry looking over at Jo, probably raising his hands in the air in frustration. Then, she speaks, "Malcolm, it's Jo. I don't know how much you've thought about this. You sound very emotional right now, and from what you've described of this man, this policeman..." She says the word with disgust. I can tell she's angry too. I feel as though I can almost hear her thoughts formulating, on the other end of the line. "We just want you to be safe. We just want to make sure you're going to be okay, both of you."

I love the sound of her voice. I love the steady tone of it. I imagine her eyes, pleading as she speaks to me, trying to reason with me in her own way. "Jo, I'm going for her. We're going to get her."

There's a moment's pause, before she speaks again, and I realize by the tone of her voice that she knows. She knows we have no choice. We have to get the little girl out. "You need to call Brennan, Malcolm. Tell him what's going on there. When will you call us back? When will we hear from you?" She'd decided. In her own way, she's reasoned it out, and decided that it's best for us to keep going, to go and get Emily.

I'll call him now, when I hang up, and I'll contact you two tonight. I really will. Don't worry. I need you both to know where we are, and what's going on." I mean it. I don't want Terry here, but I need his support, and maybe even at some point, his refuge.

"If we don't hear from you, you stupid shit...You call me. Call me as soon as something happens." Terry's excited, still not convinced, but I know that Jo has somehow calmed him down, and for now he's given in, accepting that I have it under control.

I hang up the phone and look over at Heather. She still looks scared, but there seems to be a little more light in her eyes. I take it as hope, and lean over and kiss her forehead.

Heather showers while I call the lawyer. When I tell his secretary that Terry Allister, has referred me, she says that Mr Brennan has been expecting my call, and I'm connected immediately. I ask him questions about birth records, and paternity rights, and I ask him to look up an old record of a child who was born ten years previously. He tells me that it isn't really his area, but he'll try and get me the answers. He gives me his mobile phone number, and tells me to call him back in a few hours. He says that he wants to help, and that he'll help anyone who's a friend of Terry's.

As an afterthought, before hanging up, I ask him about the penalties for kidnapping, and child abduction. After a lengthy pause he asks me if I want to repeat the question. I decline. It doesn't matter.

I don't know exactly what I'm going to do, but I know that we have to move forward. I order food from the hotel kitchen, and we eat ravenously. Heather touches the marks on my face gently, while I try to navigate my soup spoon past my puffed-up lips. I try not to think about her bruises. It brings the anger too close. I focus on moving forward, not looking back.

I shower my sore, stiff body and try to feel fresher, try to feel awake while Heather dresses and packs some of the leftover food in our bag. The afternoon has turned to night, and the snow lazily starts to drift down again. I can almost feel the coldness as I look outside at the dark purple sky, and see the people walking in the streets, pulling their jackets tighter around themselves. "Doesn't it ever stop snowing here?" I mean it. It's unlike my mild Vancouver climate.

"For three months, then it starts again." She says it quickly, as though it's a practiced answer, one that the locals probably tell strangers.

We look at each other and laugh. It's the first time in days that I've felt like laughing.

She sits away from me, on the small chair in the room, while I dress, and get ready for our journey back down the highway. She starts to speak in a slow steady voice.

"I didn't know where to go at first. I thought about going back to the motel. Then I thought about coming back for you, but I really wasn't thinking straight at all, so I just drove and drove. I know the roads. I know them from growing up here, but none of them looked familiar to me. Nothing made any sense."

"Emily didn't ask any questions. She just sat there, and after a while she reached out her hand, and held mine." Heather stops, and shakes her head. "It was almost as though she was trying to comfort me."

"We heard sirens, everywhere we went, everywhere. They wouldn't stop. I knew it was us. I knew they were looking for us. We drove out to the hills, and then past them. I just didn't know where to go. After a while, I just gave up. I pulled over to a construction site. They're building homes, out past the hills. There's big piles of dirt, and half finished buildings. We sat there, we talked. I thought we'd be hidden. I thought that no one would see us."

I hold onto my jacket, and sit on the edge of the bed, listening to her, remembering that I would have been shivering in the old barn at about the same time.

"She was comfortable with me, Malcolm. She didn't ask where we were going. She just seemed happy to be with me."

She stares forward, looking down, but not focusing. Her face is hard, the same hardness that I saw in the motel room, the night she came back from her father's house, the night he slapped her.

I don't want to ask. I don't want to ask if Emily is going through the same things Heather went through as a little girl. Heather looks at me for a long time, before continuing. "She didn't have to tell me, Malcolm. I knew, I just knew. She cried and cried. I wouldn't make her tell me. I couldn't. I held onto her, and told her that everything was going to be okay. I told her that I'd look after her."

She doesn't have to tell me anymore. I know the rest. I heard most of it from the radio in the police station. They found her. She tells me that they surrounded her with police cars, and took Emily from her arms by force. Somebody must have spotted them parked there, and called the police. The officers were rough with her. They called her a lunatic, threatened her. They talked about what prison does to someone who steals children, other people's children.

One car took Emily away, and Heather was kept in another with two officers. They were heading for the police station when a message came through on the radio, to re-direct them to Thornside. The instructions were to take her to Thornside hospital, instead of the station.

"I didn't understand. I was frantic, just wanted to get Emily back. I kicked at the doors and punched the windows so much that they restrained me, put me in handcuffs."

"The cops left me at the hospital. They took me to that room you found me in, and handcuffed me to the bed. After a while a nurse or orderly came, and injected me with something. I tried to struggle, tried to resist, but it didn't work. I had no strength left to fight with. I know that I slept because when I woke up he was there, standing over me, waiting for me to wake up. I was terrified. I felt like it was before. I felt like a child living in his house again."

I can feel the anger start to rise in me again, as she continues to speak.

"He didn't talk, he just hit me. He just kept hitting me. His eyes were crazy, just like I remembered, and he was too angry to talk. I could tell."

I remember him hitting first, and then speaking. I remember what he did to me at the police station.

"He wanted to know about you. About whether you knew, and if we'd planned on taking her together. I told him I'd lied to you and you didn't know anything. He didn't seem to believe me, but after a while he stopped asking me, hitting me. He sat down in the chair and it was crazy. It was almost like he started to smile, this strange mad, smile."

I'm holding onto the edge of the bed tightly now, trying to stay focused and not let my anger take over. I can see the snow through the window, from the corner of my eyes. It's falling heavily again. Everything is turning white outside.

"He looked at me and called me a slut, told me that I'd messed up, should never have come back. Then, he sat and didn't say anything. It was like he was just thinking. After a while, he came over and stroked my forehead. It made me sick to feel his hand on me. He told me that it was going to be okay, that everything would be okay."

She looks up at me, focusing on my face. There are no tears, just anger, and all of a sudden, I know that I really did rescue her from the hospital. I don't know how he would have done it, but he never would have let her leave there. He never would have let her come for Emily. He knew she'd never give up.

I think about how lucky we've been, how our timing has been so close. We were just a few steps ahead of him all this time. He let me leave the police station, and then must have gone to the hospital to see Heather, before coming to the motel to get me. He couldn't afford to have me out there, knowing his story, knowing what he'd done. He could deal with Heather anytime. He had her tucked away in the hospital, drugged. My mind races thinking of all the possibilities when the silence is broken by the loud ringing of the bedside phone.

The man at the front desk wants to see me, wants me to come to the desk to clear something up. The number on my credit card has been written down wrong. It's just a silly mistake. If it isn't too much trouble, can I just come and see him for a moment. It won't take long; he keeps apologizing.

We have to check out anyways. I leave her in the room, sitting on the edge of the bed, ready to go. I'm three steps down the hall when the realization hits me. I think about the man's voice. I think about the indifference he'd shown when I checked in. I'd been just another customer. But, it's different now. There's panic in his voice, and I remember. I remember that nobody had written down my credit card number. It had been put through their machine. There's no room for error there.

I turn quickly in one swift motion, and throw open our hotel room door. Motioning for her to be silent, I roughly grab her with one hand, and our small bag in the other. Looking down the hall, I see nothing, hear nothing. I pull her in the other direction, towards the sign that says, 'Emergency Exit'.

My feet don't feel like they're touching the floor, as we almost glide in mid air, towards the exit. I push open the heavy fire door, and we're pressed back by the cold air rushing in. There are some parked cars out back, and a man in a hotel uniform, leaning against a wall, smoking. He turns away when he sees us, uninterested. I pull Heather to the corner of the building, leaving her there. I squeeze her body one last time, and can feel her shivering from the cold, as I make my way around the corner, looking for the truck.

I can't see a police car or Postman's truck. There are other vehicles in the parking lot, people scraping windshields, moving the snow from their hoods. I slide into Michael's old truck, and quickly turn the engine over. I let the windshield wipers remove as much of the snow as they can, and drive back to where Heather waits.

The man, still smoking, stands shaking his head at us now, while Heather jumps in beside me. He makes a motion with his arms, as though he's telling us to clear the snow away from the windshield, but I can't. I don't have time. I can barely see out of the front window. I spin the truck around, back to the front entrance, and some of the loose snow falls off the hood and roof, giving us some visibility.

There's only one way out. We have to pass the entrance to the hotel. I can see the front desk through the big hotel windows. For a moment, I think that I may have been wrong. I think that perhaps the desk clerk really did need to see us. Maybe I've over reacted. But then I see it. He did have spare keys. His large, winter-ready vehicle is parked at an angle, right at the front door. The vehicle I took the keys from is sitting there. We don't slow down. I don't want to see Postman inside the front lobby. I drive as quickly as I think I can without drawing attention to ourselves. The truck's rear tires gently slide sideways, and I right them immediately, as we pull out of the parking lot, and back onto the main road. I wonder what he'd planned to do. Had he intended to grab Heather while I went to the desk, or was he going to try and get both of us at the same time? Even without a police car, he still has a gun and a badge. That would have been enough to get us into his car. I take some solace in the fact that there are no other cars around his, and that he's driving his own car. He's alone.

CHAPTER 30

I passed the snowplough the night before when I was travelling in the other direction, so I know that the highway has been cleared, but unfortunately the new snow has covered it back up just as fast.

I strain my eyes and push my neck forward, trying to see through the falling snow. Heather looks behind us and reaches outside, around to the back windows of the pickup, clearing them, trying to rub the ice from them. I pass other cars that almost seem to be standing still as they crawl safely along the road. The drivers look over at me in bewilderment. I suppose they wonder why anyone would drive so fast on such a treacherous night. We move along, and I watch the odometer slowly add a mile, then another, then another, and still there's no one following us.

The snow doesn't slow down. It's relentless. As we move farther along the highway, there are no other cars. I see the flashing hazard lights of cars that have pulled over and decided to wait out the storm. They're parked precariously close to the outside ditches of the road. I take my foot off the accelerator as I pass them; trying to slow down, not wanting to touch the brakes of the old truck, as it coasts past them safely. I can see clearly out the rear view mirror now, and the windows are clear of snow and ice. There's no one coming, no one back there. I try to relax, try to release my grip on the steering wheel.

"I'll keep looking back. You look forward." She says it without moving her head. I steal a glance at her as she keeps her vision trained on the view through the back window. She seems afraid again. We escaped from him one more time, but it was close. I could almost feel him back there at the hotel, feel his horrible presence.

I nod my agreement to her and try to keep my eyes looking ahead. I take my foot from the gas pedal a little, slowing down, staying safe. The side ditches are always there, almost moving towards us as we move forward. If I let my concentration lapse for a moment, I begin to slide towards the edges. There are no tracks in the road in front of me, to lead us. There are no other vehicles ahead, leaving a trail. It's just white. Everything is white. I can tell the curve of the highway from the way that the snow has fallen on the sides. It's like driving through a tunnel, with the snow banked on either side of us. Occasionally, there's a gap, and it looks as though the road has veered off, but it's just an area that the wind or terrain has cleared of snow. There are no cliffs or mountains, just flatness with long, empty fields on either side. I slow down again as the snow in front of me seems to cause a solid white blanket. It lets me see through it for only a moment, and then closes down again, furiously, silently falling.

"I don't see him. He can't have followed us. Nobody's getting through in this." I try to console her, reassure her. Her body relaxes, and she lets it fall against her side of the truck's bench seat. I hadn't realized how tense she'd been, sitting upright looking back at the snowy highway, watching for her father.

We have to stop. I have to pull over. There's no visibility, no way to see. No matter how hard I strain my eyes, I still can't make out what's ahead or behind us. The last vehicle we'd seen was pulled over to the side of the road miles back, waiting out the storm. I let the truck slow down on its own and slide into the banks

299

of snow that are built up on the shoulder. The engine runs and the heater blows warm air onto the windshield. The snow falls with its gentle strength all around us, covering everything. The windshield wipers intermittently swipe it away, as it tries to cover the front of the truck.

I shiver even though it's warm inside the cab. I shiver from the stress, the fear, and from looking out at the cold night. My body feels like it wants to shake and convulse. I'm tired of it all, tired of chasing and of being chased. She reaches over and touches my shoulders, smoothes my hair, looking at me with her blue, blue eyes. "I'm sorry. I'm sorry for all of this. I didn't want to do this to you, and I didn't want to lie to you." She looks stronger as she says it. There are no tears.

I don't think I really addressed it totally in my head until then, until I hear the remorse, the sorrow in her voice. The anger at her father was driving me. The anger had stopped me from thinking about the lies she'd told me. "I knew that something didn't add up. I just knew, but I didn't want to acknowledge it. I think I wanted to be the hero, for once I thought I could be a hero, a hero for you, for Hardly. I don't know, for somebody." I think about my friend for a moment, before continuing. "So, I didn't ask. I didn't ask the questions that I should have, and I just accepted what you told me."

"You don't need to be a hero, Malcolm. I know you. You wouldn't have let this happen, Malcolm. You're not letting it happen; you're doing something about it." She's not the confident girl from the party, or even the determined girl from the lake at the end of the world. She's different now.

We sit in the truck, touching each other, shivering, even in the warmth, watching the snow, wishing that it would slow down, stop. In the movie of my life that plays in my head, it's always been easier than this, always simpler. The girl never lies. The girl is always perfect, and I'm always the hero. But, in the movie of my life that plays in my head, I always have to wake up. I always have to open up my eyes and face reality. This time I have my eyes wide open, and the girl is sitting right beside me, waiting for me.

"You can't lie to me. You have to tell me, even if it hurts to tell. That's the only way I can do this, Heather. It's the only way it'll work." I can hear the rattle of the truck's heater. I can see the snow accumulating on the windshield and then getting wiped off. I can feel the aching on my face from the beating, but none of it matters. I'm sitting at the crossroads, willing to change course, and all I really want to hear is her answer.

"I won't lie to you. I'll trust you. I should have trusted you." She says it with honest conviction. Her eyes are warm. Her face that's been bruised and slapped and hit by her father, looks at me without the cheekiness and confidence that it had when we first met. It's different now. Although we've gotten to this point separately, I feel with her now. I feel as though we're together again.

I think of my Dad, and how much he'd like her. I think of Emily and what we still have to do. As I reach over to pull her close, there's almost a sense of relief, in both of us.

There's a slight slowing in the snow. The steady, monotonous falling has decreased now and is more sporadic. We have to move, we have to get to Emily before Postman. I still don't know what we're going to do when we get there, but I know that we have to get to her. I ease the truck back out onto the road and press on the accelerator, pushing it forward. The back wheels spin and then grab the road. Heather settles into the seat, staying close to me, touching me.

The exit for the second highway that takes us to Woodbine is still far ahead. We have several miles of long snow-covered highway to cover before we reach it. I try to relax. I let my foot push on the pedal until we find a safe, steady pace. The snow still comes down, but it's manageable now, easier to see. The old truck stays solid on the snowy highway. I stop looking back. I ignore the rear view mirror. I want to reach over and touch Heather, tell her that it's going to be okay, tell her that we'll be with Emily soon, and then it happens.

I see the blur of light, from the corner of my eye, and I know that it's him. Heather is screaming. I can see her mouth open wide. I can feel the panic coming from her. But, I can't hear her. All I hear is the steady hum of the truck's heater and roar of his engine as it nears us. He must have been driving at a tremendous speed. His vehicle is behind us. I can't look back. I want to see him. I

302

want to see his face, his fury, but I have to keep my hands on the wheel, and my eyes on the road in front of us.

She stops screaming, but keeps sobbing, without crying, making low convulsive noises. I can feel her bobbing back and forth on the seat, terrified. "Don't let him. Don't let him. Please, don't let him." I know that she's thinking about Emily. The words mean nothing, but her fear is overpowering. The whole inside of the vehicle seems to be alive with her panic and desperation. It's almost as though I can smell it.

He's almost beside us now, and I feel his big, strong vehicle make contact with the side of the truck. He's trying to force us into the ditch, trying to get us to stop. I have no choice. I hold onto the steering wheel as hard as I can and press the accelerator, willing the old truck to stay straight, as it surges forward. It slides. The rear wheels slide to one side, and I have to hold onto the wheel as though I have the entire weight of the vehicle in my bare hands. I can hear his engine, up beside me now. The snow makes no sounds. The night is silent, other than the humming of the two vehicles. He squeezes up beside us. The hard, packed piles of snow seem to pin us together, towering from either side, but still we move forward.

I don't let up on the gas. I keep accelerating, keep pushing on, but it doesn't matter. He's there. When I speed up, he's on our tail, pushing up beside us. I can't outrun him. And, when I slow down, he lies back, playing, toying with us. The truck will only go so quickly, and its traction is limited. I get a few feet ahead of him, and it feels as though we can outrun him, then suddenly, he's up beside us again. His vehicle is bigger, heavier, made for this type of terrain. It feels as though he's daring me to drive faster.

Heather is more focused now, holding onto the seat, her eyes constantly watching him, telling me where he is. "He's almost beside us. He's coming up now. He's going to catch us."

I let my tense, tired foot slip from the accelerator for a moment, and allow him to catch up to us. I wait to look over, wait until I know that I'll see him.

I need to look at him, to see his face. His black, tinted window slides down as he speeds up beside us. He has the same look, the maniacal look that he had in the police station. There's no rage or anger that I can see, just insanity. He's laughing now, enjoying himself. Our two vehicles barely have enough room, as we squeeze through the piles of snow that are in the ditches on either side of us. He slides his vehicle over and pushes toward us. I can hear the sound and feel the metal on metal, as his car hits the truck.

Every time he does it, I hold onto the wheel, trying to hold our ground, but the truck still moves, sliding over towards the ditch. I keep pushing the pedal down harder, and he keeps pace with us. He has his window down, and looks over, watching us, silently goading us. He doesn't seem worried about the road, the snow. He looks almost nonchalant at first, but then as our speeds increase I can see him hold onto his wheel harder, and stare more intently ahead at the road. I have no choice. I have to try it. I have to try and force him to make a move.

The exit to the highway that leads us to Woodbine is ahead. I know he can see it too. He must have driven this route hundreds of times. I push forward, increasing our speed. The truck is almost uncontrollable. I see the exit getting closer and closer. He's still beside us, maintaining his speed too. We're closer now, and the truck keeps going faster, not wanting to give up. I can sense him watching me as he drives alongside. I can feel him beside me. The snow is piled on either side of the short exit. There's no room for two vehicles to get through. I wait until I see the curve of the road, the incline, the hill leading onto the other highway. I wait until I can almost feel the piles of snow, leaning dangerously into the road. Then, I do it.

I take my foot off the accelerator. Firmly, I push on the brake pedal, and Postman keeps speeding forward, towards the exit. The back wheels lock up, and we start to turn. Heather flies forward, and her head bounces on the dashboard. I miss the first spin as the truck violently turns around. It's too rapid, too quick. It turns us out of control, and I pray that all of our wheels stay on the road, away from the ditches. I don't know where Postman is. I can't see him as we circle around.

I try to catch the next one, and fight with the steering wheel for control. It tugs at us, pulling at my whole body. It takes every bit of strength in me, to keep looking forward, and hold onto the wheel. I have no concept of which direction we're in, or whether

we're moving forwards or backwards. It doesn't matter. I just need
to straighten us out, to get us to stop moving. There is no sound, no
noise. We seem to be travelling slowly and quickly, at the same
time, as we turn in circles on the snowy road. I can see the built up
snow in the ditches sailing past us, and feel it falling all around. It
only takes a few seconds for us to stop, but it takes minutes to pass
in my head.

I'm shaking, vibrating, and I can't let go of the wheel, but we
stop. We're facing back down the highway that we've come from,
propped up against a wall of snow, protected from the ditch. I jump
as she strokes the back of my hands, and gently pulls them from
the steering wheel. There's blood dripping from her head, and her
eyes are wide and panicked, but we're okay. I pull her towards me,
and hold her. She doesn't cry. She just lets me hold on, rubbing my
back, trying to alleviate the fear from both of us.

There's a sharp thud behind me on the truck door, and a
clump of snow falls from a pile that we're perched against,
shocking us back into reality. I look back towards the exit where
we let him pass us. There are no signs, no other vehicle. There's no
one else on the road.

We didn't gain much ground as we spun around. I can see
the exit clearly from where we sit, and still there's no sign of him.
We wait. I expect to see his car come flying back; driving the
wrong way over the exit, trying to find us again. I expect to see
him coming straight at us, but still there's no one, just the silent
falling of the snow.

We're lodged against a snow bank, and have dug ourselves into a rut. I try to move us forward, but it's no use, we're stuck. I rock us back and forth, jamming the transmission from drive, to neutral, to reverse, over and over again, until finally we jar loose and find some traction.

I carefully turn us around, watching for him. It feels like he'll come from anywhere, from any direction. I can't chance us driving to the exit and having him flying over it, forcing us off the road. I pull over as far as I can, and put the truck into park. I need to look. I need to get up over the exit, and see if I can see him, see if I can see his vehicle. The snow will be silent. He won't hear me. I just need to know if it's safe to keep driving through the exit. I need to know where he is.

"This is crazy, Malcolm, you can't. Don't go out there." She grabs at my arm, trying to hold me back, as I try to explain to her that I just need to see. I need to see where his car is.

I give her all the options. "We can't keep driving. If he is sitting just on the other side of the exit, he'll come at us as soon as we get onto the top of it and force us off of the road." She keeps holding onto my arm as I try to explain to her. "We can't go back. We'd be driving the wrong way in white out conditions. And, I can't stay here. I need to know where he is."

I can't see any other way. The highway is empty again. There's just us and whiteness everywhere. I need to know what happened to him. He increased his speed just as we slowed down and must have hit the incline for the exit at a tremendous acceleration. I pull away from her, almost roughly, then, seeing the bloody forehead and her worried look, reach over and touch her once more. "Remember what I told you, remember what I always say when I come and kiss your head. Why did I do it? Why do I always turn around and come back and kiss you?"

Her eyes tear up and I see my Heather; I see her as the girl in the boots with the green hair, and I see her as a little girl, all at the same time. I know that she's thinking of our life, our real life back home, or maybe our life at the lake at the end of the world. "I know. I know." She answers, shaking her head.

"I do it because I can, not because I have to, just because I can." I reach over and kiss her forehead just as I've done so many times, before opening the truck door.

The coldness of the night hits me immediately, and sends a shiver right through my body. I hear her locking the door behind me, as my feet crunch down into the snow, and I start walking towards the exit. It's snowing heavily still, but I can see the tracks of his vehicle. They keep going towards the exit, and don't stop, continuing up to the top of it. Still, there's no car, no sign of Postman.

I walk, over at the side, barely skirting the piles of snow by the ditch, watching for him, listening, imagining where I'll jump to if he suddenly comes barrelling over the road. Carefully, I make my way up the incline, keeping my feet firmly in the deep snow, glad of the traction. The tracks kept going, and don't come back. He somehow made it over the hill, and around the curve. I keep straining my ears, trying to listen past my own breathing, for any sounds of his vehicle. I steal a look back at Heather. Her face is pushed up against the windshield, watching me, as the snow quickly covers the old vehicle once more.

I crouch down, as I reach the crest of the hill, trying to make myself appear smaller. I keep to the edges, to the ditch, but his tracks still move forward. He didn't stop, didn't brake. I suppose he was going so fast that he just powered right over the top of the hill, probably not even touching the ground.

The curve of the hill is covered in snow, and the banks at the side lessen, then heighten again. It isn't until I walk right around the curve that I see him. I see the blackness of it, sticking out of the snow. I quickly cross over the road and see Postman's vehicle lying on its roof, upside down, directly in the middle of the ditch, at the side of the road. There are no skid marks, no signs of slowing down. He can't have had time. He must have known that the exit curved. All the times that he must have driven this road, yet he still didn't make the curve. He kept driving straight, and with the speed, he hadn't been able to navigate it and ended up powering through the snow pile and into the ditch.

I stand for a moment and can see the wheels spinning still as it sits upside down. I carefully make my way down the curve and over towards this car. I still see no sign of the man. The driver's side of the vehicle faces me, and there are no footprints, no signs that he's gotten out of the door. I strain my eyes through the still heavy, falling snow, trying to see him. The silence is eerie. It seems as though there should be people. It seems as though there should be someone around, someone helping, but there's no one, just the steady turning of the car's wheels as it lies on its roof.

I slide, and then right myself, as I get closer, and still I see no footprints. I climb over the lowest spot in the snow bank, all the while trying to see over it, watching for any movement. I look back over at the exit, thinking of Heather sitting there. As I look at his car, I slide down the other side of the bank into the ditch. Then, I see him. He's still in the car. I make my way towards it, and see his head, his face, upside down, in the car seat.

I get closer and cautiously kneel down, peering forward to get a better look inside the vehicle. He's no longer a threat to us. He's hanging from his seatbelt, blood pouring from his head and his mouth. His right arm isn't a part of his body anymore, as it hangs unnaturally away from him, and his left hand holds onto his neck which also has blood coming from it and seems to be broken. The windshield is cracked and the steering wheel bent from where he must have bounced off them during the impact. His eyes are open, and his head is twisted towards the side window. He looks at me, not blinking. His head doesn't move; he just keeps holding onto his neck, trying to stop the bleeding. The window is still open, and I can hear him. There's no smile now, no deathly goading. There's just his steady plea, as he stares at me, through the same eyes that terrorized his daughter.

His breathing is wheezing, and it sounds as though he's only exhaling, as he keeps saying over and over again, "Please, please help me, please, please help me."

I keep looking in the window at John Postman as he lies there helplessly. I see the blood coming from his neck and his hand holding onto it, trying to stop the bleeding. His eyes are not the eyes of insanity any more. They're the eyes of a dying man. I put my hand on the door handle and hold onto it, as his eyes follow me, willing me to help him. I keep holding the handle, watching him, watching his crazed eyes, as he continues to plead. I can hear his breath as it escapes from his lungs, as he keeps saying, "please, please help me," over and over and over again.

I think of Emily, and I think of Heather, and I think of Hardly, my friend, Hardly. And, I think of the years of your life that you don't ever get back. I look at John Postman once more, as I release my grip on the handle of his door, and turn and walk away, leaving him to die.

She's already coming towards me and is halfway from the truck to the exit. Her arms are swinging back and forth, trying to keep her balance as she tries to walk along the slippery road. Her eyes are huge, with a crazed look. "I couldn't wait. I had to know that you were okay. I'm sorry. I didn't wait." She says it desperately, almost apologetically, and stands with her arms open, waiting for me to reach her.

I slide the remaining way down the incline, towards her, and embrace her so heavily that we swing around, and land on the snowy highway. I kiss her face, her bruises, her bloody forehead, and tell her that it's going to be okay, before lifting her up, and getting us back into the truck.

I push on the accelerator and get us going fast enough to get over the incline and onto the highway for Woodbine. I don't try to stop her from seeing his car. I know she'll look. She has to. "I don't understand? Where is he? What happened?" I look over and see that his door is partially open. Somehow, he managed to pop the door open, probably by weighting himself against it, trying to save himself. He has to be still in the vehicle. There was too much blood, too little life left in him.

"He's dead. There was nothing left of him, Heather. He was dying. There's nothing we can do." As I say it, I realize that I left a man to die at the side of the road. The image of John Postman, pleading for help as I decided whether or not to open his door, is burnt into my mind. I shake my head and try to concentrate on the highway in front of us.

Heather unsnaps her seatbelt and moves over towards me, curling her head into my lap. It's several miles before I realize that the sound that I'm hearing is her and not the noises from the truck. She's crying again, crying muffled sobs, as though she's trying not to let me hear. She holds onto my knees, as I drive, holding against

312

them firmly and sobbing. Her father is dead, or dying, but still we don't stop or go back. We just drive on, over the snowy roads. I don't ask her if she's thinking about the fact that her tormentor, the man that caused her so much pain and grief is dead, or if she's thinking that she doesn't have a father anymore. I just keep driving, watching the road, trying not to think about the way Postman was holding his neck trying to stop the bleeding as he begged me to help him.

I take my hand from the wheel and stroke her hair, pulling it back from her face, trying to comfort her, and then quickly I grab on again, holding us onto the road. We're just a few miles from Woodbine when the road becomes clearer, less snow covered. And, as we see the sign for the exit, the storm almost seems to stop. The blinding snow that covered the highway now falls at a slower pace. There's a car in the ditch by the exit, and a truck trying to pull it out. Two men look over and wave, shaking their heads as we drive past them, obviously wondering how we made it over the stretch of road that we just left.

"Will she be alone? Do you think there will be anyone else in the house?" It doesn't matter anymore. We've walked into so many situations in pursuit of Emily, since coming to Woodbine, that one more won't matter, but I ask anyway.

"My guess is that he just left her. She didn't say that there was anyone else living with them, but I don't know." She sits up, and dries her eyes while speaking. She watches the road in front of us, as though willing us to move faster, and get closer to Emily.

We pass the motel, and I see that all the lights are off. The rental car is still there, in front of our old room. It's late, after midnight now. Claude, and his girlfriend, will be in the back, out of sight, hoping that there are no more visits from crazed policemen.

I know the way. My sense of direction is back. It's easy to remember the streets of a small town. They all have some kind of a logical progression to them, and I can remember the day she showed me her old house. I park in the driveway this time, instead of down the street. There is a porch light on, and a faint glow coming from the big window at the front.

"Maybe you should go in by yourself, Heather. She doesn't know me. I don't want to scare her. You can call out to me, if there's somebody else in the house. I'll just stay here." I still haven't seen Emily. At the library, I focused on the other little girl, and didn't see her, and she didn't see me. It makes sense to me, but Heather keeps shaking her head.

"No, you don't get it, do you?" She reaches out and touches me tenderly, holding my hand. "I should never have left you, should never have let you do any of this on your own." She keeps looking at me. Her mouth starts to say the words, but then she stops, until finally they just come out. "You're stuck with me, remember. I don't want to do any of this without you, anymore."

I take her hands, and put them on my face, enjoying the touch, and feeling that maybe our nightmare is beginning to come to an end. We get out of the truck and make our way to the front door of her childhood home.

The blinds are drawn, and all we can see is light coming from somewhere in the front room. We softly knock on the door, and Heather quietly pushes it open. She calls Emily's name, softly, carefully. I hear every board creak under my feet, as we make our way to the front room of the old house. The room looks like a business man's study. There are large overstuffed leather chairs and conservative-looking, sturdy tables, stacked with reference books and magazines. There's a reading lamp, burning in the corner, and underneath it there's a little girl, curled into a ball, laying across a couch, eyes open wide, watching us.

She is Heather. She's a small, beautifulversion of Heather. There would have been no doubt that day outside of the school. If we'd seen her, we would have recognized her. She lies there, shivering, under the blanket, and I can see the fear in her eyes, as she looks from Heather to me, and back again.

Heather crawls towards her, telling her that it's going to be okay, staying low, then kneeling and holding her arms out towards the little girl. Emily allows her to come closer. She lets her touch her, pick her up, pull her close, and then she speaks in a hushed, frightened tone. "I'm waiting for my Dad. I'm waiting for *him* to come home." She says the word as though we should know the significance, as though we should know how important it is for her to wait for him.

Heather pulls herself up, onto the small couch, and cradles Emily in her arms, stroking her hair back, the same way I did to her back in the truck. The little girl looks at Heather, and then over at me, not quite understanding what's happening. "It's okay honey. That's Malcolm. He's with me, he's been helping me. He's a nice, nice man."

I try to look as nice and safe as I can, as I sit down on one of the big chairs, giving them the space that they need. It feels good to let my body sink into the comfort of the chair, and allow myself to breathe at a normal rate. I watch as the two of them sit, holding each other, looking into the others eyes. They talk about waiting for him to come home, about what it feels like. They talk about his hands slamming down on the table, and the way that he looks at them, frightens them. It's a private conversation, and I sit there, not moving, trying not to listen.

Emily cries soft, muted little tears. She cries as though she's trying to cry without anybody hearing her. Heather tries to stay strong, and holds onto her, as the little girl drifts into sleep. I help her balance herself and Emily, as they walk up the stairs to the little girl's bedroom. She lies down beside her, without releasing her. I stand there for another minute, until I hear Heather's breathing change, and I know that she's asleep, beside her daughter.

I use Postman's phone to call Brennan, the lawyer, waking him up. He's been busy working on the question that I asked him earlier, and has the answer. I'm so happy that I almost want to wake Heather up to tell her, but I don't. I let her sleep. I let her sleep, and protect Emily, and then I lie down on the living room couch myself.

CHAPTER 31

Something wakes me, but I'm not sure what it is. The sun is shining through the big front window, and I open my eyes just in time to see the police car carefully making its way down the street. There are two of them in the car. I recognize Ellison right away. He's driving, and when they park in the driveway, he stays sitting in the driver's seat. The other officer is older. I can see the grey hair sticking out from under his hat, and I recognize the authoritative way he talks to the younger officer. It isn't until he gets out, and makes his way up the front path, that I know for sure that it's Macklin, the sergeant from the police station.

He walks directly into the living room, as though he's been here many times before, and laboriously makes his way over to one of Postman's big leather chairs, letting his body fall into it. Slowly, he takes off his cap, and brushes his hair back, watching me the whole time, seemingly unsurprised that I'm sitting there.

He doesn't speak right away. It's as though he's catching his breath, waiting. "I know you were there. I know it was you, both of you." He looks around, as though he's searching for Heather. There are heavy bags around his eyes, and he has the tired and defeated look of a man who's seen too many troubles.

I suppose there are lots of ways that he could know. The tracks from our truck would have been covered by the falling snow immediately, but there are other ways. We'd been driving erratically on a dangerous highway, and other vehicles saw us. Any one of them could have called and reported us as being unsafe. And, there were the two men from the entrance to Woodbine who saw us leave the highway, and drive into town.

I don't answer him. I don't know what to say. We sit, staring at each other. Ellison is still sitting in the car, his head laid back on the seat. They must have been out all night, probably called out to look at John Postman's body.

It doesn't feel like I'm talking to a policeman, as his backup sits outside, seemingly disinterested in what's going on inside the house. If they were going to arrest us, or charge us, he would have come in. I'm sure he would have. No, it feels more like I'm talking to somebody who's been in the same battle that I have. I'm just not sure yet whose side Macklin is on.

"Is he dead?" I need to know. I remember the open car door as we drove past. I wonder if some way, somehow, he made it. Maybe he had a radio in the car. Maybe he was able to radio for help. Maybe John Postman is still alive.

He doesn't seem to hear me. His eyes look around the room as he starts to talk. It takes a few minutes of him speaking before I

318

realize what's happening. I feel the same way I did that day in Michael's office. I'm listening to a confession, again. This time it's Macklin's.

"He was a great cop, John Postman. He saved my ass on more than one occasion. He never hesitated, never, ever hesitated, to get involved. He'd put himself on the line for his officers any day of the week. They say not a lot happens out here in the sticks. Well let me tell you, that's bullshit, complete bullshit. John Postman looked squarely into the eyes of many a man who might have pulled a trigger on him, and never, ever flinched. Never."

He looks over at me, then, quickly away again. "That day at the station, the day he gave you a beating, that wasn't him. That wasn't the cop that I knew. He came unhinged. He never did that in all the years I knew him."

Heather is in the doorway now. She must have woken up at the same time as I had. She slowly makes her way into the room, and sits beside me, never taking her eyes from Macklin. She speaks to him carefully, as though she's remembering. "I know you. I used to know you. You worked with my Dad. I forgot all about you."

It feels strange to be sitting in his house, talking about him. It feels like he should be here too.

Macklin looks at her, silently acknowledging her. His eyes are hard at first, but as he continues speaking, they seem to soften, almost watering up. He isn't hearing us. He has his own agenda. "We didn't know. We didn't know for sure, and we didn't ask." He

319

pauses as though trying to think of what to say next. "You left, so that part was easy. Young people leave town. They go away. They move. That was no big deal. But Emily, lovely little Emily, that was harder." His face is pleading now, and he's gripping his hat in his hand.

I hold Heather back. Her body tenses up and she's leaning forward, as though she wants to attack Macklin.

He's started now, and can't stop. I'm right. It is his confession. "He called her his daughter. Emily was his daughter and he'd be raising her. I asked him, who's the mother, John? Have you been hiding somebody away from us? Do you have a woman on the side? Who's the baby's mother? If it's Heather's and she got in trouble with some boy, then tell me. I can understand that. Heather went out and got pregnant. It's not ideal, but it happens. It happens all the time. But he wouldn't tell me. He just kept saying that he was doing the right thing, and that he was the father. How was I to know? How could I have known?"

I keep holding onto Heather, as I lean us back on the couch. "I don't get it Macklin. Known what? What is it that you're trying to say?"

He's lost now, staring at the floor. "It never did make sense. I'm a cop for Christ sakes. I know when something doesn't add up, but I never questioned it. I never pursued it." He pulls his body up straighter and releases the grip on his hat, as though he just remembered that he's a police officer. "After what he did to you at the police station, and the way he pursued Heather, how he had to find her, it just wasn't right. It wasn't him. I did some research. I had to find out."

He found out. Macklin found out what Brennan, Terry's lawyer, told me a few hours earlier.

"I checked the birth records. Emily Postman was born on July 10th, 1987 in Stoney Plain, Alberta. The father is listed as John Postman. He was right about that." He pauses. He doesn't want to say the words, "But the mother, the birth mother is listed as Heather Postman."

Heather looks at me, asking me with her eyes, and I give her the news that I received the night before. "It's true. I called Brennan last night, after you fell asleep. He's right. You're the legal mother. We'll be able to take her. We can get Emily out of here. Nobody can stop us."

Postman must have wanted to make sure that he had legal rights over Emily, so he listed himself on the birth certificate. But he also had no choice when it came to the mother. Heather gave birth to Emily, and she did it a long ways away from Woodbine. He had no choice. He had to list her as the actual mother.

She holds onto me for a while, and we watch Macklin. He just sits there, looking like he's waiting for something.

"I almost told you once. I was just a little girl, but it had started already. I thought about how safe you looked, how trusting. But then I'd see you with him, I'd see you all laughing together. I could see the way you looked at him. You looked like you were afraid of him too." She lets out a short laugh. "Maybe you were, maybe you all were. So, I kept it to myself. I never did tell you what he was doing to me."

I release my grip on her and let her get up and stand over him. Macklin raises his eyes to look up. I know what he wants. He wants what all of us want. He wants to be able to sleep, and breathe, and not have regrets, about the things that you don't do. His eyes are wet now, as he speaks to her. "I'm sorry. I didn't know. I never knew for sure."

And she gives it to him. She gives him his absolution. She lays her hand on his shoulder, and gently squeezes it as he lets his head drop towards her hand. Her head is still turned away, as though she can't look right at him, but she lets the man breathe. And then, she leaves us to go upstairs to her daughter. Nothing else really matters to her now.

"The other cop, Ellison, why did he help us at the hospital? Does he know too?" I still have blanks to fill in.

He comes back to normal a little, trying to be a policeman again. "I told him to. I posted him in the hospital. I knew that you'd come for her. I knew that you'd be there at some point, and I told him to let you take her. He didn't argue. He just followed my orders. I didn't know that it would end like this, but I knew that I had to do something."

We sit facing each other for a few moments, then he gets up, still trying to look like a policeman, before going back out to face his junior officer. As he stands to go, he finally responds to my question, although I know the answer already. "And yes, he's dead.

322

John Postman died in an accident on the highway sometime late last night."

I cut him off, anticipating his question. "Yes, we'll be going. We'll be flying out immediately. And, of course, we will be taking Emily."

He nods at me as he leaves, but still looks lost. He looks like Michael the day that I left him at the side of the highway. I wonder if Macklin has a family to go home to. I wonder if he has a way to be happy, a way to forget about the mistakes that a man can make.

I watch their car drive off, and listen to the sounds of the old house. After a while I walk halfway up the stairs, and listen to Heather and Emily talking. I can't hear the words, but I can read the tones. I can hear Emily asking short, quick questions, and Heather answering in a kind, reassuring voice. From time to time, there's crying from Emily, until Heather talks to her again, telling her how much she loves her, and that everything is going to be okay.

The arrangements happen so easily and quickly that it feels as though someone is looking after us. I leave a message for Michael, telling him where he can collect his truck, and then I pick up the rental car back at the motel. I don't go in the room. I don't want to see it. I can imagine the mess that he would have made when he saw that I wasn't there, and I don't want any more reminders of John Postman, and what he did. I look over at the motel office, as I drive back to pick up Heather and Emily, and resist the temptation to go in and return Claude's key to the laundry room.

It's an incredibly satisfying sensation to be driving out of Woodbine, knowing that we never have to go back there. Emily has three large suitcases, packed with the belongings that she wants to keep, and Heather and I have our small carry on travel bag, that's starting to look very travel worn. We tell Emily to take only her favourite clothes, and that we'll get her new ones when we arrive at our destination. Surprisingly, she doesn't ask many questions. She just keeps holding onto Heather's hand and watching me from a distance. It might be my imagination, but I almost think that I can see her breathing a little easier too, as the car pulls out of town and we head for Toronto airport.

It's easy to buy Emily a ticket and get her on a plane. When I call Brennan, and tell him what we're doing, he assures me that we'll have no problems, and he's right.

She's never flown before and chooses the safeness of the aisle seat, with Heather in the middle and my big frame squeezed up against the window. I look over at her from time to time, and smile, trying to get a smile back, but she just nuzzles her head into her mother's side. It doesn't matter. She's in the right place. All of us are in the right place.

As the plane touches down, Heather looks over at me, and her face can barely stop beaming. "Are you sure Malcolm? Are you sure about this?"

I stare out the window at the cold dreary rain, lashing against the side of the plane. "It's too late now anyways, even if I'm not. But yeah, I'm sure."

Both of them are there, standing side by side. Hardly is leaning precariously on his crutch, and when he sees us, starts awkwardly trying to hop towards us. My Dad doesn't seem to notice anything other than me, though. His eyes lock on mine, and he hugs me with the same strong arms that he's always had. "It's good to have you home, son. Good to have you home." He's smaller than the last time I saw him but he's still the same. He's still my Dad.

In the movie of my life that plays in my head, there are no more temporaries, ever. The hero finds the girl. He knows exactly where his home is, and little girls never get hurt. When I called my Dad from Postman's house and told him a little bit about what we'd been through he said to come home, and I didn't have to think about it at all. I knew exactly where that was.

Hardly reaches out to shake my hand, and I steady him on his crutch. "You're home now then, Malcolm. You're finally home. I was right, wasn't I? It's inside of you. It's always inside of you."

I nod back to my friend and let him lean against me as my dad hugs Heather and kisses her on the cheek, the way the Scots do. He tells her that she's welcome here, welcome in his home. Then, he leans down to Emily's height, and holds out his hand to shake hers. "And who do we have here? Who is this young lady?"

She holds out her little hand and lets him shake it. For a moment it's as though she's forgotten everything that's happened to her, to all of us. She looks at my dad, staring hard at him. He's just a harmless old man. He could be anybody's grandpa or anybody's dad, and with his Scottish accent and his kind, sweet grin, he charms the little girl. She pulls her hand away from him, but she's smiling, smiling like any other little girl, and showing off her very own, perfect little half dimple.

Martin Crosbie Media Information

In a press release, Amazon referred to Martin Crosbie as one of their success stories of 2012. His self-publishing journey has been chronicled in Publisher's Weekly, Forbes Online, and Canada's Globe and Mail newspaper. Martin's debut novel, MY TEMPORARY LIFE, has been downloaded over one hundred and fifty thousand times and became an Amazon bestseller. He is also the author of:

My Name Is Hardly-Book Two of the My Temporary Life Trilogy

Lies I Never Told-A Collection of Short Stories

How I Sold 30,000 eBooks on Amazon's Kindle-An Easy-To-Follow Self-Publishing Guidebook 2014 Edition

Martin was born in the Highlands of Scotland and currently makes his home on the west coast of Canada.

Twitter https://twitter.com/Martinthewriter

Facebook https://www.facebook.com/martin.crosbie.3

Martin's website http://martincrosbie.com/

Martin's email address martin@martincrosbie.com

Amazon Author Page http://tinyurl.com/la5t9eg

Martin's self-publishing journey has been documented here:

Publisher's Weekly Apr/2012 **http://tinyurl.com/cq9ygdd**

Globe and Mail newspaper Apr/2012 **http://tinyurl.com/ks2v2e7**

Forbes Online Aug/2012 **http://tinyurl.com/k4v3pnu**

Martin is a proud contributor at Indies Unlimited:

And, an occasional contributor to the Georgia Straight
newspaper:

Martin's Books:

**My Temporary Life-Book One of the My Temporary Life
Trilogy**

Published Dec. 19, 2011

Publisher-Martin Crosbie

Romantic Suspense

Available on Kindle

Amazon US **http://tinyurl.com/l9xshv6**

Amazon UK **http://tinyurl.com/mxaxtlm**

Amazon Canada **http://tinyurl.com/lgpycef**

Malcolm Wilson learns that everything is always temporary.
Growing up, he's raised by a promiscuous mother who can't stay
out of trouble, his best friend is a thirteen-year-old alcoholic, and
the masters at his tough Scottish school are always raising their
canes in his direction. When he becomes an adult, he escapes, and
chooses the safe route, watching the rest of the world from a
distance. Everything changes the day he meets the beautiful,
alluring, green-haired Heather, and when he learns of Heather's
own abusive childhood and the horrific secret she's been carrying,
Malcolm makes a decision-this time he's not backing down,
whatever the cost.

The first book of the MY TEMPORARY LIFE Trilogy deals with friendship, love, and what it means to be a hero. It was a top-ten Amazon bestseller in all categories.

What readers are saying about *My Temporary Life*:

There were moments of magic, scenes filled with foreboding, passages that were poetic and ruminative, others that were breathtaking. The masterful handling of Malcolm's mother, was brilliant. There were many scenes, especially toward the end, that were fast-paced and made the book impossible to put down.

Susan Russo Anderson-Amazon review

I have to say I have not read a book that took me on such an emotional ride in many years. I just finished it and I'm still reeling. I am typically a romance/fantasy reader but this is definitely going on my favorite books list. Martin Crosbie will be on my watch list of authors in the future. This was an incredible story to read.

Patricia Paonessa-Goodreads review

Mr. Crosbie's first novel is a wonder! Once I started, I couldn't stop. I just HAD to find out what happened next. His characters are so believable and I felt a real connection to his hero's kind heart and the difficulties he faced while growing up and throughout his life. I completed the novel in just a day and was sad to have it end.

Flavia Joy-Amazon review

My Name Is Hardly-Book Two of the My Temporary Life Trilogy

Published Dec. 10/2012

Publisher-Martin Crosbie

Historical Fiction

Available on Kindle

Amazon US **http://tinyurl.com/jw7mf72**

Amazon UK **http://tinyurl.com/lkr3w3u**

Amazon Canada **http://tinyurl.com/n8hmu6u**

A beautiful girl is missing, and may or may not want to be found, a soldier on his last and most dangerous mission, and a vow made to a dying friend. Northern Ireland, in 1996, was one of the most dangerous places in the world. The government called it a state of unrest, the people who lived through it called it the time of "The Troubles".

Gerald "Hardly" McDougall is a forgotten man. He's abused, bullied, and left behind. The only escape left is to join the British Army. At first, he's a reluctant soldier, then everything changes when tensions in Northern Ireland escalate and the Army need a man with a particular set of characteristics. Hardly's re-assigned and sent into the heart of the troubles, living in the same houses as the IRA soldiers he's fighting against.

MY NAME IS HARDLY takes the reader on a twenty year journey through Hardly's life--from the beginning, when he leaves Scotland and joins the Army, to the tragic final days when his time as a spy in Ireland has to come to an end.

What readers are saying about *My Name Is Hardly*:

Martin Crosbie's remarkable storytelling talent is apparent throughout his most recent novel, "My Name Is Hardly." The story seized me from the first paragraph and held me relentlessly until I'd come to the novel's thoughtful and moving conclusion.

Kathleen Lourde-Amazon review

I have no doubt that when the last piece is in place, Crosbie's work will stand tall as exemplary literary fiction, and a reproach to those who mourn the decline of the "gatekeepers" of commercial publishing. Any gate too small to let in Martin Crosbie should have been blown up a long time ago.

Steven Hart-Goodreads review

Lies I Never Told-A Collection of Short Stories

Published April 13, 2013

Publisher-Martin Crosbie

Short Story Collection

Available on Kindle

Amazon US **http://tinyurl.com/q7w7vu3**

Amazon UK **http://tinyurl.com/l3ksbky**

Amazon Canada **http://tinyurl.com/mvew4r6**

"It's what we do. We make our own beds. We become thirty and then forty and we

divorce and re-marry and visit our children on weekends, and work at jobs we

never dreamed of doing, and have too many relationships with people we don't

like, and on the outside we look like any other forty-year-old hero. We're not

though, because it never goes away. No matter how hard we try to hide it, inside

we're still seventeen, sitting at the river, looking for the girl with the brown

eyes."

In this collection of short stories, Martin Crosbie, the bestselling author of "My Temporary Life", presents us with a glimpse into the rear-view mirror of life. Crosbie's writing is quiet, so quiet that when the crash comes you suddenly realize you've been gripping onto the edge of your chair, living the story right along with the main character. In this intensely personal collection, he writes about relationships, sex, children, infidelities, guilt, and sometimes, the absence of guilt.

Lies I Never Told includes four new, original stories, one previously published short story, and the first chapters of his Amazon bestselling novel "My Temporary Life" and the follow-up "My Name Is Hardly".

What readers are saying about *Lies I Never Told-A Collection of Short Stories:*

Could not put this book down. I am amazed at the depth of feeling and emotion in his words. All of the stories are so different yet so connected at the emotional level. My only disappointment is that the stories were not longer. I really hope that this book is just a prelude of the novels to come. Martin grabs me from the first line and takes me on an emotional journey with all his characters.

Debbie Dore-Amazon review

Where Martin Crosbie found his voice is a mystery. His ability to create stories (here very brief ones) that explore the psyche of his chosen stand-in trope in such a way that within a few sentences you are so aware of the character's life and feelings that he seems to be sitting beside you, in conversation with only you.

Grady Harp (Hall of Fame reviewer)-Goodreads review

How I Sold 30,000 eBooks on Amazon's Kindle-An Easy-To-Follow Self-Publishing Guidebook

Published Sept. 4, 2013

Publisher-Martin Crosbie

Self-Help-Sales and Marketing

Amazon US **http://tinyurl.com/ppxud2p**

Amazon UK **http://tinyurl.com/ne7jnmc**

Amazon Canada **http://tinyurl.com/ozf24m3**

*Outlines the methods that the top 5% of successful self-published authors utilize to produce their eBooks in a professional, cost-effective manner

*Shows what happened after Amazon changed the rules and what you need to do right now to adjust your strategy

*How to adopt the philosophy that will allow promotional opportunities to come to you

333

*What you need to know in order to position yourself for a run at the bestseller lists

In February 2012 Martin Crosbie's self-published eBook My Temporary Life hit Amazon's top ten overall bestseller list. The next month Amazon posted a press release revealing that Crosbie had made $46,000 in one month, with one book. Previously to this, his novel was rejected one hundred and thirty times by traditional publishers and agents.

In the months that followed, My Temporary Life and its sequel have been consistent sellers, often sitting atop Amazon's rankings. Crosbie's story has been mentioned in Publisher's Weekly, Forbes online, and other media outlets around the world. In fact, Amazon referred to him as one of their 2012 success stories in their year-end press release.

How I Sold 30,000 eBooks on Amazon's Kindle-An Easy-To-Follow Self-Publishing Guidebook tells the story of how he became a full-time writer, detailing the specific steps he took to find and connect with his readers. Plus, it describes how to adjust and tweak your strategy as Amazon changes their systems.

What readers are saying about *How I Sold 30,000 eBooks on Amazon's Kindle-An Easy-To-Follow Self-Publishing Guidebook:*
Yes, I was skeptical because I've read one or two of these books, and their suggestions are... let's just say not that good.

Last night, I skipped the intro and jumped right to the meat of the book. Chapter One was better, much better, than I had expected. But it was when he said, DON'T go out on Twitter and FB and shout "read my book" a thousand times a day that he convinced me that he was honest and knew what he was talking about.

For anyone at the publishing stage or who wants to get there, so far :-) [I will always be a hardcore skeptic] this is a good reference on what to do, on how to build relationships instead of walls. If you're not yet at the publishing stage, start now to build an audience and support group. And Martin C practices what he preaches, especially the part about supporting other authors. He followed me back on Twitter and friended me on FB.

NSW-Amazon Review

If you are a new writer this book is a must. I wish I had it when I first started writing. It is filled with easy to read and easy to understand information. However, even if you are an already published writer this book will offer you new information you might not have known. I found it helpful in so many ways. There are also links to various other sites that offer valuable info that is very difficult to find. Basically, "How I Sold 30,000 Ebooks on Amazon Kindle," takes a lot of the guessing and hard work out of self publishing.

Roberta Kagan-Amazon Review

Please connect with Martin!

https://twitter.com/Martinthewriter

https://www.facebook.com/martin.crosbie.3

http://martincrosbie.com/

martin@martincrosbie.com

RECEIVED MAR - - 2017

Made in the USA
Charleston, SC
14 March 2017